SKYLINE COLLEGE LIBRARY

3 9368 04317392 7

ID0757864

Nazi Gold

Nazi Gold

The Real Story
of How the World
Plundered Jewish Treasures

By
George Carpozi, Jr.

New Horizon Press
Far Hills, NJ

SKYLINE COLLEGE
LIBRARY
3300 COLLEGE DRIVE
SAN BRUNO, CA 94066

Copyright ©1999 by George Carpozi, Jr.

All rights reserved. No portion of this book may be reproduced or transmitted in any form whatsoever, including electronic, mechanical, or any information storage or retrieval system, except as may be expressly permitted in the 1976 Copyright Act or in writing from the publisher.

Requests for permission should be addressed to:
New Horizon Press
P.O. Box 669
Far Hills, NJ 07931

George Carpozi, Jr.
Nazi Gold: The Real Story of How the World Plundered Jewish Treasures

Interior Design: Susan Sanderson

Library of Congress Catalog Card Number: 98-66168

ISBN: 0-88282-167-9

New Horizon Press
Manufactured in the U.S.A.
2003 2002 2001 2000 1999 / 5 4 3 2 1

CONTENTS

Part III *Allied Gold Maneuvers*

Part IV *Tip of the Art-berg*

Part V *The Insurance Rip-off*

Part VI *Coming to Terms*

"Don't you see?" he cried. "The American Standard Translation orders men to triumph over sin, and you can call sin ignorance. The King James translation makes a promise in 'Thou shalt,' meaning that men will surely triumph over sin. But the Hebrew word, the word *timshel*—'Thou mayest'—that gives a choice. It might be the most important word in the world. That says the way is open. That throws it right back on a man. For if 'Thou mayest'—it is also true that 'Thou mayest not.' Don't you see?"

John Steinbeck
East of Eden

PREFACE

For more than fifty years following the end of World War II, the nearly six billion people inhabiting the planet Earth had been surreptitiously kept in stygian darkness about one of the greatest thefts in history: the confiscation by Nazi Germany during the war years of an estimated $580 million of Third Reich Central Bank gold—approximately $5.6 billion in today's values—along with as yet undetermined amounts in other assets. Those astronomical resources were stolen from governments and their peoples in countries Germany overran.

Though victims of all religious persuasions suffered substantial losses, the Jewish people sustained by far the greatest deprivations. Nearly twice as much as originally thought, according to the 1998 United States government report, *United States and Allied Wartime and Post War Negotiations with Argentina, Portugal, Spain, Sweden, and Turkey on Looted Gold and German External Assets.* For not only were they stripped of their worldly resources—down even to the gold fillings of their teeth—but six million also were murdered in death camps.

Inarguably that savagery certainly was humankind's most heinous mass extermination ever, a slaughter which has come to be known as the Holocaust.

Among the "neutral" or "non-belligerent" countries upon which this book focuses that *accepted* the over
$300 million in stolen gold bullion (worth $2.6 billion in
today's prices) between 1939 and 1945 in exchange for critically vital goods and raw materials that helped sustain the
Nazi regime and prolong its war effort, were Switzerland,
Spain, Portugal, Italy, Sweden, Norway, and Turkey.

Even Argentina, an ocean away from the European
war, had a role in those perfidious misdeeds against the
Jewish people. That South American nation, which harbored fugitive Nazi criminals after World War II, must bear
its own guilt in the Nazi plunder of gold from the Jews.

Ironically, the role that the European nations played
in exchanging goods for Nazi gold was carried out—
despite repeated warnings by the Allies to cease and
desist—even when Germany was in retreat from steam-
rolling Allied advances on all fronts and those countries no
longer had any reason to fear aggression from Germany.

Switzerland, among all the "neutral" countries, figured most prominently in ravaging Jewish resources and is
now receiving condemnation as the greatest plunderer of
Nazi gold and other assets during and after World War II.
Unquestionably, Switzerland was the principal banker and
financial broker for the Germans in those years of
upheaval and turmoil, but, as this book shows, was not the
lone culprit.

Three-quarters of the confiscated $580 million
($5.6 billion in today's market) went to the Swiss National
Bank's own account. The rest went to the accounts of
other countries depositing funds at Bern's principal financial institution.

Spain, Portugal, Italy, Sweden, and Turkey all provided Adolf Hitler's regime with goods and capital to underwrite his country's six-year war effort from 1939 to 1945. In this book we look deeply into the roles played by these countries and show how they are implicated.

Had the "neutral" Swiss and other nations in the "non-aggression" category not engaged in this calumnious deception, the war might well have ended months, even years, sooner. The Third Reich couldn't possibly have bankrolled its purchases of war materials by itself. Germany's own monetary resources (the reichsmark) were virtually worthless in the world market where Germany was obtaining its war supplies.

After the war less than twenty million dollars in looted gold and metal was returned by the other neutrals. Switzerland only returned fifty-eight million dollars of the stolen gold it got from the Nazis.

It has been no easy task to produce this book with the real story of the *who, what, when, where, how,* and *why* gold and treasures were plundered from the more than six million victims of the Holocaust and found their way into the coffers of European nations.

The research utilized includes scores of sources that provided significant quantities of previously unavailable documents—some compiled by the Office of Strategic Services (OSS), the precursor of the Central Intelligence Agency; the United States Army; the State, Justice, Defense, and Treasury Departments; the Federal Bureau of Investigation; the Federal Reserve Board; the National Archives and Records Administration; National Security Agency; and the United States Holocaust Memorial Museum.

The American Jewish Commission on the Holocaust, formed in 1981 on the initiative of a number of the country's most prominent Jewish leaders, under the aegis of former United States Supreme Court Justice Arthur J. Goldberg, provided invaluable research and documentation for this book.

Their mission led them to conduct an objective and deeply-penetrating inquiry into the actions and attitudes of American Jewish leaders and organizations, dwelling on the Holocaust just before and during the years of World War II, when the great tragedy was in progress.

The voluminous report titled *American Jewry During the Holocaust,* prepared by former Ambassador Seymour Maxwell Finger, a professor of political science at the City University of New York, was compiled "not to make moral judgments but rather to enable later generations to learn from this experience whatever might help prevent a similar tragedy from ever again befalling the Jews or any other people."

Another monumental report added much information. *U.S. and Allied Efforts to Recover and Restore Gold and Other Assets Stolen or Hidden by Germany During World War II* or the *Eizenstat Report* has provided unlimited and invaluable insight into unpublished accounts of the sordid history relating to Nazi Gold.

In addition, *Holocaust Gold Credit to the Nation Prepared by the Research Department of the Holocaust Educational Trust in London* added important insights, as did information from "Le Monde's La Complicite Francaise dans la politique antijuive," the report on the International Conference on Nazi Gold in London, *The Bergier Report,* the *Report of the*

International Commission of Independent Experts, Senator
Alfonse D'Amato's July 1998 Banking Committee Hearing,
"Swiss Banks, the 1946 Washington Accords and Current
Developments in Holocaust Restitution," and the report
compiled by Germany's Federal Archives.

More vital information was found in the recently
released addition to the report referred to earlier, *United
States and Allied Wartime and Post War Negotiations with
Argentina, Portugal, Spain, Sweden and Turkey on Looted Gold
and German External Assets.* The complete study was man-
dated in May 1997 by President Bill Clinton at the behest of
United States Senator D'Amato, Republican of New York,
to catalogue to the fullest extent possible United States and
Allied efforts to recover and restore gold and other assets
stolen by Nazi Germany, and to determine to what extent
the recovered German assets were returned to their rightful owners—the survivors of the Holocaust as well as to
the heirs whose kin were made to pay the ultimate sacrifice
in Hitler's death camps and gas ovens.

Significantly, the seven-month government study
and its supplement, prepared by William Z. Slany, the State
Department's historian, adopts a harsh and unforgiving view
of the "initially valiant, but ultimately inadequate, steps taken
by the United States and the Allies to make assets available
for assistance to stateless victims of Nazi atrocities."

Newspaper articles, in-depth personal interviews,
and reports both on and off the record from many voices
in many nations also provided needed direction and important clues.

In addition, the revised edition of *Nazi Gold:*

Information from the British Archives provided invaluable information through their in-depth consideration of the question of whether non-monetary gold, and in particular gold taken from Holocaust victims, might have found its way into the Tripartite Gold Commission's monetary gold pool.

A variety of explanations will be addressed in this book to analyze why civilized governments have suddenly turned inquiring minds to matters that occurred during the last world war, over fifty years ago.

A primary reason is the declassification of intelligence documents in many countries around the world, including Eastern Europe, which provide concrete proof of what happened. There is also the work of researchers using computerized databases and the opening of such museums as the United States Holocaust Memorial Museum. The fiftieth anniversary of the end of the war generated new interest as well as the fact that 600,000 Holocaust survivors have reached the end of their lives and the next generation wants to understand their past. Working on behalf of the survivors, the World Jewish Congress led by Edgar Bronfman, Israel Singer, and Elan Steinberg have brought the issue to the foreground. Impetus has also come from Lord Janner who advanced the idea for the London Conference; a bipartisan group in the United States Congress, led by Senator D'Amato and President Clinton; the Volcker Commission in Switzerland; and the World Jewish Restitution Organization. These voices among others have sought to end the too long silence concerning the real facts not only about Nazi Germany and the Holocaust but those countries and individuals who profited from its victims' possessions.

For too long, the remaining victims and their descendants have searched for justice, only to be largely ignored or lied to by the benefactors of those ill-gotten gains, the governments of Switzerland, Turkey, Spain, Portugal, Italy, Sweden, Norway, the Netherlands, and the Latin American nation, Argentina.

Argentina may deny the role it played in helping finance Germany's war, but it cannot deny that its banks received capital transfers of Swiss-held Nazi gold shipped to that South American country to support the new lifestyles of fleeing Nazis after Germany's collapse in 1945. And although long denied, the Allies—France, Britain, and America—have also reaped profits from the plundered victims.

The human factor plays a predominant role in this unfolding chronicle. How individuals and families were deprived of their possessions and their lives will add its poignant dimension to this chronicle.

The modus operandi of Nazi Germany's calculated massive and systematic plundering and the way it was designed to buttress the efforts of the orderly, intentional, and essential financing of the German war machine by using "neutral" countries as banking and financial facilities to aid and abet the Third Reich in its diabolical scheming will also be revealed.

Further, it will be exposed that the way the reichs-mark, Nazi Germany's principal currency largely unusable during the war, was substituted for by Hitler with looted Jewish gold and shipped, first, to Switzerland and then on to other countries that helped the Nazis much more than was once thought, so that Germany could obtain desperately needed war materials.

The narrative will dwell, too, upon the way the Reichsbank, the German Central Bank, knowingly and willingly received gold plundered from the central banks of neighboring countries which the Nazis overran and, in addition, had a "special record of credit and debit" called the Melmer Account, for the deposit of jewelry, watches, and even dental fillings of Jews who became victims of the Holocaust.

The way the gold from both monetary and non-monetary sources was ultimately smelted or resmelted into gold bullion and its origins effectively disguised with false markings will also be revealed. It will be shown how this bloodstained gold found its way not only to the neutral nations but even into Allied coffers.

Microfilm records at the National Archives have been utilized to reveal that on a single day of one year during that horrific period of history, an aggregate of loot was assembled from Jewish citizens that comprised 854 rings, one trunk of silver objects, and one trunk of dental gold amounting to 29.99 grams. Total worth: $1.5 million in World War II values—and ten times more by 1998 standards.

Too often, countries used neutrality to provide a pretext for avoiding moral consideration. Of course, neutrality is historically a well-established principle of international law, and smaller countries have used it over the years to protect themselves from the incessant number of European "brush" wars.

The Department of State report provides considerable insight into how the administration of President Harry S. Truman, failed in postwar negotiations to force the Swiss and other "neutral" countries to return the stolen treasure in a timely way after peace came.

The so-called 1946 Washington Agreement allowed many nations to continue to enrich themselves from their lucrative war profiteering. Switzerland, for example, emerged from World War II with its coffers filled with gold as one of the wealthiest nations in Europe. However, Switzerland, though the largest, was by no means the only guilty party.

Despite appeals from Allied negotiators to consider the moral imperatives, other countries demonstrated for all too long an obdurate reluctance to cooperate with Allied efforts to retrieve and redistribute the looted gold.

Many gave repeated protestations after the war that they had never received any looted Nazi gold. Yet, emerging reports of the "neutral" nations' culpability are incontrovertible.

According to the State Department report, Germany looted $579 million in gold during the war, about $5.6 billion in today's market. Around $400 million of that plundered gold went to Switzerland, and of that, between $185 and $289 million was for its own account in looted bullion. The rest was for the accounts of other depositor countries largely placed at the Swiss National Bank.

American leadership in the postwar negotiations to retrieve Nazi gold and other assets, while ostensibly well-intentioned, was in actuality limited. There was a demonstrable lack of senior level administration support for a tough and consistent United States negotiating position with the neutrals who had hoarded Nazi gold.

Moreover, there was an unjustifiable lack of attention to ensure the implementation of arrangements already negotiated, such as the 1946 Washington Agreement and the Tripartite Gold Commission that was established by the United States, Britain, and France to supervise restitution.

Turkey, for instance, which had millions in Nazi assets, returned nothing!

Italy, which had itself grabbed significant Jewish wealth during the German occupation of that country in World War II, did not give up the loot they acquired until many years after the end of the war, and gave only a portion of its share.

Even the Vatican had in its coffers tarnished gold.

The joint failure of these countries to make greater efforts to place the Nazi gold in the hands of the proper benefactors—families and descendants of the victims, as well as the few remaining survivors of the Holocaust—is under scrutiny.

"Wartime objectives were replaced by new Cold War imperatives," according to one of the conclusions the report cites. "For example, the Berlin Blockade in June of 1948 emphasizes this. The need to rebuild postwar Europe; the need to create NATO to contain the Soviet threat; also putting a democratic West Germany on its feet, and other security concerns with all neutral countries also took precedence."

Though facts and figures will be exposed in this book, there is a deep and abiding human element running through the entire narrative. For example, the experiences of Gizelle Weisshaus of Brooklyn, New York, who learned about the State Department report detailing how neutral countries were hoarding gold looted by the Nazis, is recounted.

"My thoughts at once turned to my many loved ones I lost to Hitler's madness," stammered the sixty-seven year old Romanian-born Holocaust survivor as she contemplated the way she'd spend her final years keeping her family's spirit alive through *mitzvahs* (good deeds) should she ever see any of the money.

"The money is not for myself," is the way Mrs. Weisshaus put it. "I need this money for charity work. There are many people who are suffering still. I know many [Holocaust survivors] today who are living on Social Security and are practically starving."

Today, former victims and their descendants are standing up to those who stole and are reclaiming their property. They are considerably unlike Dutch economics professor Victor Halberstadt's father (himself hidden by a Catholic family during the war) who, like many of the dispossessed, went back to the Amsterdam apartment the family lived in before World War II only to find a Dutch family living there using his family's furniture—and walked away glad to have survived.

Another New Yorker, Hinde Fekete, now in her fifties, was a four-year-old when she was snatched from her father's arms and sent to a concentration camp. Her family had the impression they had made it safely to Switzerland from Belgium after their homeland was overrun by the Nazis. This belief was soon shattered.

"My family was expelled by the supposedly neutral Swiss and they later died at the Auschwitz concentration camp," said Mrs. Fekete.

"Unfortunately the State Department report has come too late. It took fifty years to unmask Switzerland. And I say it's important the world knows that Switzerland was not neutral. Germany was depositing the gold in their banks, and the Swiss were depositing Jews in their gas chambers."

A third New Yorker, Elias Abraham, seventy-two, serves as another but by no means last example of Holocaust survivors who have been deprived of their family and possessions.

A Czechoslovak native who lost his brother, parents, and grandparents to the Nazis, Abraham shudders when he remembers that the two gold fillings the Nazis pulled from his mouth might have been smelted into a gold bar that's sitting in a bank somewhere.

"These countries have no right to keep that money; it should be immediately dispersed between the needy and all people who are still alive—and the sooner the better," said Abraham, who came to the United States in 1948 and refused to sign up for reparations from the German government years ago "because no money can pay for my parents' blood."

"But I have changed my mind. I just registered. I find it very important that everyone gets their money."

This then—the truth about the history, the victims' possessions and the present status of that ill-begotten Nazi gold—is what this narrative will reveal.

PART I

A Tarnished History

CHAPTER 1

Suspicions of Thievery

Gold from Austria, Czechoslovakia, and the independent city of Danzig had already been appropriated by the Nazis when Britain declared war on Germany in September 1939. According to the British Ministry of Economic Warfare based on correspondence between them, the Treasury, and Bank of England officials, ninety-seven million dollars had come to the Reichsbank just when it was almost broke. The bank had already defaulted on loans, exhausted its credit, and antagonized the international Jewish community. To gain needed materials, Germany had to barter. Her economic base, despite her efforts to boost productivity and stockpile essential raw materials, was in deep trouble. More gold was desperately needed to fund the plans the Nazis were making.

This was a goal the British had to foil.

To do it, Britain needed to monitor Germany's gold acquisitions and determine how, when, and where they would be funneled. An economic blockade, to be successful, would have to stop the Germans from purchasing vital raw materials for the production of armaments and war supplies.

There's no clear clue to pinpoint precisely when the world first became aware of Adolf Hitler's confiscation of persecuted Jewish citizens' gold.

However, March 1940 can stand as the date when the United States became "officially" aware that an atrocity had occurred on the European continent more than twenty months before the Japanese strike against the American fleet in Pearl Harbor.

On March 20 of that year a cablegram was dispatched from American personnel in Berlin to the State Department in Washington describing the forced movement of Jewish people from Germany to Poland. The wire warned that the moneys the emigrants were carrying might be confiscated at the border.

But details were woefully lacking and the true severity of the situation was never transmitted to President Franklin Delano Roosevelt, who had to rely on other sources for scanty information about Hitler's treatment of Germany's Jewish citizens. By then, World War II had been under way for almost eight months.

The United States ambassador to London at the

time was Joseph P. Kennedy, who had held the post since 1937. Kennedy had sired a family of three daughters and four sons, one of whom, John Fitzgerald Kennedy, became President in 1962.

Ambassador Kennedy, who had been openly advocating a wish to see the United States avert any confrontation with Nazi Germany and, indeed, was promoting a policy of appeasement, was stunned when Hitler unleashed his ground and air forces against Poland in the invasion that exploded into war.

A few days earlier, Kennedy had been handed a secret message from Alex Kirk, the chargé d'affaires at the United States Embassy in Berlin, that there would be war within a week. The note was conveyed to London by Kennedy's son Jack. The future president was returning to England after being dispatched by his father on a "fact-finding tour of Europe to determine the feelings of the populace about Germany's seeming bent to start a war for territorial gains that it had long coveted."

The elder Kennedy's stance in favoring an alliance with Germany was well known by then. That posture, as the ambassador viewed it, "would lead to international peace and prosperity and result in having America become the largest beneficiary of such a move... To put in a billion or two now will be worth it, for if it works we will get it back and more."

Meanwhile, England's Prime Minister Neville Chamberlain who had done nothing about Hitler's invasion of Poland was succeeded in office by Winston Churchill. With the declaration of war by England, the German Luftwaffe began round-the-clock bombing of Britain.

Hitler's air attacks followed a series of catastrophic events put into motion by the Axis powers, including the collapse of France and the Russian invasion of the Baltic Republics and of Rumania. Britain literally stood alone in Europe as the last democracy that was actively resisting the swiftly charging ground and air forces of the Third Reich.

Although Churchill's intrepidness against the Nazi hordes and his oratory inspired the people of England and of America, Ambassador Kennedy still tried to convince President Roosevelt that England had no chance to survive the war. He persisted in his entreaties that the United States make a deal with Hitler to settle the conflict.

Even before the invasion of Poland, as was explained, the White House was receiving small bits of information about the forced movement of Jewish people from Germany to Poland as well as warnings that the moneys and other valuables they were carrying were possibly being confiscated at the border by storm troopers. Although the German government offered assurances that no steps were being taken to confiscate the property of enemy aliens of Jewish origin, it was reliably established that German Jews as well as Jewish citizens of countries overrun by Nazi forces were not that fortunate.

Long before the Reich Citizenship Law of 1941 was codified, the working principles of the law had become common practice: All German Jews who left Germany were deprived both of their citizenship and their property.

The restrictions that were incorporated into that law applied to all Jewish people being deported to Poland

and German-occupied territories of the Soviet Union, as well as Jews who escaped to Allied or neutral countries.

In the findings of the study *U.S. and Allied Efforts to Recover and Restore Gold and Other Assets*, Department of State chief historian Slany spoke understandingly about "the unique circumstances of World War II [whereby] neutrality collided with morality; too often being neutral provided a pretext for avoiding moral considerations. Historically a well-established principle in international law, neutrality served through centuries of European wars as a legitimate means by which smaller nations preserved their political sovereignty and economic viability.

"But it is painfully clear that Argentina, Portugal, Spain, Sweden, Switzerland, Turkey, and other neutral countries were slow to recognize and acknowledge that this was not just another war. Some never did. Nazi Germany was a mortal threat to Western civilization itself, and had it been victorious, to the survival of even the neutral countries themselves."

The thoroughly researched 212-page report contains a foreword written by Under Secretary of Commerce for International Trade Stuart E. Eizenstat, who was appointed by President Bill Clinton to be special envoy of the State Department on property restitution in Central and Eastern Europe. Eizenstat's first effort was to appoint Dr. Slany, the State Department historian, to conduct the study.

Slany immediately recruited eleven principal participants to carry out the mandate "to describe to the fullest extent possible, United States and Allied efforts to recover and restore gold and other assets stolen by Nazi

Germany, and to use other German assets for the reconstruction of postwar Europe.

"It also touches on the initially valiant, but ultimately inadequate, steps taken by the United States and the
Allies to make assets available for assistance to stateless
victims of Nazi atrocities.

"America itself remained a non-belligerent for over
two years following the outbreak of the war in Europe,"
Eizenstat wrote.

"Restrictive United States immigration policies
kept hundreds of thousands of refugees from finding
safety in the United States, most tragically exemplified by
our refusal to allow the [mercy ship] *St. Louis* to dock with
its cargo of refugees—many of whom perished after the
vessel was forced to return to Europe.

"Nevertheless, the United States froze German
assets in April 1940 (twenty months before entering the
war), conducted little trade and commerce with Nazi
Germany, and generously assisted Britain, the Soviet Union,
and the anti-Nazi cause—despite fierce domestic opposition—through programs like Lend-Lease."

CHAPTER 2

Nazi Carnage on Latvia

On July 1, 1941, the Nazis marched into the Latvian seaport of Riga but did not destroy the city as the Krauts serving in the Kaiser's armies had done in September 1917 during World War I.

Hitler's Panzer divisions had no need to level the city this time around. The Soviet Union, which had annexed Latvia in 1939 at the beginning of World War II in a quid pro quo with Germany and made it an "independent state" of the USSR, had its armies in flight after Der Fuhrer stabbed ally Josef Stalin in the back and declared war on him.

Now the region's riches—wood pulp, paper, cellulose, matches, veneered goods, paints and varnishes, textiles, boots, shoes, and so many other products needed for the Nazi war effort—were ripe and ready to be plundered from its storehouses and factories. As were all the worldly goods of Riga's Jewish community—the people's jewelry and cash, household furnishings, clothing, and even the gold in their teeth.

Reva Shefer at age seventy-six has vividly searing recollections of the day the Nazis stormed into Riga.

Reva was nineteen years old then and her memory was scarred all at once by the trauma of seeing her father taken from their home in his pajamas and shot on the street outside.

Immediately after, her grandfather was hauled away and locked up with hundreds of other men in the landmark Great Choral Synagogue, an architectural masterpiece and a community retreat that harbored what had been Riga's thriving Jewish populace. His fate remained a mystery to Reva for three days. Then the awful truth about his ultimate future flickered before her terrified eyes as the Nazis set the synagogue ablaze and killed all who were inside, then let the magnificent structure burn to the ground.

Only Reva, her mother, grandmother, and younger brother were spared—for the time being. They were herded into Riga's ghetto, where they existed until the Germans materialized in full force on December 7 and hauled everyone they hadn't yet executed to concentration camps.

"We were surrounded by drunken police shouting

at us and throwing things," Reva Shefer recalled. "We were not people. Anybody could do anything they wanted to us.

"That night, as they emptied the ghetto and we walked five abreast down the middle of the road, I broke free with my brother and two others. We ran and hid in a shack that had recently been deserted.

"For some reason, we weren't found. I remember that night and what I felt—the awful fear of having to wonder how soon we'd be caught and made to pay the penalty of escaping from our Nazi captors.

"Fortunately, we weren't found and for the next few days and perhaps it was weeks—I just cannot remember for how long we played the cat-and-mouse game with the storm troopers.

"When we finally eluded our pursuers, we set about trying to keep out of their sights for good. For the next two years I managed to hide in twelve different places around Riga, almost always with the help of Latvian gentiles.

"For those two years I never walked in the light of day. I slept on tables, under beds, and even in the forest. I feared every sound, every knock at every door, every glance I received.

"I just cannot—I don't want to—tell you everything that happened during those two dreadful years. I simply don't want to give you the horror..."

The occasion for Reva Shefer's voluble outpouring about the suffering she endured at the hands of the Nazis was occasioned on November 18, 1997, when she was summoned with her husband to make their presence felt at a glorious old building in Riga that was once the central Jewish Theater in the Latvian capital and then became the home of the Institute of Marxism-Leninism under Soviet rule.

Reva Shefer and her husband awakened in a high state of excitement that morning of November 18—actually, hours before dawn. Reva showered in the comfortable apartment she shares with her husband, then began dressing in the wardrobe she had been selecting to wear for the past several days.

She stood before the dresser mirror and slipped into a plaid tartan suit. When she felt comfortable with its fit and appearance on her slender frame, Reva wiggled her feet into a pair of black orthopedic shoes.

She then stood up and took her husband's arm. The couple was driven to the Jewish Theater and escorted to the podium, where the Communist symbol of the hammer and sickle is still etched in the wall but which has been overshadowed by a Star of David that now commands the eye's attention above the dais.

Other victims of Nazi persecution—all of them survivors of the Holocaust—had gathered at the Jewish Theater to take part in the ceremonial rite that would, in a few days, lead to their own remuneration from the Swiss government for their sufferings.

It had been more than a year since Switzerland's seemingly indelible image of neutrality in World War II and probity in matters of finance was shattered by disclosures that its banks laundered stolen gold for the Nazis. Mrs. Shefer and the others who'd been invited to this community center were earmarked to receive reparation payments for suffering they endured during the Holocaust.

The Swiss government, which had been attacked widely in the preceding months for its hypocrisy, venality, and unwillingness to admit its role as a banker for Nazi gold, had finally relented to a degree by caving in to world opinion and taking the first visible steps at making amends.

The Swiss set up a fund of $200 million through an arrangement with a consortium of its banks and businesses that was to provide each of 27,000 eligible Holocaust survivors in Eastern Europe with up to $1,000 each.

Of course that figure is a mere drop in the bucket compared with the findings of how much Nazi gold the Swiss banks held as a "neutral nation" in World War II. But it was a start.

"This distribution is a positive step," declared Gideon Taylor of the American Jewish Joint Distribution Committee, which had undertaken the task of allocating the funds to eligible recipients.

"We are now moving from the realm of discussion to that of action," he stressed.

That fund, unfortunately, was the only visible part of Switzerland's attempt to make amends. Other than the still-ongoing historic study and findings by the United States that shook up the Swiss and made them begin to come clean, the Alpine nation was moving toward making reparations with what could only be described as considerable lethargy.

In Switzerland, there was only one government

commission assigned to investigate the banks and one other to examine the Swiss war record.

Both were performing dismally. Neither investigative body had produced a single finding in the year or so that it had undertaken its probative duties. The same can be said about attempts to resolve the obligations of the other "neutrals"—Sweden, Spain, Portugal, Italy, and Turkey, as well as France and Argentina—who have been sitting on Nazi gold received in exchange for vital raw materials and/or art treasures for more than a half century.

The *Washington Post's* John Goshko reported that, according to the June 2, 1998 report by Stuart Eizenstat:

- Portugal and Spain provided nearly all of Germany's tungsten used to produce weapon-grade steel.
- Sweden supplied iron ore and ball bearings.
- Turkey, in some war years, provided 100% of Germany's chromite to harden steel for making armor.

In fact, five neutral countries handled $500 million in assets for the German government, and $300 million ($2.7 billion in today's dollars) was routed through Switzerland to pay Portugal, Spain, Sweden, and Turkey for German supplies and armaments. Part of the gold used to make these payments was looted from the wedding rings and gold teeth of Holocaust victims.

As for Reva Shefer, she was handed a $400 check from Switzerland for the suffering she endured during the Holocaust.

That was the very first payment by the Swiss in

response to the disclosures of the last year—and others were to be made in Riga in the days and weeks ahead.

Was the $400 payment to Mrs. Shefer enough?

The question was put to Rolf Block, the fund's president.

"What could ever be enough?" he responded. "But it is a start, and for those survivors living on fifty-dollar-a-month pensions, it may not be as little as you might think."

Although Riga was once a center of world Judaism, Reva Shefer was among only eighty Holocaust survivors still alive in Latvia—and in line to receive reparation payments from the Swiss.

In 1935, nearly 50,000 Jews lived in Riga alone—almost 13 percent of the city's population. Most were killed in the concentration camp that Reva escaped at Salaspils—or were slain in the forests outside the city where they had sought refuge after eluding arrest.

The $400 check handed to Reva Shefer was deemed to be minuscule considering the suffering she had endured in having to "live like an animal in the ghetto, losing most of her family to the Nazis, and having had to spend two years hiding in cellars, toilets, and forests to stay alive.

"The amount means nothing," Mrs. Shefer stated as her rich voice wavered only briefly. "I care about the fact of it. No matter what it took, finally, after all these decades, somebody is saying, 'You suffered and we know it.'"

Mrs. Shefer's reserve wasn't shared by all who attended the ceremony in the Jewish Theater.

Seventy-two-year-old Margers Vestermanis, chief of the Jewish Documentary Project in Riga, said there was not then, nor will there ever be, a reason to celebrate restitution.

"I cannot be excited today," he told the 150 persons gathered at the event, "because I have to remind you that more than a half century ago, when millions were being slaughtered by the Nazis, the world pretended that it did not see.

"The world pretended not to see the mass graves, the crematories, the camps. They did not see our suffering and our death.

"But the world did see something. They saw our property, and without any shame they went to take it, to grab it."

There was no response from the Swiss, who obviously were the primary targets of Vestermanis's wrath. But there were some final words from the slightly-built and lustrously gray-haired Reva Shefer.

When asked what she would do with her money, Mrs. Shefer responded without any tinge of regret, "I hoped I'd be able to buy my first washing machine. But they cost more than four hundred dollars. So I guess I'll keep washing the clothes by hand."

What Reva Shefer had left unsaid when she relived the first days of her close encounters with the Nazis was this poignant anecdote that was related by a historian familiar with the way this courageous woman managed to escape with her life:

"Mrs. Shefer survived the most perilous moment of her captivity by slipping away from a column of prisoners being herded to the forest of Rumbula outside Riga, where 25,000 Jews were shot on November 30 and December 8, 1941...."

CHAPTER 3

A Twofold Attack

In 1875, Deutsche Reichsbank, Germany's national bank, was founded. It remained an independent institution until Hitler came to power in 1933. At that point, he proclaimed a new banking act so that he could appoint his own representatives to the Reichsbank Board of Governors.

When Austria was annexed in 1938, the Reichsbank took over the gold reserves from the Austrian national bank.

Then, when Danzig was occupied, the Reichsbank took over its gold reserves. Although it was not known at the time, in January of 1939 the president of the Reichsbank, Hjalmar Schacht, and several board members wrote Hitler that there was no longer currency or gold reserves at the bank. Soon after, Hitler put the Reichsbank wholly under his control.

From the earliest days of World War II, the United States and its Allies realized the importance to the German war effort of imports from the "neutral" and "nonbelligerent" nations of Europe and elsewhere.

Germany's industrial production and military capacity depended on vital materials, such as bearings and iron ore from Sweden, precision tools and ammunition from Switzerland, chrome from Turkey, and wolfram (tungsten ore) from Portugal. The Third Reich depended on the non-warring nations for badly needed supplies for its war economy.

"The arrangement for paying for these imports also drew increasing attention from the United States and its Allies, as did the Allied effort to counter those arrangements," according to the Department of State's findings in *Property Restitution in Central and Eastern Europe.*

The United Kingdom instituted a program to obtain goods from the neutral countries and turned over its management to the Ministry of Economic Warfare (MEW).

American efforts in this endeavor were started in 1940, more than a year before the Japanese attack on Pearl Harbor, after President Roosevelt recognized the need for the United States, although still "neutral," to lend a big hand to Britain in carrying out an effective economic blockade on Germany.

"Both United States and British authorities were determined to minimize Axis opportunities to benefit from the large amounts of gold and United States currency held in occupied countries as well as in Switzerland, Sweden, Spain, Portugal, Turkey, and Argentina," the *Property Restitution* study continued.

The main concern of the Treasury Department in the early years of the war was to prevent the Nazis from using the financial resources of the United States to finance their military campaigns and occupation costs.

One way to achieve that goal was to regulate monetary transactions in foreign exchange or property dealings in which any foreign party held an interest.

To assist the Treasury Department in that task, President Roosevelt issued Executive Order 8380 on April 10, 1940. It froze Norwegian and Danish assets in the United States as soon as Norway and Denmark fell to invading German armies.

Eventually, every country in Europe except Great Britain was included in that executive order, as well as China and Japan. The Foreign Fund Control (FFC), established in 1940 with the Office of the Secretary of the Treasury and made a separate bureau within the Treasury Department in September 1942, administered the freeing of controls and the permitted use of frozen assets only with a license granted by the department.

No citizen or company from those countries could use funds or properties in the United States without a Treasury Department license. Only after the governments of "neutral" Sweden, Spain, Portugal, and Switzerland gave the United States assurances that they would forbid transactions involving blocked countries or individuals did the United States permit transactions that involved any of those "neutral" countries and their citizens.

Tangier did not come under the Spanish general license and so remained blocked as part of France, which like the other countries had been taken over by the Germans.

Turkey and Argentina did not lend assurances that they would cooperate in the offer advanced by the United States and thus were not granted licenses.

The Soviet Union—as yet not stabbed in the back by its "ally," Germany—received a general license without providing such assurances. The Federal Reserve monitored transactions (over $5,000 for Switzerland) under Treasury Department supervision.

The bootlegging of foreign moneys—especially French francs—into and through Switzerland began as early as the spring of 1941, according to records kept in Bern and stingily yielded to the United States during postwar investigations on behalf of victimized Jews.

Those funds were destined for transfer to the French colonies via Lisbon. Jewish and other refugees entering Switzerland were reportedly bringing large sums of dollars with them as they fled Nazi advances in their countries.

As World War II raged in 1941, the United States Treasury Department believed that nationals of Axis countries could be selling their interests in accounts blocked in the United States to Swiss purchasers, either voluntarily or under duress, and that those funds could become available to the Axis.

While few details were forthcoming, the total foreign holdings in Swiss banks at the end of 1942 were estimated to be several billion Swiss francs, with German and old Austrian accounts estimated at more than $116 million.

And how honorable and aboveboard were the "neutral" Swedes, Spanish, Portuguese, Turks, and Argentines in their dealings with Germany and the stolen Jewish gold that they were known to have in their possession?

The issue of Nazi gold was then and is today tied inevitably to the Nazi policy to exterminate the Jews, the "Holocaust." America still felt the effects of the Great Depression in the late 1930s and followed a strict and unwavering isolationist policy in all foreign affairs. There was a mind-set in the United States which made most Americans unwilling to be drawn into European power struggles or to take sides between the tyrannical Adolf Hitler, who had come to power in Nazi Germany, and his intended victims.

Not until the Japanese attack on Pearl Harbor on December 7, 1941 did that attitude change. By then, nothing could be done by America for Jewish victims because the war in Europe was being waged by the Germans with full force and furor.

"Finally, in December 1942, the United Nations issued a brief but eloquent statement on the mass slaughter of Jews; this was a full eighteen months after it had begun.

"They made little or no attempt until very late in the war to rescue Jews from the Holocaust, and in some cases actually obstructed such attempts by others.

"There was great concern about where they [the U.N.] could put any massive number of Jewish refugees. Their attitude on the subject was construed by the Nazi authorities as tantamount to acquiescence."

The relevance of the gold taken from Holocaust victims to Hitler's war effort was of concern to the Allies from very early in the war.

"The Reich Citizenship Law of November 25, 1941, codified actions that were already commonplace in depriving all German Jews who left Germany of their German citizenship and declaring their property forfeited. This decree applied to Jews being deported to Poland and German-occupied territories of the Soviet Union, as well as to those Jews who had escaped to Allied or neutral countries.

"By late 1942, German authorities were beginning to confiscate property from all residents of occupied countries who had fled abroad. All visible wealth was confiscated, with the exception of a small percentage, usually between 10 and 12-1/2 percent, that the emigrant was permitted to retain and export abroad. In addition to providing foreign exchange for the Axis war effort, there was mounting evidence even in 1942 that individual members of the Nazi party personally profited from carrying out this confiscation."

Despite a half century of research, no single document has yet come to light to provide clear evidence that Adolf Hitler gave a written order for the Holocaust. Without that crucial paper, generations of historians, in the words of Alan Cowell, correspondent of the *New York*

Times in Bonn, "have veered from the right-wing revisionism of David Irving of Britain, who sought to discount Hitler's role, to a belief, embraced by American scholars like Richard Breitman and Daniel J. Goldhagen, that Hitler made the decision in early 1941—a thesis supported by the systematic killing of Jews later that year."

Cowell, whose dispatch ran in the *Times* on January 21, 1998, took note of the eminent German historian Hans Mommsen, who described Hitler as "a weak dictator," then cited the Holocaust as "the result of a horrendous bureaucratic process unfolding with its own momentum."

Generations of German students had learned that the detailed planning for history's biggest genocide first emerged from a conference of senior Nazis in a villa at Wannsee, near Berlin, precisely fifty-six years earlier, on January 20, 1942.

"But now," Cowell reported, "a thirty-four-year-old German scholar, Christian Gerlach, has set off a debate among historians with a new and contentious theory, based on a notation by Heinrich Himmler, the SS chief, discovered in previously secret Soviet archives and on other documents. The documents supposedly establish that Hitler did, indeed, make a personal decision to put to death German and all other European Jews under Nazi occupation, and announced it to his most senior Nazi followers on December 12, 1941."

In a recently published article, Gerlach argued that the decision was touched off by America's entry into the war after Pearl Harbor, at which time Hitler "decided it was time to redeem a prophecy made in early 1939 that a new

world war would mean the annihilation of all Europe's
Jews, not just those in the Soviet Union."

Gerlach argued further that the Wannsee conference
was called "to make clear that German Jews, many of whom
had already been deported to concentration camps in Eastern
Europe, were also to be included in the 'Final Solution.'"

Two other studies establish blame for the Holo-
caust: *American Jewry During the Holocaust* and *U.S. and Allied
Efforts to Recover and Restore Gold* (The Eizenstat Report).
The conclusions in each instance are not at great odds.

Compare these resolutions for their striking simi-
larities from each of the studies:

American Jewry: "The record shows that all Allied
governments were well aware of Hitler's extermination policy [as early as 1939] but, for a variety of reasons, were generally reticent and evasive about calling attention to the fact
that his target for genocide was the Jews."

As cited in earlier passages, it wasn't until
December 1942 that the fledgling United Nations issued its
alert bearing on the mass slaughter of Jews, which came
fully eighteen months *after* the killings had begun.

The U.S. and Allied Efforts report: "As early as March
1940, reports of forced movement of Jews from Germany
to Poland warned that the moneys they were carrying might
be confiscated at the border. Although the German government provided assurances that no steps were being
taken to confiscate the property of enemy aliens of Jewish
origin, it was already clear that German Jews as well as
Jewish citizens of countries overrun by German forces
would not be so fortunate..."

And they were not. They were slaughtered en masse. According to Christian Gerlach's profound presentation about the way the "Final Solution" came about:

"In mid-to-late 1941, a general order for the murder of German Jews had not yet been made." (Even though thousands of German Jews had been deported to concentration camps in Eastern Europe, and some had been killed even as Soviet Jews also were being methodically massacred).

"However, on December 18, 1941, Himmler met with Hitler and later noted that the discussion had covered 'The Jewish question/to be exterminated as partisans,' according to a document found in Soviet archives."

In his report from Bonn, *New York Times* correspondent Alan Cowell sums up his own introspection of the issue in these words: "Some historians believe that Himmler's remarks could have alluded to the way Hitler wanted to publicly depict the systematic killing of Jews.

"At the same time, the discovery of the Himmler note in the Soviet archives is seen as significant because of the overwhelming lack of documented evidence connecting Hitler to the Holocaust."

While a scholar such as Christian Gerlach has been able to put together with considerable substantiation when and how the Holocaust originated, the same cannot be said about the State Department's report, *U.S. and Allied Efforts to Recover Gold and Other Assets."*

That study fails totally to take into account when America first became aware of the way Hitler was killing Jews and seizing their gold and other assets. It adroitly sidesteps the issue with this carefully coined phraseology: "The immediate problems of caring for and providing for the victims of Nazism overshadowed in their immensity the issues that make up the subject of this report.

"Outstanding private historical scholarship has been carried out in recent years on United States refugee policy in World War II. Notwithstanding, an accurate and comprehensive review of United States Government records bearing on the tragic failure to rescue more than a few thousand victims of the Holocaust deserves to be the subject of a separate report."

Now a separate report tells the world about the way the Holocaust was carried out and the role the Swiss and other countries played in holding onto that loot of the nearly six million Jews who paid with their lives for Adolf Hitler's decision to commit the most heinous genocide in world history. Two highly authoritative sources—*American Jewry During the Holocaust* and Christian Gerlach—have set the record straight.

But they're not the only ones who have given us in-depth insights to how Hitler ordered the annihilation of Europe's Jews—and when he did so.

For instance, in 1942 and 1943 cables were intercepted from Portugal, Portuguese and Swiss bank accounts were monitored, and occasional confidential reports from His Majesty's representatives in Portugal were intercepted. One showed that an account in the Bank of Portugal could be traced to the Swiss National Bank. It showed gold which was thought to be purchases of Portuguese escudos. Another involved the sale of German gold to Swiss banks which purchased escudos and transferred them to a Lisbon Reichsbank account. Afterwards, the Portuguese bank used the Swiss francs to buy gold and put it into the Bank of Portugal account.

The whole story of how stolen gold was converted into orthodox financial holdings wasn't uncovered until the end of the war, but throughout it the British government, using the Ministry of Economic Warfare, was supplied with important information by the Treasury, the Foreign Office, and the Bank of England as well as by United States intelligence sources on how German gold was moved to neutral countries.

Another Portuguese Bank account was discreetly linked to a Reichsbank request to obtain gold that was in the Swiss National Bank and deposit it into the Portuguese Bank account.

Reports surfaced that Sweden and Spain were also pursuing similar deals. It seemed to Britain and, later, the United States, the neutrals were aiding and abetting the enemy.

Something had to be done. The British government began contacting its allies on whether a warning should be issued to these countries.

The consultation resulted in seventeen nations signing, on January 5, 1943, the Inter-Allied Declaration Against Acts of Dispossession, which the British government had championed. It stated that "the Allies intended to do their utmost to obstruct the enemy's looting." In order to do this, the Allies reserved the right to declare invalid all "transfers of, or dealing with, property, rights and interests of any description whatsoever" the property in enemy-occupied territories.

"No interest, dividends or capital repayments

would be received by or credited to persons residing in Sweden or Switzerland until collecting banks had received 'solemn and detailed declarations from selected banking institutions in these two countries, to the effect that the securities concerned are free from enemy taint.'"

In the inner circle of the Allied powers, there was little doubt that the ultimatum though politically important, could probably not achieve its goal. The truth was the Allies could do little to enforce the proviso and had to determine if the little they could do was advisable. In fact, one British official, G.L.F. Bolton of the Bank of England, thought the declaration could have the opposite effect and make the Nazis "take every possible legal step to hide or cloak the effects of their policy of looting Europe."

Nevertheless, in 1943 the Allies were trying to invoke a stronger position toward neutral countries dealing in Nazi gold. Little, however, was achieved and intelligence reports show that Switzerland continued to receive looted gold from Germany sent both to banks in Switzerland and in transit to the neutral countries. The British response was swift. G. Gibbs of MEW wrote to Sir David Waley on April 14, "We believe that it is not an exaggeration to say that Germany is in difficulties over her exchange position with most of the adjacent neutral countries and that, therefore, very shortly she will be forced to attempt to make greater use of her gold stock than she has done hitherto... There seems little doubt that Germany has sold since the war an amount equal to the whole of these stocks, and we have no reason to believe that she has added to her gold stocks by lawful means. Therefore, all the gold on which she can now lay hands may be said to be looted and they should be warned that if they accept gold from Germany they are laying themselves open to claims under the terms of the Inter-Allied Declaration of January 5."

A short while later a declaration was submitted by the Bank of England to the British Embassy in Stockholm. Although this statement did not deal with German gold exports, the American Treasury, a year later, made a more sweeping proposal about not recognizing the transference of title to looted gold disposed of by the Allies (see chapter on the United States for more detail). The neutral countries' lack of responsibility because of their illicit dealings with Germany in gold was criticized.

Warnings as well as a new declaration repudiating such trade were issued. The Soviet Union issued a similar declaration on February 23, 1944. The Swedish Ministry for Foreign Affairs was notified of it through their embassy in Moscow on February 29, 1944.

By late spring, the governments in exile advanced similar edicts. Both Norway and Belgium announced they also supported the declaration. However, the compliance proved to be more illusion than reality. Though much of this would not be known for decades, what was known convinced the Allies that the neutrals' acceptance of looted gold in exchange for war material and "laundering" of gold was like a bleeding wound afflicting the Allied drive to end the war.

In the early summer of 1944, the Allied governments, according to the British archives, made a new determination to try and control the looted gold traffic. The

Final Act of the United Nations Monetary and Financial
Conference occurring at Bretton Woods states in Article
VI that "in anticipation of their impending defeat, enemy
leaders, enemy nationals and their collaborators are transferring assets to and through neutral countries in order to
conceal them and to perpetuate their influence, power and
ability to plan future aggrandizements and world domination."

The Act called on the conference participants to
take immediate measures to prevent the transfer of enemy
assets including looted gold to their territories. Because of
this conference, the "Safehaven" program was established
to prevent the enemy from enjoying the fruits of both ill-
gotten and legitimate assets abroad.

Though that same month the British joined the
Americans in telling the Swiss they would not receive
deposit gold in which those in Germany and associated
countries had an interest, they did not require this from the
other neutrals.

The war was now moving to its final stages. Memos
from the Foreign Office to the Enemy Department
(August 21, 1944) considered the problem of compensat-
ing German Jews who had suffered property losses from
Nazi persecution or legal discrimination. The problem
proved to be a difficult one. It was impossible to turn the
clock back. Questions like, 'Will claims be individual or col-
lective ones through the courts?' abounded, but no definitive answers were found. The Swiss still didn't reply to the
Anglo-American approach.

As the summer of 1944 turned to autumn, talks
continued on what further warning and/or sanction

should be given. The British were wary of formal steps such as a demand for negotiations because the Allies would then have to come up with another plan if the country refused.

Instead, notes were sent to Portugal, Spain, Sweden, and Turkey reminding them of the resolution of Bretton Woods.

Meanwhile, the Swiss finally seemed to be willing to stop at least some of their trading in Nazi gold. On December 20, 1944, they blocked all Hungarian, Slovak, and Croatian assets in Switzerland.

The Historical Bust Society to the Soviet Empire established in 1945 can contribute one bizarre piece of information to the knowledge bank of the whereabouts of Nazi gold.

In 1945, when the Russian army entered Berlin, commandos of the NKVD, the super secret agency of the Russian elite, captured $31 million in Nazi gold (now worth hundreds of millions). Instead of turning it over to the government, they had it shipped to South America and melted down by the Historical Society to make busts of Russian leaders. The busts were disguised by being painted black, white, or brown and were shipped back to Russia.

Twenty-two of these busts are still in trust inventory. When the Society was "privatized" in 1994, they were forbidden to sell the originals. However, they now make "Registered and Numbered Replicas as well as replicas of the original one kilo Nazi gold bars" (complete with swastika and serial numbers) which they advertise can be shipped "to any country on earth on an insured basis."

CHAPTER 4

Swiss History

Of all the "neutral" nations of World War II, the one with the most pernicious role, which included the deepest and most crucial economic relationship with Nazi Germany, was, as has now been revealed, Switzerland.

The Swiss, of course, were in a precarious position once France fell, due to the fact that they were a landlocked country on Germany's border and at her mercy. The Allies were putting pressure on the neutral countries to stop or restrict their trade with Germany, but there had to be some balance in the case of Switzerland since Britain needed specialized imports and Swiss francs. Also, the Brits were wary that if too much pressure was brought to bear, Germany might occupy Switzerland as it had France, pushing Switzerland further into the Axis camp.

According to the State Department's *U.S. and Allied Efforts to Recover and Restore Gold and Other Assets Stolen or Hidden by Germany During World War II*, Switzerland's role during and after the war was "very mixed."

"Switzerland ended World War II as one of the wealthiest nations in Europe," Eizenstat writes in the foreword to the report.

"It conducted trade with the Allied countries as well as with the Axis powers. The Swiss National Bank maintained gold accounts for Nazi Germany throughout the entire war but also received deposits of the precious monetary metal from the United States, Canada, and Great Britain as well."

From the Allies standpoint, the "good guy" role the Swiss played during the war was in serving as "a key base for U.S. intelligence gathering" and as "a protecting power—most critically for its POWs."

Despite the approval of Allies, the Swiss government admitted shortly after the war that their policies on refugees during the war fell short in that innumerable amounts of displaced Jews looking to escape Nazi persecution were turned away from Swiss borders. Also, the Swiss government persuaded Nazi Germany to incorporate the 'J' stamp in their efforts to persecute Jews. The 'J' stamp allowed easy identification of Jews and in turn, made it nearly impossible for Jews to flee Germany or German-occupied countries and to find sanctuary in many other countries.

However, it must be said that "As many as about

50,000 Jewish refugees were admitted from 1933 until the end of the war.

"But Switzerland imposed on Jewish communities the burden of sustaining the Jews admitted after the outbreak of war." (Most were interned in labor camps).

"In August and December 1944, Switzerland admitted an additional 1,700 concentration camp inmates from Bergen-Belsen, and in February 1945 an additional 1,200 from Therienstadt."

However, the Swiss washed their hands of further involvement with those emigres because "various Jewish communities were required to support these additional survivors."

But no such demands were exacted on Swiss relatives of well over 100,000 non-Jewish refugees taken in after 1940. The government catered unselfishly to their wants and needs after welcoming them for settlement in the country.

At the end of 1944, "Secretary of State [Edward Reilly] Stettinius and his State Department colleagues concluded that, on balance, Switzerland's neutrality had been more a positive than a negative for the Allies during the war," the 1997 State Department study stated.

But the study found the conduct of the State Department to be totally misguided.

Labeling Stettinius's conclusion a "benign judgment," the report pointed out that the view expressed by the Roosevelt administration cabinet member was "not shared by other agencies, from the War Department and Treasury Department to the Office of Strategic Services (OSS), and the Justice Department."

Those agencies noted that in addition to its critical banking practices for the Nazis, Switzerland also engaged in direct industrial production for the Axis and helped protect the enemy's investments.

"Swiss shipping lines," the report went on, "also furnished Germany with a large number of boats for the transport of goods...[and] also allowed an unprecedented use of its railways to link Germany and Italy for the transport of coal and other goods.

"Switzerland provided Germany with arms, ammunition, aluminum, machines, and precision tools, as well as agricultural products.

"Swiss convoys [with immunity from aerial attack by Allied forces because of its neutral status] carried products from Spain across France through Switzerland to Germany.

"Swiss banks serviced Nazi markets in Latin America.

"This conduct continued even as the Germans retreated and the threat of invasion [of England by Nazi troops] evaporated.

"As late in the war as early 1945, Switzerland vitiated an agreement it had just reached with the United States to freeze German assets and to restrict purchases of gold from Germany."

Switzerland's indifferent and unconcerned attitude persisted in the postwar negotiations, and it was in that period which the State Department study, in the words of its historian William Slany, "is most incomprehensible."

The report's most damning findings against the

Swiss to surface are: "The Swiss teams were obdurate negotiators, using legalistic positions to defend their every interest, regardless of the moral issues also at stake. Initially, for instance, they opposed returning any Nazi gold to those from whom it was stolen, and they denied having received any looted gold. The Swiss contended that they had purchased it in good faith, that it was war booty obtained in accordance with international legal principles by the Third Reich during its victorious campaigns, and that there was no international legal principle which would entitle the Allies to recover and redistribute Nazi assets."

That stance flew squarely in the face of all that is honest and righteous, for the amount of Germany's gold reserves before the war was well known. The evidence presented in the State Department report is eminently clear and incontrovertible.

The Swiss National Bank and private Swiss bankers knew, as the war progressed, that the Reichsbank's own reserves had been depleted and that the Swiss were handling vast sums of looted gold.

Intelligence reports indicate the Swiss were totally aware of the Nazi gold heists from central bank reserves of neutral and occupied countries.

The ever-so-difficult-to-pin-down Swiss were finally corralled in 1946 with an agreement hammered out between the Allies and the Swiss at a gathering in the United States in Washington, D.C.

The accord obligated Switzerland to transfer 250

million Swiss francs ($58.1 million) in gold to the Allies for
the reconstruction of war-torn Europe, of which a portion
was to be redirected to the assistance of stateless victims,
for the most part Jews.

In that same agreement, the Swiss committed
themselves to identify dormant accounts that were heirless
and could be used for the benefit of Nazi victims.

That $58.1 million in German-looted gold to be
turned over to the Allies was far less than the range of
$185-to-$289 million in stolen funds the State and Treasury
Departments estimated was stashed at the end of the war
in the Swiss National Bank vault in its own country's
account.

An additional $120 million of German-looted gold
was also estimated to be on deposit for other countries at
that time. But the Swiss were not forthcoming about the
possible availability of those funds for the "humanitarian"
purposes they consented to participate in.

The $58.1 million finally coughed up by Switzerland
was promptly paid to the Tripartite Gold Commission
(TGC) for redistribution to claimant countries.

"But the other part of the Accord," according to
the State Department's report, "the liquidation of hundreds of millions of dollars in German assets, was neither
promptly nor even fully implemented." In an effort to
avoid fulfilling their part of the accord, the Swiss prolonged the process by raising arbitrary questions and bela-
boring fine points of the agreement. They also demanded
concessions from the United States including the unblocking of the same German assets the Swiss were supposed to
liquidate.

"They refused to make an exemption for the assets of surviving Jews from Germany and heirless German Jewish assets, and continued to make them subject to liquidation," William Slany's study reported.

"They refused to recognize any moral obligation to return looted Dutch gold when evidence became available after the conclusion of the 1946 negotiations."

By 1950 United States mediators grimly concluded that the Swiss "had no intention of ever implementing the 1946 Washington Accord."

Secretary of State Dean Acheson was then compelled to remark: "If Sweden has been an intransigent negotiator, then Switzerland was intransigence 'cubed.'"

While the United States was trying to make the Swiss acknowledge the Nazi gold stockpiled in their banks, action was taken in September 1946 to carry out a mandate of the past January's Paris Reparations Agreement reached by representatives of the United States, Britain, and France and which was called the Tripartite Gold Commission (TGC), to be headquartered in Brussels, Belgium.

Its task was to review and adjudicate claims from governments (not individuals) for the restitution of looted monetary gold recovered in Germany or acquired from the "neutrals" in their negotiations with the Allies.

The TGC was to ensure that each claimant country would receive restitution from the gold pool assembled by the Allies for the Commission in proportion to its loss of monetary gold at the hands of the Germans during the war.

Immediately after the TGC's establishment, ten nations made claims for the looted Nazi gold: Albania, Austria, Belgium, Czechoslovakia, Greece, Luxembourg, the Netherlands, Poland, Yugoslavia, and finally and ironically, Germany's wartime ally, Italy.

The Commission made its first distribution of $143 million from the gold pool in October 1947. Allocations went to Belgium, the Netherlands, Poland, and Yugoslavia.

France, one of the participants in the Tripartite's formation, did not file as a claimant but was entitled to receive reparations in the same manner as the ten other nations who filed for compensation.

A second round of allocations was made by the TGC between 1958 and 1966. A payment went out to Albania as recently as October 1996.

Overall, payments of 329 metric tons of gold, initially worth $380 million (today $4 billion) have been made to the claimant nations. Of that amount, $264 million came from the Foreign Exchange Depository (FED) that was formed in 1945 as a section of the Office of Military Government United States (OMGUS) by the American occupation force in Germany.

The FED was given supervision over the Reichsbank building in Frankfurt and made custodian of some 400 million reichsmarks in gold that the bank had hidden in the Merkers salt mines which were discovered by American troops who overran Germany in 1945.

Between 1945 and 1948, the FED collected, guarded, inventoried, and distributed to various countries nearly $300 million in gold bullion and gold coins ($2.9 billion today).

The FED worked with Allied governments, occupation authorities, and the Tripartite Gold Commission in inventorying that collection (consistent with official definitions of monetary and non-monetary gold), and making disbursements as agreed.

Just when it seemed everything was settled and terms had been arranged to have the Swiss release their ill-gotten Nazi gold, a voice against the terms of the Allied-Swiss agreement was sounded by United States Senator Harley Kilgore, who earlier had approved the pact.

Writing to President Harry S. Truman, Kilgore argued that the agreement "violates both in spirit and in form the Allies' pledge to route out Nazism and the German war potential" and would "leave intact Nazi resources and strengthen the hand of Nazis and Nazi collaborationists in Switzerland, and eventually in all neutral and Allied countries."

That was Kilgore's first volley. He had more to complain about, much more....

CHAPTER 5

A Bonanza—
The German Salt Mines

The effort to restore the Nazi gold to its rightful owners wouldn't have been possible at all had it not been for the intrepidness of United States troops in their mop-up operations during the last days of the war in April 1945.

Barely two months earlier, in February 1945, as the Allied forces closed in on Hitler's beleaguered troops, German officials took steps to relocate all German gold reserves in their possession to various remote hideaways south of Berlin.

About 400 million reichsmarks in gold were shipped

to the Merkers salt mines in Thuringia in the southwest region of eastern Germany and stashed in the labyrinthine mazes of that underground complex.

In addition, fifty million reichsmarks in gold were distributed to branch offices of the Reichsbank in central and southern Germany. Both the Merkers treasure and most of the lesser holdings were recovered by United States Armed forces in the closing days of the war and transported to Frankfurt am Main for what was intended to be purposes of "security and central accounting." According to MEW, the salt mine bonanza probably represented about 20 percent of all gold held in Germany.

When American troops stormed the Merkers mine, they found a spectacular and substantial stash, totaling two thousand containers filled with German Reichsbank gold, foreign currency, and other valuables.

Word was flashed to the Treasury Department in Washington about what the soldiers had found. Treasury Secretary Henry Morgenthau was advised by his top aide, Frank Coe, that the recovered bullion must be placed in a "reparations fund" until final plans were drafted to dispose of it.

Morgenthau didn't immediately respond to Coe's advisory, opting to "take the recommendation under advisement."

The preliminary part of the report, *U.S. and Allied Effort to Recover and Restore Gold,* states, "The Reichsbank treasure discovered by the United States Army in the salt mines at Merkers consisted of more than just gold bars and currency. Lying in one area of the mines were eighteen bags of silver and gold alloy bars and 189 parcels, boxes, suitcases, and trunks containing jewelry; gold and silver articles such as watches, wedding rings, cigarette cases, compacts, spectacle frames, candle sticks, and Passover cups; hundreds of pounds of dental crowns and fillings; and gold and silver coins.

"Also captured at Merkers was Albert Thoms, head of the Reichsbank's Precious Metals Department, who identified the 207 bags and containers as comprising the 'Melmer' account belonging to the SS [the German Secret Police, also known as Storm Troopers].

"The implications of this SS horde were immediately recognized. Brigadier General Frank McSherry suggested that 'this SS property contains evidence which might be useful in the prosecution of war criminals' and had the bags and containers stored in a separate room in the vaults of the Foreign Exchange Depository."

Over the next two years, British and American forces investigatory teams did a thorough examination of Reichsbank records and interrogated German officials involved in the thievery committed against Jews and Gentile "enemies" of the Third Reich and pieced together the story of the Melmer account. Most important sources of information were Thoms, Reichsbank Vice President Emil Puhl, and SS-Hautsurmfuhrer (Captain) Bruno Melmer, all of whom were interrogated by or at the request of the United States Army's Finance Division.

What they found was gathered together chiefly at Frankfurt.

According to records from the Nuremberg Trials, the FED's Central Files, and questioning of Puhl, who also provided sworn statements, this is the sum and substance of the way Hitler's secret police processed the loot they extracted from their victims:

Puhl claimed that sometime in the Summer of 1942, Reichsbank president and Reich Minister of Economy Walter Funk informed him of an agreement between Reich chieftain of the SS and its police force Himmler and Reich Finance Minister Lutz Schwerin vonn Krosigk, which sanctioned the Reichsbank to receive shipments of confiscated jewelry and securities from the SS.

After converting these shipments into cash, the bank was to use the funds to finance Germany's industrial enterprises.

Funk instructed Puhl to make the necessary arrangements for these shipments with Oswald Pohl, head of the SS Economic Administrative Main Office (SS-WVHA). After meeting with Pohl, Reichsbank Vice President Puhl relinquished responsibility for dealing with the shipments to Otto Frommknecht, the Reichsbank's director for cash and vault, and to Frommknecht's subordinate Thoms, the head of the bank's Precious Metals Department.

In his interrogation by the United States Army, Pohl confirmed that he met with Puhl in the summer of 1942, and the two worked "in the utmost secrecy in arranging for gold, jewelry, and foreign currency to be deposited in the Reichsbank—while gold teeth and crowns taken from concentration camp victims were to be melted down and the gold ingots transferred to the Reichsbank."

After those arrangements had been agreed upon, all subsequent shipments from the East and from concentration camps were forwarded to the Reichsbank.

As head of the Precious Metals Department, Thoms was able to provide many details about the SS shipments to officials of the Finance Division, which employed him to examine the captured Reichsbank records for traces of the looted central bank gold.

Thoms recalled that, again in the summer of 1942, Frommknecht sent him to Puhl, who informed him that the SS was about to begin delivering shipments to the Reichsbank that would contain not only gold, silver, and foreign currency, which was in the Reichsbank's area of competence, but also jewelry and other types of property whose disposal would be the Reichsbank's responsibility. Puhl also told Thoms that in the interest of secrecy the Reichsbank must dispose of those items itself.

Shortly after that meeting, Pohl's deputy, SS-Brigadefuhrer (Brigadier General) August Frank informed Thoms that an SS officer named Melmer would deliver the first shipment in a truck.

The shipment arrived on August 26, 1942, and other deliveries quickly followed.

The tenth delivery, in November 1942, was the first that included dental gold, and subsequent shipments contained even larger amounts of similar grisly metal.

The deliveries were first deposited into an account designated "Melmer." The Reichsbank then sorted and inventoried the deliveries before disposing of them.

Gold and silver bars and currency were bought by the bank at full value from the SS and small items like gold rings were sent to the Prussian Mint for smelting.

Jewelry and larger foreign currency were dispatched to the Municipal Pawnshop, which sold the better items abroad for foreign currency and sent most of the rest to the Degussa firm for resmelting.

Degussa, the Deutsche Gold-und Silber-Scheidean-stalt, was a large German industrial enterprise that engaged in the refinement of precious metals and manufacture of alloys and chemicals, including hydrogen cyanide, the poison used in the gas chambers at Auschwitz-Birkenau. (Today, the Frankfort-based firm and world's leading manufacturer of dental alloys, is facing a lawsuit filed in late August 1998 by Holocaust victims' families and survivors for billions of dollars.)

During the war, Degussa was allowed to keep a certain amount of gold for industrial purposes, but any gold exceeding the permitted amount was sold back to the Reichsbank and credit for the proceeds was deposited in the SS account.

Thoms noted that a few of the deliveries contained stamps or other designations indicating that they came from concentration camps or from the cities of Auschwitz and Lublin.

Reichsbank records confiscated at Merkers by the Army and studied by the Finance Division provided additional support for the claims of Thoms and Melmer about the way gold and other assets were appropriated by Hitler's Storm Troopers.

On June 5, the Four Powers in occupation of Germany—the United States, Great Britain, Russia, and France—issued a declaration assuming supreme authority in Germany. How to find, identify and gain control of looted gold dominated that year. During July and August 1945, at the Potsdam Conference, these powers appointed the Allied

Control Council in Berlin to claim custody of German-owned assets in other countries not already under Allied control. The Soviet Union would be able to claim property only in Bulgaria, Finland, Hungary, Romania and the eastern part of Austria. The Western Allies would take control of German property in former neutral nations.

A gold pool was established for the looted monetary gold recovered from Germany and the neutral countries. Later, it was distributed to formerly occupied countries. The idea of this so-called gold pool, an American suggestion, was taken up in November and December at the Paris Reparation Conference. Eighteen countries attended and formally agreed that the United States, Great Britain and France would administer the pool, and its work was to be carried out by a specially appointed commission—the Tripartite Gold Commission.

Preparatory to that same conference, the British view was that identifiable gold should be given back to the owner while what was left should be put into the reparations settlement. However, according to the minutes of the meeting, the British representative was forced to compromise and accept the French and American view that because of the problems in identifying gold "all gold found in Germany should be divided between the countries which had the right to restitution, in proportion corresponding to their losses."

It was decided to fund at least twenty million dollars of aid to the victims of the Nazis who were now homeless so that they could receive some part of the German reparations. In order to accomplish this, the non-monetary gold found as well as some other German assets would be used.

By 1946, the United States Military Government
knew from available records and from interrogations that,
beginning in August 1942, the Reichsbank received and
converted gold and other valuables that the SS had looted
from Jews the Nazis enslaved and murdered in Poland
and from Jewish and non-Jewish concentration camp
inmates.

In fact, Puhl's role in arranging for "the receipt,
classification, deposit, conversion, and disposal of properties taken by the SS from victims exterminated in concentration camps" formed the basis for his indictment in 1946
before the United States Military Tribunal at Nuremberg,
which subsequently sentenced him to five years' imprisonment.

The source of the gold and other valuables in those
shipments was clear from the "Reinhardt" designation of
the file in which Melmer kept the correspondence relating
to his deliveries to the Reichsbank. The name of this file
referred to Operation Reinhardt, the SS program for
exploiting Jewish property and labor and murdering millions of Jews in killing centers in Eastern Poland.

The Allies learned about the details of Operation
Reinhardt shortly after the war, and documents linking
Oswald Pohl with the Reinhardt program contributed to
the decision of the United States Military Tribunal at
Nuremberg to sentence him to death.

The Reichsbank's Precious Metals Department
records captured at Merkers included receipts for at least
some of the SS shipments whose contents had been disposed of or "processed," although the receipts didn't

include the value of the "non-currency" contents of deliveries that were disposed of through other agencies.

Based on those receipts, the Foreign Exchange Depository concluded that there were seventy-eight deliveries of which about forty-three were fully inventoried by the Reichsbank, which put the total value of the inventoried deliveries at 23,455,781.96 reichsmarks, of which RM 1,866,329.18 were gold coins, and RM 3,018,623.13 gold bars.

Thus it was possible to say that approximately $1.6 million in gold coins and bars were received by the Reichsbank in the first forty-odd deliveries of Melmer (SS loot) received.

The bottom line in all these gymnastics bearing on Nazi gold was repeated time and time again by the thieving Nazis.

So that in the end, they had deposited the grand total of $255.96 million worth of stolen gold in the Reichsbank and the other repositories it chose toward war's end as a safe haven for the loot in order to keep it out of the hands of victorious Allied captors.

Comparisons of captured records from the Berlin Reichsbank and United States Army inventories at the Frankfurt Reichsbank show without equivocation that approximately 98.6 percent of the $255.96 million worth of gold had been found and secured.

The question is, what happened to the 1.4 percent of that precious metal that remained unaccounted for? Three million was stolen and unaccounted for somewhere between the Berlin and Frankfurt terminals. To learn the answer, the Paris Conference on Reparation is pivotal:

Part III of the Final Act
of the Paris Conference on Reparation
(Monetary Gold)

A. All the monetary gold found in Germany by the Allied Forces and that referred to in paragraph G below (including gold coins, except those of numismatic or historical value which shall be restored directly if identifiable) shall be pooled for distribution as restitution among the countries participating in the pool in proportion to their respective losses of gold through looting or by wrongful removal to Germany.

B. Without prejudice to claims by way of reparation for unrestored gold, the portion of monetary gold thus accruing to each country participating in the pool shall be accepted by that country in full satisfaction of all claims against Germany for restitution of monetary gold.

C. A proportional share of the gold shall be allocated to each country concerned which adheres to this arrangement for the restitution of monetary gold and which can establish that a definite amount of monetary gold belonging to it was looted by Germany, or, at any time after 12 March 1938, was wrongfully removed into German territory.

D. The question of the eventual participation of countries not represented at the Conference (other than Germany but including Austria and

Italy) in the abovementioned distribution shall
be reserved, and the equivalent of the total
shares which these countries would receive, if
they were eventually admitted to participate,
shall be set aside to be disposed of at a later date
in such manner as may be decided by the Allied
Governments concerned.

E. The various countries participating in the pool
shall supply to the Governments of the United
States of America, France and the United
Kingdom as the occupying Powers concerned,
detailed and verifiable data regarding the gold
losses suffered through looting by, or removal to,
Germany.

F. The Governments of the United States of
America, France and the United Kingdom shall
take appropriate steps within the zones of
Germany occupied by them respectively to
implement distribution in accordance with the
foregoing provisions.

G. Any monetary gold which may be recovered
from a third country to which it was transferred
from Germany shall be distributed in accordance with this arrangement for the restitution
of monetary gold.

**Part I, Article 8: Allocation of the Reparation
Share to Non-Repatriable Victims of
German Action
(Non-monetary Gold)**

In recognition of the fact that large numbers of

persons have suffered heavily at the hands of the
Nazis and now stand in dire need of aid to promote
their rehabilitation but will be unable to claim the
assistance of any Government receiving reparation
from Germany, the Governments of the United
States of America, France, the United Kingdom,
Czechoslovakia and Yugoslavia, in consultation with
the Inter-Governmental Committee on Refugees,
shall, as soon as possible, work out in common
agreement a plan on the following general lines:

A. A share of reparation consisting of all the
    non-monetary gold found by the Allied Armed
    Forces in Germany and in addition a sum not
    exceeding twenty-five million dollars shall be
    allocated for the rehabilitation and resettlement
    of non-repatriable victims of German action.
B. The sum of twenty-five million dollars shall be
    met from a portion of the proceeds of
    German assets in neutral countries which are
    available for reparation.
C. Governments of neutral countries shall be
    requested to make available for this purpose (in
    addition to the sum of twenty-five million dol-
    lars) assets in such countries of victims of Nazi
    action who have since died and left no heirs.
D   The persons eligible for aid under the plan in
    question shall be restricted to true victims of
    Nazi persecution and to their immediate fami-
    lies and dependents, in the following classes:
    (i) Refugees from Nazi Germany or Austria

who require aid and cannot be returned to their countries within a reasonable time because of prevailing conditions.

(ii) German and Austrian nationals now resident in Germany or Austria in exceptional cases in which it is reasonable on grounds of humanity to assist such persons to emigrate and providing they emigrate to other countries within a reasonable period.

(iii) Nationals of countries formerly occupied by the Germans who cannot be repatriated or are not in a position to be repatriated within a reasonable time, In order to concentrate aid in the most needy and deserving refugees and to exclude persons whose loyalty to the United Nations is or was doubtful, aid shall be restricted to nationals or former nationals of previously occupied countries who were victims of Nazi concentration camps or of concentration camps established by regimes under Nazi influence but not including persons who have been confined only in prisoners of war camps.

E. The sums made available under paragraphs A and B above shall be administered by the Inter-Governmental Committee on Refugees or by a United Nations Agency to which appropriate functions of the Intergovernmental Committee may in the future be transferred. The sums made available under paragraph C above shall be administered for the general purposes referred to in this article under a program of administration to be formulated by the five Governments named above.

F. The non-monetary gold found in Germany shall be placed at the disposal of the Intergovernmental Committee on Refugees as soon as a plan has been worked out as provided above.

G. The Intergovernmental Committee on Refugees shall have power to carry out the purposes of the fund through appropriate public and private field organizations.

H. The fund shall be used, not for the compensation of individual victims, but to further the rehabilitation or resettlement of persons in the eligible classes.

I. Nothing in this Article shall be considered to prejudice the claims which individual refugees may have against a future German Government, except to the amount of the benefits that such refugees may have received from the sources referred to in paragraphs A and C above.

To implement the ideas agreed upon in Paris, there would have to be agreements with every one of the neutrals holding German assets. These neutrals were invited to a March meeting to be held in the United States in Washington, DC. Another agreement was signed in May.

Sweden and Switzerland, which held the largest assets, would, according to the plan, be dealt with first.

Thereafter, Portugal, Spain, and Ireland would be handled, and, finally, Turkey and Argentina.

On May 31, 1946, negotiations with Sweden began in Washington. While the Allies tried to formulate a joint Swedish-Allied control of German assets, the Swedes rejected joint control, as they had been doing. They wanted any control mechanism to be solely in their hands. The major powers, however, pressed their ideas. The final agreement provided for requisitioning, examination, and liquidation of German assets in Sweden through the auspices of the Foreign Capital Control Office. The agreement disposed of $378 million of liquidated assets: One hundred fifty million dollars was to be put into a Swedish Riksbank account to purchase essentials for the German economy. One hundred twenty-five million dollars was in financial aid, and fifty million dollars of this was to go to the International Refugee Organization in London for reparation and the resettlement of non-repatriable victims of the Nazis.

Sweden, at the end of the negotiations, announced that they would return gold which had been stolen from occupied countries—according to the Allies, all gold that was acquired after January 1943 was to be considered looted since it was their contention that all legitimately acquired gold reserves of the Germans had been utilized by this date. "The Allied line of reasoning," detailed the report of the proceedings, "was based on the following points: Before the seizure of the Austrian central bank's gold, Germany had not more than approximately USD 100 million in gold at its disposal.... With the addition of approximately twenty-three million acquired legitimately from the Soviet Union before the outbreak of the war and the fifty-three million taken from Austria and the thirty-three million from Czechoslovakia, this last portion seized forcibly, Germany began the war with some 210 million in gold."

And yet, because Germany kept meticulous records of all the gold it confiscated between 1933 and 1945, the total amount of gold now known to have been looted is $8.5 billion. Of this, one-third or $2.6 billion came from individual victims and private businesses.

"The precision is down to a single bar of gold," said Elan Steinberg, Executive Director of the World Jewish Congress which probed Nazi Germany's wartime financial transactions. Today there is no doubt that more than was originally thought, 75 percent of the current valuation of the $5.2 billion, was shipped first to Switzerland and then to other neutrals and Axis-friendly countries in order for the Nazis to buy strategic goods and services.

CHAPTER 6

"Justice, Decency, and Plain Horse Sense"

Senator Kilgore was playing hardball when he urged President Truman to renounce the Allied-Swiss agreement, basing his main argument on the understanding that the Germans had looted more than $700 million in Europe, that $400 million in gold was transferred to Switzerland, and that it was reasonable to estimate that Switzerland received at least $200 to $300 million in looted gold from countries conquered by the Nazis.

He expressed further dismay over the way Allied-Swiss negotiators agreed that $130 million in looted gold

bars had been received by Switzerland, that $88 million was
the amount they retained, and that they assigned merely $58
million to the Allied gold pool.

Then Kilgore unleashed what many Jewish organizations agreed were the harshest—and most profound—
words yet uttered by any political leader on Capitol Hill,
"Justice, decency, and plain horse sense require that the
Allies hold Switzerland responsible for all of the
$300,000,000 of looted gold which they accepted from the
Nazis and reject their proposition of settling for twenty
cents on the dollar."

The senator also categorically rejected the terms of
the Allied-Swiss agreement that would split the Nazi assets
in Switzerland on a fifty-fifty basis. He contended that such
a division would profit those Swiss who dealt with the
Nazis during the war and might safeguard the assets of
wealthy German industrialists who aided Hitler.

Left entirely to the Swiss was the management of
the divestiture of the assets, which presumably allowed
Nazis and Nazi collaborators to regain "cloaked" portions
of the $1,500 million in Swiss assets frozen during the war
in the United States.

Kilgore also doubted that the "riches earmarked to
reach the Swiss people" would really be paid to them.
Instead, he feared the money would "enrich only the Nazi
collaborationists and ensure that Switzerland remained an
outpost of Nazism."

And lastly, the agreement would establish a pattern
that allowed other former neutral states to serve as safe
havens for Nazism.

In closing his letter to Truman, Kilgore uttered a final, impassioned plea to hold out respect for those nations who paid with their citizens' lives in fighting the forces of the Third Reich. "Mr. Randolph Paul, the principal American negotiator, has personally informed me that he does not believe it possible to secure from the Swiss, by negotiation, any more stringent terms with respect to seizure and elimination of Nazi assets in Switzerland.

"I believe that this is probably the case. And accordingly I urge that all negotiations be broken off and that the United States take the initiative in bringing this matter to the attention of the United Nations as a matter of the highest order of security to the nations which sacrificed so much in blood and treasure to defeat Nazism and Fascism in the field of battle."

President Truman acknowledged Kilgore's letter on May 27 and sent a copy to Treasury Secretary Fred Vinson with the comment, "I don't know where he gets his information, but I thought it might be worth looking into."

Yet Vinson never replied to the president. Shortly thereafter he was named by Truman for appointment as Chief Justice of the United States Supreme Court.

That left the matter in the hands of Vinson's successor, John Snyder, to deal with Kilgore's protest of the settlement reached with the Swiss. Snyder spent hardly any time responding to the president with his view that "an agreement with the Swiss has been struck and there's no reason to abrogate it at this stage."

Truman then dashed off a letter to the senator making it clear that he accepted the agreement.

"As you know," Truman wrote, "the Allied Delegations, after long deliberation and mutual consultation, decided to and have accepted a compromise settlement. Accordingly, the question cannot now be reopened.

"The factors which impelled settlement on the basis of the final Accord—which I believe were thoroughly explored with you before action was taken—seem to me to indicate strongly the wisdom of this step."

Senator Kilgore was a minority voice of complaint from the Senate about the terms of the Allied-Swiss agreement on the dispensation of Nazi gold.

But there was another voice of protest that was directed to Truman seeking a presidential denouement of the pact with the Swiss. Representative Joseph Clark Baldwin also turned to the nation's chief executive with a request to abort the agreement in a telegram to the White House on July 13, 1946.

"I am profoundly disturbed by the agreement which netted only $58 million out of a reliably estimated $800 million of gold looted by Germany. I urge you, Mr. President, to order investigations. Surely the situation warrants both Executive and Congressional investigations."

A response was communicated to Baldwin by Dean Acheson, then assistant secretary of state who would later step into General George C. Marshall's shoes as acting secretary of state in 1950.

"With respect to the looted gold problem, there was no reasonable evidence that Switzerland had purchased $300,000,000 worth of gold looted by Germany," wrote Acheson.

"As you will realize, there is necessarily difficulty in proving just what amount of gold purchased by Switzerland was in fact gold which had been looted by Germany," continued the new secretary, who appeared totally unfamiliar with the subject of which he spoke.

"It was conceded that about $88 million of gold originally belonging to the Bank of Belgium had been acquired by the Swiss National Bank. Yet the Swiss vigorously contested liability, on grounds that they had made their purchases in good faith. Under these circumstances, the Allied negotiators agreed that settlement for $58.14 million worth should be accepted—particularly since the French Government, which was the largest loser to the Germans, held this opinion."

It was never determined on what basis Congressman Baldwin calculated the Swiss portion of looted gold at $300 million, nor was there any information about why those officials who prepared Acheson's letter disregarded or discounted the estimate of $289 million of German looted gold, which was drawn up in February by their State Department colleague Otto Fletcher.

On November 11, 1946, a portentous postscript on the way the negotiations were carried out in Washington, D.C. received a strident appraisal by Dr. Walter Stucki, head of the Swiss delegation to the conference in the nation's capital.

Shortly after returning to Basel, he delivered a diatribe about his disappointment over the outcome of the recent discussions.

The United States Consul in Basel, Leland

Harrison, whose lengthy service in that post extended from September 1937 to October 1947, characterized the speech as "a presentation by a disappointed and bitter man." Then he went on to digest what Stucki's lament to his listeners in the Swiss government was all about. "Stucki asserted that the principles advanced by the Atlantic Charter had been violated by the very Allied nations that had promulgated the Charter.

"Can one still speak of equality today, considering everything that has happened of late, the veto rights of the Great Powers, for example?'"

Harrison went on with his report of Stucki's obviously vapid lament against the United States and its Allies, "Turning to the Currie agreement [Lauchlin Currie had headed a United States mission to Switzerland to conduct economic negotiations bearing on financial matters growing out of settling the way Swiss-held Nazi gold was to be distributed], Stucki described the setting of the negotiations. Stucki said Switzerland was in the position of a [single small] nation confronting three great powers with sixteen other states arrayed behind them.

"Stucki claimed that in 1935 the Swiss could still say 'no' to the solicitations of a Hermann Goering, but in the dangerous political isolation in which Switzerland found itself at the end of hostilities in a world lacking material and moral foundations, our 'no' could not have avoided consequences of such action because the pressure on us was heavy. Stucki followed in a sarcastic vein with a series of accusations he imagined the Allies had made against Switzerland, such as being characterized as a 'haven of Fascism.'

"When the Swiss first learned of the Currie Mission, these negative sentiments were far from their minds. In fact, the just-concluded liberation of France had raised hopes that shortly proved futile.

"Without identifying those 'hopes,' Stucki pointed out that at the time Swiss imports were at their 'lowest figure.' He enumerated the measures taken by the Swiss Government as a result of the Currie mission and other forms of Allied pressure.

"Under the circumstances, 'what were we to do?' Stucki asked rhetorically; Switzerland could not have dealt with the trial of nerves that would have ensued if an agreement had not been reached.

"According to Stucki, definitive measures against the Axis had not been taken earlier (although they were under consideration for some time) because Switzerland lacked coal which was only to be had from Germany.

"He continued by pointing out that the Germans understood the situation and did not consider Swiss blocking actions as an 'unneutral act.'"

Consul Harrison reported lastly that Stucki's speech "was well received but recognized as the presentation of an embittered civil servant who had not received a posting commensurate with his performance on behalf of the Swiss nation."

More recently, the Swiss have heard the relentless attacks of New York Senator Alfonse D'Amato. For a long while, they appeared to pay no more attention to his cry.

Finally, an Associated Press dispatch out of Bonn

on April 1, 1997, announced that Swiss officials "proposed creating a $4.7 billion fund to pay back Holocaust victims."

It came in an address to the Swiss Parliament by President Arnold Koller, who outlined a plan "to use proceeds from the sale of huge Swiss gold reserves to compensate Jewish victims of the Nazis and others in need."

His stunning pronouncement caused world gold prices to plummet instantly and left many members of Parliament in a catatonic state of shock, inasmuch as Switzerland's previous president opposed creation of a compensation fund and slammed Jewish-advocacy groups with charges of "blackmail" for asking that gold stolen from victims of the Holocaust be paid to its survivors and the descendants of the six million whose lives were taken by the Nazis.

Koller's proposal to make amends with the Jewish advocacy groups and meet their demands at long last amounted, in truth, to measurably inadequate compensation from the huge stores of gold the Swiss were known to have amassed during the war—an estimated $5.6 billion.

However, it seemed intended to blunt the scathing United States report about to be released that would establish the way the Swiss bought or stored that $5.6 billion in gold and other assets solely from the Germans—virtually all of it snatched from Europe's persecuted Jews.

The Swiss, according to the United States State Department, were well aware—and were very wary—of the recent investigation that Under Secretary of Commerce Stuart Eizenstat undertook to unearth the Alpine nation's role in stashing, then holding onto the Jewish gold.

President Koller's proclamation, though only a

beginning, was met in the United States with congratulations. The individual most stunned by the news was Senator D'Amato.

"I think it's an amazing admission of responsibility," D'Amato stated. "This is the first time that we've seen that kind of an admission, and I think it will go a long way to begin the healing process. I think it is a significant undertaking—and a departure for those who, a short time ago, accused us of blackmail."

According to the road map laid down by President Koller, the proposed fund for restitution was to be processed by a newly-organized "Swiss Foundation for Solidarity," which was to dole out annually several hundred million dollars "in interest" on the $4.7 billion—starting within two years.

The Swiss did not immediately outline how recipients of the money were to be chosen.

The fund would constitute an additional, but significantly smaller humanitarian financial portfolio established by Swiss banks for payback. The Swiss National Bank was the first to give $71 million to that fund for "poverty-stricken" Holocaust victims.

World Jewish Congress President Edgar Bronfman, the distillery tycoon, praised the Swiss for their "historic endeavor to confront the past" and for their "laudable goal of making moral and material restitution to those who suffered under Nazi persecution.

"We hail President Koller's announcement as representing a victory for the Swiss and Jewish peoples," Bronfman went on.

Koller advanced the view that his gesture "rein-
forces Switzerland's humanitarian tradition and proves our
gratefulness for having been spared during two world
wars."

Other Jewish leaders endorsed Bronfman's praises of
Koller's proposal.

"This is first and foremost a victory of the moral
position for which we have fought all along," declared
Avraham Burg, of Israel's Jewish Agency, which launched
the probe into Holocaust victims' bank accounts shortly
after the end of the war but had been stonewalled by the
Swiss.

Another notable leader, Howard Squadron, past
chairman of the Conference of Presidents of Major
American Jewish Organizations, stated, "Finally, the Swiss
have seen that there's a responsibility here, and they have
acknowledged it in a dimension that is well beyond what
had previously been talked about.

"They've demonstrated that they really extended
themselves to meet their responsibility and they should be
complimented for it."

Mel Urbach, a lawyer representing the World
Council of Orthodox Jewish Communities, lauded Koller
for "recognizing the seriousness of the claimants and the
survivors and for taking a bold move in offering such a significant amount of money."

However, Rabbi Marvin Hier, dean and founder of
the Simon Wiesenthal Center, stated, "Outgoing Swiss
President Jean-Pascal Delamuras accuses Jewish groups of
'extortion and blackmail'—and of masterminding a plot

to bring down the Swiss banking establishment—after demands are made on behalf of Holocaust victims for compensation of plundered assets housed in Swiss banks."

CHAPTER 7

Well-known Facts

Informed American Jewish leaders knew about the concentration camps virtually from the beginning. They soon learned about the Wannsee Conference of January 20, 1942 in Germany, where the decision to annihilate the Jews of Europe was formalized.

They knew it from the correspondence from Rabbi Michael Ber Weissmandel (from Slovakia) by 1942, and certainly from the correspondence of Gerhart Riegner, from the World Jewish Congress, and the Sternbuchs (Orthodox) from Switzerland as well as many other sources, including Bundist reports from Poland, not to mention the accounts in the general and Jewish press.

In the report *American Jewry During The Holocaust*, the truth about the conditions that faced European Jewry were explicitly set forth:

"In the archives of most of the major Jewish organizations there are large scrapbooks and files with thousands of clippings, and many reports from Switzerland, London, and Palestine with details of the extermination process.

"Often these reports contain copies of accounts (letters and documents) received from occupied territories under German official or actual domination—Italy, Vichy (France), Poland, Hungary, Slovakia, Rumania, and Germany itself.

"If the Jewish Agency's representative in Switzerland, Richard Lichtheim's letters and reports were published, it would suffice to show how much and how early the Jewish leadership knew of what went on. The same would be true of a collection of Riegner's reports and letters."

The conclusions cited in *The American Jewry* study illustrate the reception given to the most terrifying episodes of the "Jewish Experience" encountered during the critical hours of its existence in America.

"For the American public at large," the report states, "the very enormity of Hitler's crimes, exceeding normal human comprehension, may have diminished the reaction. People react, selectively, to man-sized threats. It is not giant tragedies that plumb our emotional depths; it is, rather, the plight of single human beings.

"In a week when three thousand people are killed in an earthquake in Iran, a lone boy falls down a well-shaft in

Italy and the whole world grieves—six million Jews are put to death, and it is Anne Frank, trembling in her garret, who remains stamped in our memory."

If all those findings were true, then why couldn't America's Jewry, living in total freedom from government oppression, face up to the challenge of a horrific truism?

According to the findings of *American Jewry During The Holocaust,* "Even as late as December 1944, 12 percent of Americans believed that the mass murder accounts about Jewish slayings were untrue, 27 percent believed only about 100,000 people were involved, and only 4 percent believed the truth—that more than five million Jews had already been put to death."

Significantly, the study also determined that the media sources in the U.S. "were hampered by wartime limitations on communications and that they could have no reporters in Nazi-occupied territory where the criminal slaughter of the Jews was taking place."

Another factor weighing against the presentation of a full picture of Nazi criminal slaughter of Jews was the skepticism that greeted reports of atrocities in wartime: that they were often exaggerated. That belief was recorded by history, such as the many false stories about German savagery in Belgium during World War I.

Yet, in truth, the World War II atrocities were even worse than the reports about them—but the media were still reacting to their earlier experiences.

Nevertheless, one scholar, Dr. Sol Chaneles, whose 1939 paper, "America First, 1939: How The News Media Reported The Destruction of European Jews," clearly made a point of stating that the *New York Times* provided extensive coverage of Nazi persecution as early as 1939— along with several American Jewish daily newspapers and periodicals, which also carried detailed accounts about the bone-chilling mass murders.

"Those publications all had reported that two million Jews had been exterminated and about four million were threatened with a similar fate," continued Dr. Chaneles. "While many Americans, including Jews, could not believe the reports...Jewish leaders certainly did."

Chaneles ended his criticism by asking, "Why didn't this problem of credibility elicit from [American Jews] a mighty public relations effort to convey the truth to the largest number of Americans, including [all other] Jews?"

While Chaneles didn't provide a response to his query, another scholar, the legendary Polish hero of World War II, Dr. Jan Karski, offered convincing testimony that established an awareness about the systematic destruction of the Jewish people of Europe on the part of the free world's Jewish leadership and governments and international institutions.

Dr. Karski said so in a 1981 address at the International Liberators Conference (ILC) when he related how in September 1943 he left on his last mission on behalf of the underground to the Government in Exile in London.

Before his departure, he admitted he bribed SS guards of the Warsaw ghetto to smuggle him in so he could observe first-hand what was occurring there.

When he returned to the free world, he unloaded his findings about the cesspools in Poland that he trod, and also managed to latch onto the ears of world leaders such as British Prime Minister Churchill, President Roosevelt, leaders of international organizations, and the Vatican—as well as other shapers of public opinion.

This scholar further spoke to the most prominent Jewish leaders and vast public audiences. During the war, Karski published a book, a selection of the Book-Of-The-Month Club, and he wrote articles in 1943-44 in the most prestigious newspapers and magazines in America and Great Britain.

However, of all the significant strides he made in putting across his reports on the tyrannical treatment of Jews in his homeland, nothing quite compared with the last paragraph of his address to the ILC in 1981 when, with tragic sarcasm, he expressed his bewilderment about the vacuous responses to his repeated and widespread alarm signals: "Later, however, when the war came to its end, I learned that the governments, the leaders, scholars, writers did not know what had been happening to the Jews. They were taken by surprise.

"The murder of six million innocents was a terrible secret.

"The Second Original Sin had been committed by humanity; through commission, or omission, or self-imposed ignorance, or insensitivity, or self-interest, or hypocrisy, or heartless rationalization.

"This sin will haunt humanity to the end of time. It does haunt me. And I want it to be so."

Rescue activities were not handicapped by a lack of knowledge on the part of America's Jewish leadership about atrocities perpetrated upon their European brethren under Hitler's domination.

No study ever authorized in the United States to obtain an accounting of the actions and attitudes of American Jewish leaders and organizations about Hitler's extermination of Jews can compare with the one delegated by the American Jewish Commission on the Holocaust, formed in 1981 on the initiative of virtually every prominent Jewish leader in America.

The underlying thrust of that study was "not to make moral judgments but rather to let later generations profit in the hope that the experience might help prevent a similar tragedy from ever again befalling the Jews or any other people...."

So explained former United States Supreme Court Justice Arthur Goldberg, who, after accepting the chairmanship of the commission, invited thirty-two distinguished Jewish leaders from virtually every walk of American life to serve as officers and members.

The fruit of the four-year study was the publication of the commission's findings in the voluminous work titled *American Jewry During The Holocaust—A Report By The Research Director, His Staff And Independent Research Scholars Retained By The Director For The American Jewish Commission On The Holocaust* [referred to herein for brevity as *American Jewry During The Holocaust* or simply *American Jewry*].

Justice Goldberg felt very strongly about the study to which he lent his name. He stated, "It is a striking fact that in the voluminous published material on the Holocaust, not a single book deals primarily with the role of one of the most important groups involved: namely, the leaders of the major American Jewish organizations.

"The role of every other key group and leader has been thoroughly studied: Franklin D. Roosevelt and the State Department; Winston Churchill and the British Foreign and Colonial Offices; the Vatican and other Christian church authorities; the International Committee of the Red Cross—and, of course, Hitler, the Nazi hierarchy, and the rulers of other Asia powers and of the Nazis' satellites and conquered countries.

"No comparable study of the role of American Jewry exists."

Director of the study, Dr. Seymour Maxwell Finger, was faced with a lack of funds that prompted the dissolution of the commission until January 1983, when Goldberg guaranteed the necessary funding that led to the completion of the final draft and its publication in March 1983.

American Jewry During The Holocaust did not stir emotions or provoke widespread comment at the time—nor since. To some observers of the scene the reason for its tepid reception was likely brought about by the conclusion that the commission reached—the question of whether American Jews had knowledge of what was happening in Germany and European countries under Hitler's boot—and whether they could have done anything about the situation.

This is not a trick question yet it commands a "yes" response to the first query, whether American Jews knew what Hitler was up to, and "no" to the latter question of whether they could have done something about the situation, since a number of prominent Jews were closely associated with President Roosevelt.

Among the Judaic workhorses in or allied with FDR's Administration were Samuel Rosenman, the President's chief speechwriter; U.S. Supreme Court Justice Felix Frankfurter; New York Senator Herbert H. Lehman; and American Federation of Labor president Sidney Hillman.

But it was not their wont to speak out for European Jews in those perilous times, according to the commission's findings.

"In general...they saw their role principally as patriotic Americans bolstering a president carrying the heavy burden of overcoming a great depression and fighting World War II. They did not speak out strongly for special action on behalf of the Jews of Europe."

Much of that silence was provoked by Western powers who were in a "long and feckless flight from reality"—most especially the French and British, who were "exhausted and demoralized by the heavy cost of their 1918 victory [in World War I]."

Their policy toward Hitler at the outset of his emergence into prominence was based on "wishful thinking," the commission found.

"They discounted frank declarations of his aims and did nothing effective to stop his treaty-breaking rearmament program and his bloodless, step-by-step territorial advances in 1936-39."

Britain compounded the inability of the European

community to deal with Hitler from strength on May 17, 1939, when the government issued a White Paper, cutting back sharply on—and agreeing to end entirely within five years—Jewish immigration into the Palestine Mandate that Britain propounded as early as the 1920s as a means of implementing its intentions to establish a Jewish homeland in that Middle East enclave.

"It was clearly an attempt to compete for the favor of the Arabs, then under increasing influence from Germany," the report declared further.

"Thus the appeasement of Hitler, which had already put millions of European Jews in peril of their lives, was further compounded by a step which cut off all but a relative handful of those same Jews from their most likely avenue of escape.

"This policy—to which the United States made no strong objections—was to become a serious stumbling block to the rescue of Jews from the Holocaust."

"Up to 1941 Hitler's policy was to rid Europe of its Jews, not necessarily to kill them. Starting in 1933 the Nazis used 'laws' and decrees along with officially stimulated violence to identify, terrify, extort from, and dehumanize the Jews under their control.

"Thus, the Nazis deprived them progressively of rights, dignity, economic and professional opportunities, property, freedom and finally, life itself."

The world, since those years, has asked repeatedly why, when the Jews felt the agony of persecution did they not get away from their tormentors?

A number of reasons kept Jews—especially the

older ones—in residence in Germany, Austria, Poland, and
other countries that had come under the domination of the
Third Reich.

"They were reluctant to leave friends, family, and
familiar surroundings," *American Jewry During The Holocaust*
concluded in its report, "they were inclined to clutch at
straws of hope that the madness would pass.

"Moreover, to leave Germany a Jew initially had to
give up 80 percent of his property and savings, and later all
except 250 reichsmarks [$100 in late 1930's equivalent cur-
rency].

"Finally, most potential countries of refuge were in
the throes of the Depression and put up formidable barriers to immigration or even temporary haven."

That predicament became clear in July 1938 at the
thirty-two nation conference on refugees at Evian, France,
where it was established that governments in the free world
that would admit Jewish refugees were pitifully few compared with the numbers who needed rescue,"

The commission then concluded that area of its
findings by declaring this shocking bottom line: "Those
restrictive policies, which were exploited in Nazi propaganda,
encountered little dissent from Roosevelt's Jewish advisers,
who were keenly aware of widespread opposition to the
influx of multitudes of new immigrants [into the U.S.] at a
time of massive unemployment."

All those circumstances combined and conspired to
hold down the prewar flight of Jews from Nazi-controlled
regions.

In 1933, the year Hitler came into power and

thundered that he would rid Germany of all its Jews, the exodus that followed amounted to only 37,000 "pariahs" as the one-time paperhanger called them, fled the country, with its most prominent escapee being the renowned scientist Albert Einstein, who made his way to America.

In the next five years, to the end of 1938, only a total of about 150,000 Jews had fled Germany. Some 350,000 then remained—half of them over the age of 45, since it was the younger generation that emigrated at the urging of their elders.

In that same year, especially after the brutal Kristallnacht rampage—and the prewar months of 1939— some 200,000 additional Jews fled, while approximately the same number of Austrian Jews came under German rule after the March 1938 Anschluss.

The report, *American Jewry During The Holocaust* advanced the theory that the Western governments contributed to the Third Reich's ultimate goal to exterminate all Jews from the European landscape. It states, "With the outbreak of war in September 1939, an already alarming picture changed drastically for the worse. Hitler's empire expanded drastically, absorbing additional millions of Jews in Poland immediately, and soon afterward in other parts of Europe.

"Simultaneously, the doors of escape were locked from the inside as the Nazis closed their frontiers, which thereafter could only be passed with help from the outside.

"Although Western governments at last somewhat relaxed their barriers against immigrants and refugees, no country even then would go as far as to open its borders to

large-scale resettlement of European Jews—their only
hope, as it turned out, of escaping virtually total destruction.

"Hitler's formal decision in 1942 to slaughter all
Jews coming under Nazi control—the 'Final Solution'—
was taken only after it had become evident that other countries were not prepared to accept them in sufficient numbers to accommodate his fiendish goal of ridding Europe
of all Jews by terror, extortion, and expulsion."

For what consolation it may be to the surviving victims of The Holocaust and their descendants, the report
points out in its conclusion, "Jews were not the only victims of the Nazis. More than 20 million Russians, Poles,
and others were killed, but only the Jews were slaughtered
systematically, simply for the 'crime' of being Jewish."

To understand how American Jewry responded to
The Holocaust and to the policies of the United States
government, a brief glimpse must first be taken into the
nature of Jewish organizational life in this country from
the days of the *Landsmannschaftena* (mutual aid societies of
Jews from particular European towns or districts) to the
present.

Jewish organizational life in America had not been
monolithic in those times, and certainly wasn't so in the
period that was the concern of that eminent group of
scholars who prepared the study, *American Jewry During The
Holocaust*.

It's important to note that the American Jewish
community of 1939-45 wasn't the fellowship as we know it
today.

It had little power.

Most Jewish citizens were, first and for the most part, second generation Americans, still trying, laudably, to meet altruistic goals they had set for themselves. They were neither affluent nor influential. The Jewish organizations actively pursuing those high aims were mainly small, under-staffed, and under-financed.

However, most Jews were preoccupied with domestic problems, such as the Great Depression and World War II. More significantly those of combat age served in the armed forces, while others were in vital positions in the business community or defense work.

The American Jewish Congress was the leading organization in America before the outbreak of World War II that had for many years been looking after the interests of Jews in this country. The outbreak of war caught them, as it had other related organizations in the country, unprepared to meet the crisis that had befallen European Jewry.

It was affiliated with the World Jewish Congress, its parent organization launched in 1936 under the leadership of the legendary Rabbi Stephen Wise, one of the most ardent campaigners in the world against bigotry and anti-Semitism.

With a two-fisted leader named Gerhart Riegner, who got wind of Hitler's plan for the "Final Solution" from his "watchdog's post with the World Jewish Congress branch in Switzerland," he was able to cable to the United States a warning about that never-before-publicized Nazi plot to murder all Jews under German control.

According to Riegner, the extermination "with one blow" was to be carried out in the autumn of 1942, ostensibly with the disfiguring and deadly prussic acid (cyanide); soon after to be supplanted by the "more humane" gas ovens.

His message was sent to the World Jewish Congress branch in the United States—and by extension to the American Jewish Congress.

In that time frame—1942—only six major organizations operated in the United States on behalf of protecting Jewish people's rights:

1. The prestigious and heavily-bankrolled American Jewish Committee.
2. The American Jewish Congress, an affiliate of the World Jewish Congress.
3. B'nai B'rith and its closely allied sister organization, the Anti-Defamation League, which served as America's principal watchdog against anti-Semitism.
4. The Jewish Labor Committee, representing 756 separate labor groups.
5. The Orthodox Committee (Agudath Israel).
6. The most-recently formed rescue agency Vaad Hatzalah.

Engaged in heavy-duty work, these organizations performed feats important to the daily lives of Jews in America, devoting themselves to good works in behalf of Jewry in the United States.

Riegner's message was immediately relayed to the State Department, but the immediate reaction in Washington was to say it doubted the veracity of the report. Consequently, the State Department censored the communiqué that was to have been passed on to Rabbi Stephen Wise.

Much of the State Department's reluctance to surge forward and seek further information on the threat to Europe's six million Jews was brought on by Undersecretary of State Sumner Welles, who took at face value what his staff told him, "There's nothing to that report."

Nevertheless, on his own, Welles sought independent verification of the report. He asked the WJC not to inform the media about the message from Riegner until "I can tap the Vatican for substantiation."

Uncomfortable with what his ears told him, but not wanting to lose the WJC's only sympathetic audience in the State Department—as well as his main conduit to Riegner in Geneva—Rabbi Wise simply waited.

The tormented WJC president, who shared his exchanges privately with Welles as well as other related information at meetings with Jewish organizational leaders, didn't rest on his efforts with Welles.

Rabbi Wise wanted more movement on the part of Washington officials. Thus he appealed to an American Jew who held one of the nation's most exalted positions: Felix Frankfurter, the renowned U.S. Supreme Court justice.

In his message to Frankfurter, who had been named to the nation's highest court by FDR, Wise appealed for a way to reach the President's ear.

"Please consider informing the Chief...the foremost and finest figure in the political world today, about the plight of Europe's Jews...."

Justice Frankfurter subsequently responded to Rabbi Wise and informed him what FDR's response was.

FDR repeated exactly what Undersecretary Welles had told the rabbi, "Jewish refugees are not being slaughtered.... They are being put into labor camps and used to perform forced labor...."

Wise was aware that the President couldn't have gotten his information through any contact with Hitler, since the rabbi knew how much the German dictator despised FDR, his arch enemy despite the fact that even though the United States had declared war on Germany at the same time it started hostilities against Japan after the Pearl Harbor sneak attack on December 7, 1941, the American government was merely on the verge of sending troops to the European continent, and had thus not yet met Nazi soldiers in combat. In fact, the Navy, Marines, and Army were then occupied island-hopping the vast Pacific and thrashing the combat troops draped in the military uniforms of the Empire of the Rising Sun.

On November 24, 1942, Undersecretary Welles finally confirmed to Rabbi Wise what the latter had known all along for the better part of a year. The substance of Gerhart Riegner's cable in early 1942, Welles conceded finally, was accurate. Mass annihilation of Jews had begun in 1939, after Germany invaded and conquered Poland, and was continuing to this time not only in Poland but in other lands being conquered by the Third Reich.

Some half of the six million Jews in territories occupied by the Nazis had already been slain in a purposeful, unrelenting extermination campaign, Wise was reliably informed from Geneva.

The terms of Germany's "Final Solution to The Jewish Question" had finally broken through to the Washington bureaucracy and come into the open. Now it could be told to the American public.

With three million Jewish lives taken by Hitler's monstrous design to exterminate that race, the remaining Jews were also doomed to be murdered by the end of the war on the Nazi dictator's orders.

With that dreadful fate awaiting what was left of European Jewry, eight American Jewish organizations came together at Rabbi Wise's request. Calling themselves "The Joint Emergency Committee On European Jewish Affairs," the alliance recommended various courses of action that it proposed be taken—but it could offer no plan of attack until the organization could have a meeting with FDR.

Some days after a personal appeal by Rabbi Wise, the President received the organization's chief spokesman and four other members of his group for an interview that ended with the President pledging to do "all in the Administration's power to be of service to your people in this tragic moment."

Dr. Finger summarized the outcome of the meeting with FDR in the White House, "Those present in the Oval Office found Roosevelt's response encouraging. Yet FDR spoke only of postwar retribution. As with the Allied War Crimes Commission, he had allowed the issue to come to a head before making a move of no consequence, although he possessed information on The Holocaust well before Wise's November 24 statement.

"Roosevelt assured Speaker of the House Sam Rayburn, in addition, that restrictive immigration laws were

Congress's sole responsibility for retaliatory bombing on the ground that 'the victims' would only be 'entirely safe' with the thorough defeat of the Axis.

"This position, to be held consistently thereafter in World War II, was considerably easier than grappling with the vexing, urgent problem at hand."

On December 17, 1942, the democracies did acknowledge the incredible reality of the German murder plot, and affirmed their resolution "to press on with the necessary practical measures" to halt this "bestial policy."

Yet, like FDR, "The UN Declaration on Jewish Massacres" remained silent on possible relief and rescue.

Upon receiving a long dispatch from Riegner about worsening conditions in Poland and other conquered lands, the American Jewish Congress organized a "Stop Hitler Now!" rally in Madison Square Garden.

Thirty-seven thousand aroused citizens—more than twice the 16,000 seating capacity of the sports arena—turned out for the March 1, 1943, assemblage that heard World Zionist Organization president Chaim Weizmann bemoan the apathy of the Christian world toward the plight of Europe's beleaguered Jews.

Warm messages of support were also sounded at the rally by the Archbishop of Canterbury and Arthur Cardinal Hinsley of the New York Archdiocese of the Roman Catholic Church for immediate action to save innocent human beings.

An eleven-point program of rescue was adapted, calling for:

1-2. Make approaches to the German government

and its satellites to permit Jewish emigration (out of all Third Reich territories).

3. Allow establishment of refugee sanctuaries.

4-5-6. Permit greater entry of immigrants into the United States, Great Britain, and Latin America.

7. Open the gates to Palestine beyond the narrow limits authorized by the 1939 White Paper (which set severe limits on Jewish settlements in that Mid-East territory that historically was a Jewish homeland).

8-9. Establish United Nation financial guarantees for feeding and rescue.

10. Appoint an appropriate intergovernmental agency to implement the program.

11. Name a tribunal that would ultimately bring the criminals to justice.

The following day, Undersecretary Welles publicly declared that the detailed program was receiving "the most serious and sympathetic consideration from both President Roosevelt and the State Department."

That same week, the State Department let it be known that an Anglo-American conference "would shortly focus on the refugee question."

But the Conference on Refugees, held in Bermuda in April 1943, only demonstrated what The Holocaust Commission study termed as a reflection of "the true intentions of the Anglo-American Alliance." It went on to complain: "Nothing was done and no plans were announced to carry out any of the eleven points in the Madison Square Garden Program."

It became clear that America's Jews—and most certainly their rapidly-diminishing brethren across the sea—had been deep-sixed by the do-nothing governments of the United States and Great Britain. Their hypocrisy was just as unforgivable to this country's saddened and distraught Jewry as was their feebleness in taking a single step to halt the carnage Hitler was heaping on European Jews.

Not until early 1944, after the International Committee of the Red Cross and the Swiss and Swedish Governments—under the repeated pleadings of Rabbi Wise and the War Refugee Board—had stepped in and saved many thousands of Hungarian Jews, did America and Britain utter a word about the calamitous treatment of the Jews under Hitler's heel.

Only then did Roosevelt and Churchill voice their first and only protest to the Nazi dictator, who by that time was deeply entrenched in his bombproof bunker at the chancellery in Berlin, too far gone in mind and spirit to pay heed to the call. For, on April 30, 1944, with Allied armies surrounding his last bastion, the Nazi tyrant put a gun to his head and committed suicide.

"One can only speculate as to how many might have been saved if the Allied governments had made similar statements soon enough and persistently enough and if the WRB had been established earlier," concluded Professor Finger in his study *American Jewry During The Holocaust.*

The last words recorded in that study sum up the inordinate number of "what-might-have-beens" had

American Jewry begun its pleas to save Europe's Jews years sooner than when it did sound off: "The fact must be faced that what the millions of Jews of Europe needed, and only a small proportion of them got, was rescue.

"Until late in the war, when Zionism began to dominate Jewish efforts—without achieving its hoped-for major impact on the rescue problem—Jewish efforts were predominantly aimed at traditional refugee relief; indeed, the distinction between refugee relief and rescue were often blurred, both by Allied governments and the Jewish organizations.

"The typical beneficiary of the American Jewish organizations then operating in Europe was a person who had escaped from Nazi-dominated parts of Europe, was living in a less-than-legal status in a strange country, and needed food, clothing, and shelter.

"But the problems facing millions of European Jews at that time was precisely how to become refugees— that is, how to escape from Nazi areas where they were in daily peril of physical attack, deportation, and death.

"Only a small proportion could hope to escape by clandestine means. Escape on a large scale was conceivable only if authorities in the Nazi-allied countries could be induced to permit it to happen. The crucial need was to apply whatever pressure or inducement might cause these authorities to resist Nazi orders for deportation of Jews, to stop physical mistreatment of Jews on their own territory, and to consent, openly or secretly, to a mass exodus of Jews to Allied or neutral countries. And there was a corresponding need to persuade Allied and neutral countries to let them in.

"This crucial need was not met."

The report continues, laying blame on the Allies for being too slow and cautious in taking action, thus losing any chance to successfully keep the "Final Solution" from following its "relentless course." Although the main goal of the Allies was maintaining their own interests and winning the war, according to the report, neutral countries followed the same path of indifference when it came to the plight of Europe's Jews.

For example, the report explains, Switzerland closed its borders to Jews that were seeking refuge, forcing them to return to what would be certain death. Yet, shockingly, Switzerland later admitted that allowing these people to enter the country would not have put Swiss security at any risk.

The report also offers scrutiny of the Soviet Union's role, which it describes as "one of total indifference." Despite the fact that he was kept abreast of the situation by his informants throughout Eastern Europe, Stalin did nothing to help or save Europe's Jews. And when he did help Jews during Russia's victory against Germany, it was only "as an incidental by-product of his own war aims.

"The Soviets did, however, evacuate large numbers of Jews along with other civilians as they retreated before the Nazi invasion in 1941. And, like the Western Allies, they liberated Jews and other inmates from concentration camps as they pushed Nazi troops back again in the campaigns to defeat Nazi Germany."

Yet there was an unwillingness on the part of

Soviets, as well as Western Allies, to even admit to the existence of a genocide of Jews. Of the Soviets, the report states, "Even today they suppress references to the fact that the people slaughtered at Babi Yar were Jewish and carry out a vicious 'anti-Zionist' campaign."

The report goes on to outline the many arguments that have been set forth to defend the action—or lack of action—of the Allied and neutral countries. "It has been pointed out that during the years after Dunkirk and Pearl Harbor the Allies were on the defensive worldwide, had great armies to raise, great battles to fight, and great losses and suffering to endure, and hence could not attend to all the woes of a world at war." Claims continue with the argument that later on, when the war changed and the Allied forces were winning, all efforts needed to be focused upon defeating Germany and its allies.

Another argument is that leaders and politicians of the Allied nations—though not anti-Semitic themselves—had to consider the underlying anti-Semitic beliefs of the citizens of their countries. It is argued that they could not take any strong or decisive action to aid the persecuted Jews of Europe because they did not want to stir up anti-Semitic sentiments or tensions in their own backyards or among their troops in a time when a united front was most critical.

The proof of this concern, it is argued, is that many people did not even believe that Hitler's "Final Solution" existed or was as horrific as some claimed it to be. This was only bolstered by the fact that tales of atrocities committed by Germans during World War I were later proved to be false.

Another claim is that all of the previously referred
to arguments defending the Allied nations' position are
irrelevant anyway. In fact, it is claimed, in the end, there was
little if anything the Allies could have done to save or help
the Jews for two reasons: "the merciless nature of the Nazi
regime" and the fact that Europe's Jews were spread out all
over the continent's vast terrain.

With these arguments considered, the report continues, "The point most relevant to our inquiry, to which the facts
reviewed above overwhelmingly attest, is this: The governments allied against Hitler were well and currently informed
about the tragic fate of the Jews, certainly by 1942, and did little to mitigate it.

"It would be grossly unjust and inaccurate to go
further and charge that responsible Allied leaders actually
shared the Nazi aim of extermination and, as Goebbels
wrote, were 'happy' to see it carried out; after all, Jews in
the Western democracies continued to enjoy full rights of
citizenship and many held high positions."

However, the report refutes, "the evidence is con-
clusive that the United States, Soviet, and British governments did not look on the Jews as allies in the common
struggle, nor gave a high priority to their rescue. Like governments generally, they gave top priority to their national
interests, particularly during a war for their own survival.
There was, indeed, great danger that the Allies might be
defeated by the Axis powers, and it is understandable that
the enormous tasks involved in waging the war preoccupied
the wartime leaders—Roosevelt, Churchill, and Stalin.

"Had the war been lost, there would be even fewer

Jews surviving in the world and no Israel. Yet facts are facts, and the fate of European Jewry was not uppermost in their minds."

The record reveals that all Allied governments had considerable advance information about Hitler's policy to exterminate Jews but, for a variety of reasons, were generally reticent and evasive about calling attention to the fact that his target for genocide was the Jews.

Finally, in December 1942, the fledgling United Nations, as they began to call themselves, issued a brief but eloquent statement on the mass slaughter of Jews; this was a full eighteen months after the killings had begun.

In the report, Justice Goldberg states, "They made little or no attempt until very late in the war to rescue Jews from The Holocaust, and in some cases actually obstructed such attempts by others.

"There was great concern about where they could put any massive number of Jewish refugees. Their attitude on the matter was construed by Nazi authorities as tantamount to acquiescence."

According to *American Jewry During The Holocaust*, "This Allied attitude was foreshadowed well before the extermination program began. We have already referred to the prewar unwillingness of Western governments, as late as 1938, to admit large numbers of Jewish refugees.

"After war began in 1939, foreigners in Britain who were nationals of countries under German control— including Jews, despite their status as persecuted victims and pariahs in the Nazi states—were classified as 'enemy aliens' and even, for a time, placed in detention camps.

"In effect, British officialdom—a quarter of a century after calling for creation of a 'Jewish national home'— was unable to perceive the Jews as a nation of people. Instead they were treated as nationals of the states which had stripped them of all their rights.

"The British government, in pursuit of its aim to conciliate the Arabs, invalidated all certificates of entry into Palestine that had already been issued to Jews.

"As enemy aliens, Jews were also generally barred from entering territories of the British Empire."

The report goes on to state that even though some Jews were admitted into Britain and the United States as refugees, both governments either obstructed Jews fleeing from German-controlled territory during the "phony war" period (1939-1940).

"In 1942 and thereafter, when the plight of Europe's Jews had become truly desperate," the report continues, "the British and American official attitudes remained much the same. The two governments had first-hand intelligence on the Jewish condition in Nazi-occupied lands and were currently informed on steps to carry out the 'Final Solution.' Many reports in 1942 came from deportees who had escaped from the death squads."

In May 1942 the Jewish Socialist Party of Poland, the "Bund," sent a report to London informing the world that the Germans had 'embarked on the physical extermination of the Jewish population on Polish soil.' The report provided precise data on the places and dates of executions and the number of Jews involved, totaling about 700,000. This was followed by Gerhart Riegner's cable from Geneva to Washington that alerted Allied governments and Jewish leaders of the same—Hitler's "Final Solution."

Once Riegner's report was released to the public by the Jewish Telegraphic Agency the following month, additional reports came out that mirrored his findings. Rabbi Wise found that his worst fears were realized. He began working on an analysis of the role Hitler's "Final Solution" played in each effected European country. The twenty page report, *Blueprint for Extermination*, was presented to President Roosevelt on December 8. Armed with this in-depth record, the United States and the Allies, took no action.

On December 17, 1942, the date of the one and only Allied statement of protest, Nazi propaganda minister Josef Paul Goebbels wrote in his diary, "'At bottom... I believe both the English and Americans are happy that we are exterminating the Jewish riffraff.'"

The *American Jewry* report further reveals that there was overwhelming evidence of Britain and America's effort to avoid involvement in the matter. "It is notable... that both the British Broadcasting Corporation and the United States Office of War Information reported the Nazis' mass slaughter of millions of people beginning in 1942, but did not mention that the targets of this horror were Jews."

Even more significant is the fact that the death camps, whose inmates were chiefly Jewish, were never sub-jected to Allied bombing. On several occasions synthetic oil, rubber, and other war production plants in the large com-plex at Auschwitz were bombed, but the death camp and gas chambers were left untouched—except once, by mistake.

One Auschwitz survivor has testified that he and others hoped to be bombed by the Allies, not only because there might be a chance of escape in the confusion but because even if they themselves were killed they might first have the consolation of seeing Germans killed—and in any case it was better to die by bombing than be gassed.

Erich Kulka, another inmate at Birkenau, the part of the Auschwitz complex where most of the gassing and cremating took place, later told the historian Martin Gilbert, "'We saw many times the silver trails in the sky.... All the SS men would go into the bunkers but we came out of our huts and prayed that a bomb would fall, or soldiers and weapons will be parachuted, but in vain.'"

Despite the hopes of imprisoned Jews, bombings of the horrific camps never came. However, "it is worthy noting that the Allies had detailed maps of the entire Auschwitz complex, which had been provided by Weissmandel, the heroic rabbi in Slovakia. It should also be noted that the Allies, even after they attained mastery of the air over Europe, did not threaten the Nazis with retaliatory bombing if they did not desist from the mass slaughter of European Jews."

"On the Acquiescence of this Government in the Murder of European Jews," a memorandum discussing the United States' attitude of indifference, dated January 19, 1944, was written by Josiah E. Dubois, Jr., then assistant general counsel for the U.S. Treasury Department. The memorandum, addressed to Secretary of the Treasury Henry Morgenthau Jr., "to substantiate the charge of acquiescence—in contrast to mere inattention or indifference—"

gave specific facts about State Department actions and summarized them as follows:

"(1) They have not only failed to use the Governmental machinery at their disposal to rescue Jews from Hitler, but have even gone so far as to use this Government machinery to prevent the rescue of these Jews.

"(2) They have not only failed to cooperate with private organizations in the efforts of these organizations to work out individual programs of their own, but have taken steps designed to prevent these programs from being put into effect.

"(3) They not only have failed to facilitate the obtaining of information concerning Hitler's plans to exterminate the Jews of Europe but in their official capacity have gone so far as to surreptitiously attempt to stop the obtaining of information concerning the murder of the Jewish population in Europe.

"(4) They have tried to cover their guilt by:
   "(a) concealment and misrepresentation;
   "(b) giving of false and misleading explanations for their failures to act and their attempts to prevent action; and
   "(c) the issuance of false and misleading statements concerning the 'action' which they have taken to date."

On the other hand, the *American Jewry* report offers examples of what the United States government did do to help Jews. "In justice it should be recalled that United States policy on this question was not completely static throughout the war. An important development was the creation of the War Refugee Board (WRB)... this body succeeded in relaxing the application of curbs on the sending of money abroad, and on contacts with enemy authorities, in such a way as to facilitate rescue efforts by the American Joint Distribution Committee and other Jewish organizations.

Roosevelt created the WRB by Executive Order 9417 on January 22, 1944. The instructions accompanying the order were sent to U.S. diplomatic posts abroad by the State Department. "On receiving this instruction in Ankara, Turkey, the same Ambassador Laurence Steinhardt who, earlier in Moscow, had actively obstructed the granting of visas to such people, now worked aggressively to carry out his new instructions—prodded by the WRB representative in Ankara, Ambassador Ira Hirachman."

The new policy was too little, too late, because by mid 1943, most of Poland's Jewish population were dead or in concentration camps, as well as were Jews in Germany, Luxembourg, France and Belgium. "The 'Greater German Reich,' as these latter countries were called, had been declared *Judenrein* (purged of Jews) and, in the Soviet Union, Jews had been killed in great numbers."

Yet the new policy was not a complete loss; a large number of Hungarian and Rumanian Jews were saved from death at the hands of Germans in 1944 and 1945.

The report concludes on this issue with a thought on what could have been. "It should be noted that during the last three years of the war nearly 400,000 German prisoners of war were interned in camps across the United States. Most were used in civilian industries, particularly agriculture, to alleviate labor shortages. This makes it difficult to argue that the tens or even hundreds of thousand Jews who might have left Europe in that period, notably from Hungary and Rumania, could not have been similarly interned to save them from death."

Justice Goldberg, in *American Jewry During the Holocaust*, states, "The American Jewish Commission on the Holocaust was formed in 1981 on the initiative of a number of American Jewish leaders. It was created with a view to conducting an objective inquiry into the actions and attitudes of American Jewish leaders and organizations concerning The Holocaust during those years of World War II when the great tragedy was impending and in progress.

"The underlying aim of the initiators of the project was not to make moral judgments but rather to enable later generations to learn from this experience whatever might help prevent a similar tragedy from ever again befalling the Jews or any other people."

With startling insight, Justice Goldberg continues, "It is a striking fact that in the voluminous published material on the Holocaust, not a single book deals primarily with the role of one of the most important groups involved; namely, the leaders of the major American Jewish organizations. The role of every other key group and leader has been thoroughly studied: Franklin D. Roosevelt and the State Department, Winston Churchill and the British Foreign and Colonial Offices, the Vatican and other

Christian church authorities, the International Committee of the Red Cross—and, of course, Hitler, the Nazi hierarchy, and the roles of other Axis powers of the Nazis' satellite and conquered countries.

"No comparable study of the role of American Jewry exists." Goldberg concludes, "It is not my intention to detract from the factual character of the report.... But one conclusion is beyond contradiction. The Holocaust—the planned, deliberate murder of six million European Jews by Adolf Hitler and his minions—was an unprecedented crime against humanity. Nothing comparable has ever occurred or must be allowed to happen again."

CHAPTER 8

Victims' Gold

Aside from monetary gold confiscated from central banks of countries occupied by Germany, valuables of a different magnitude, including currency, wedding bands, watches, and religious items were stolen from victims of Nazi persecution. Gold confiscated from individuals was taken from victims of Nazi concentration camps and death camps, at national borders from Jewish people attempting to escape Hitler's war machine, from Jews being transported to Polish ghettos, and from residents of countries occupied by Germany. In an article in the Jewish Telegraphic Agency by Daniel Kurtzman, "nearly one-third of all gold looted by the Nazis came from individual victims and private businesses."

A well-orchestrated system of collecting, classifying and selling gold looted exclusively from victims of Nazi death camps was implemented in 1942 and overseen by SS Captain Bruno Melmer. Valuables, clothes and women's hair were confiscated by Nazi soldiers or were collected by Jewish prisoners who were forced to service the gas chambers and crematoriums. The valuables were then transported to the Reichsbank by Melmer and deposited in an account in his name and divided on the basis of value.

According to the Report: *SS Loot and the Reichsbank by Colonel Bernard Bernstein dtd 30 October 1945*, records and receipts divided the shipments of gold into the following categories: Foreign Exchange, Gold Bars, Silver Bars, Alloy Bars, Gold and Silver Coins, Purses, Knives and Forks, Jewels, Pearls, Gold and Diamond Rings and Watches, Dental Gold, Broken Gold, Silver, and Expenses. Currencies, gold and silver coins, gold bullion and securities were incorporated into the bank's holdings. Jewelry and larger items made of precious metals were taken to the Berlin Municipal Pawn Shop. There, the items were again divided. The more valuable items were sold abroad in exchange for foreign currency, which was more useful to Nazi Germany than its own currency. The remainder of the items were sent to Degussa Smelting Company and turned into gold bars to be returned to the Reichsbank. Smaller items were sent to the Prussian State Mint, where they too were smelted into bars. The bars were then returned to the Reichsbank, where they were combined with the monetary gold that originated in the central banks of occupied countries. The gold was then sold to either Germany's commercial banks, Deutsche and Dresdner Banks, or to the central banks of other countries, primarily Switzerland and Italy. The common practice of assigning pre-war dates to looted gold that was smelted into gold bars was implemented in an effort to disguise it from the central banks and Allied powers.

Because the Nazis kept meticulous records of gold transactions, an accurate estimate of the total amount of looted gold that came from victims of Nazi atrocities can be determined. According to Elan Steinberg, executive director of the World Jewish Congress, "the precision is down to a single bar of gold." Records kept by the Office of the Military Government United States (OMGUS) reveal that the Dresdner Bank received seventeen gold bars that were "not of a high fineness level," while the Deutsche Bank received twenty-two such bars. Four bars from the Melmer account were sent to Rome, and at least three bars were confiscated by United States forces and turned over to the Tripartite Gold Commission for the Restitution for Monetary Gold and deposited in the gold pool. Switzerland also received at least 120 kilograms of gold from the Melmer account according to an Associated Press article.

One of the key German financiers handling operations overseas, and having strong ties with Nazi officials, Hermann Josef Abs, was also the head of Deutsche Bank's Foreign Department. In an AFP article, it is concluded that during the war, the Deutsche Bank bought 4,446 kilograms of fine gold from the Reichsbank. Because of the precise records kept by Bruno Melmer, the origin of gold ingots bought by the Deutsche Bank can be traced back to gold and jewelry stolen from victims of Nazi death camps.

Indistinguishable from monetary gold that originated in the central banks of occupied countries, victim gold could only be identified through chemical analysis. If, when the gold was smelted, the amalgams used during processing the gold into dental fillings or jewelry was not removed, it could be detected. However, origin was determined by appearance alone, and the gold was integrated into the monetary gold reserves. Proceeds from the sale of gold from the Melmer account were deposited in the Max Heiliger account, held by another member of the SS.

Jewelry from victims was also sent via diplomatic pouch to the German Legislation in Bern. There they were handed over to German agents who traded them for much needed foreign currency and industrial diamonds.

While the valuables deposited in the Melmer Account were mainly taken from Nazi death camps and concentration camps, other personal assets of individuals and private businesses were also taken. According to an article in *Time*, gold looted by Nazi soldiers was discovered by the American 90th Division. At the salt mine in Merkers, a small town south of Berlin, American troops found, "sacks filled with gold and silver coins, piles of bank notes, religious items, and more than 8,500 bars of gold. Suitcases at the back of the vault contained gold and silver objects, sacks of wedding rings, watches and gold dental work." According to recently declassified United States State Department records, gold retrieved from Merkers salt mine was transported to London and New York.

Despite the thorough records that were kept, many disappeared in the seventies, including files on the Melmer account. A Reuters article states that twenty-six Melmer folders including "incoming and delivery bookings for jewelry, other valuables and dental gold which were delivered from Auschwitz in seventy-six consignments to Berlin" were either lost of destroyed.

PART II

Neutral Gold Games

CHAPTER 9

Swiss Lucre

Though this book focuses on the actions of the nations other than Switzerland which enriched themselves on looted Nazi gold and supplied Nazi Germany with war material and capital, it is impossible to consider these actions without also understanding that, as was pointed out earlier, Switzerland stood at the center of the unsavory trade in Nazi plunder. According to the Bergier Commission Report, Switzerland was the recipient of four-fifths of all the gold the Nazis looted. Acting as banker, merchant, and international transit point, Switzerland profited on the war.

A quick backward glance at the history of Switzerland in this regard is useful to understanding how the country functioned in relation to the other neutrals and the victims of the war. Around the spring of 1941, Switzerland
began receiving the smuggled proceeds of foreign
exchange. Through Lisbon, it received large amounts of
French francs. In addition, Jewish and other fleeing people
sometimes brought with them large amounts of cash. It
was even thought by United States Treasury officials that
nationals of Axis countries whose accounts were blocked
in America were trying to sell their holdings to the Swiss. It
was estimated in 1942 that there were several billion Swiss
francs in these accounts, while German and Austrian
accounts were believed to have about $116 million. There
were other ways in which German funds were being transferred to and from Switzerland as well. The Swiss banks
were intermediaries in transferring gold to Portugal, dollar
notes were sold—some through fines extracted from
German Jews—and investments were made in the United
States and Latin America.

In 1943, Germany absorbed nearly one-third of all
Swiss exports. Even after the Inter-Allied Declaration
Against Acts of Dispossession Committed in Territories
Under Enemy Occupation or Control and other Allied
attempts to control the trade of plundered gold and other
treasure, Axis business with and through Switzerland continued as usual until the end of World War II.

Of all the "neutral" nations of World War II, the
one with the most pernicious role, which included the
deepest and most crucial economic relationship with Nazi
Germany, was Switzerland.

In the foreword to the State Department report, *U.S. and Allied Efforts to Recover and Restore Gold and Other Assets Stolen or Hidden by Germany During World War II,* Eizenstat states that Switzerland's role during and after the war was "very mixed.... Switzerland ended World War II as one of the wealthiest nations in Europe.

He continues, "It conducted trade with the Allied countries as well as with the Axis powers. The Swiss National Bank maintained gold accounts for Nazi Germany throughout the entire war" while at the same time, doing business with Germany's enemies—the United States, Canada, and Great Britain."

Despite being a neutral country, Switzerland was considered a friend by the Allies who were able to gather intelligence within Swiss borders and who viewed the country as "a protecting power—most critically for its prisoners of war."

However, Switzerland was also supplying Germany with two billion kilowatt hours of electricity every year. The Swiss rail system transported German troops and, according to recently declassified documents, German Holocaust victims as well.

Each new report heightens the figures and adds startling information. The 1997 interim report by the Bergier Commission recounts information released by the BBC that revealed that, "seventy-six percent of Nazi gold transactions went through Switzerland and the volume of trade between Swiss private banks and wartime Germany was at least three times higher than previously thought."

The Swiss National Bank took in more than $389 million ($3.5 billion today) of Nazi Gold and $64.2 million

($580 million today) of Nazi gold passed through other Swiss banks. Of the gold taken in, according to the Commission, $146 million was Holocaust victim gold and over two million of this came from Auschwitz victims whose possessions were taken way by SS guards.

However, the report was quick to point out that "The Swiss government acknowledged as early as 1952 and reiterated in 1997 there were shortcomings in Switzerland's refugee policies [during the war]." Yet the Swiss also "persuaded the Nazis to establish the 'J' stamp which prevented tens of thousands of Jews from entering Switzerland or other potential sanctuaries."

During the war, Swiss borders were almost closed to Jews from France and Belgium who were trying to escape Hitler's persecution.

It is true and to their credit that beginning in 1933 and extending to 1945, 50,000 Jewish refugees were admitted, 30,000 of which remained in Switzerland. However, after the outbreak of war, the burden of supporting these Jewish refugees—many of whom escaped with only the clothes on their backs or with very few possessions—was placed on the Jewish communities of Switzerland.

"In August and December 1944, Switzerland admitted an additional 1,700 concentration camp inmates from Bergen-Belsen, and in February 1945 an estimated 1,200 from Therienstadt."

However, the Swiss refused to become further involved with those emigrants because they expected Jewish communities to take on other survivors. Yet no such imposition was placed on Swiss relatives of the over 100,000 non-Jewish refugees taken in after 1940.

In addition to refusing the beleaguered refugees, and taking their looted valuables, Switzerland supported Germany's efforts by supplying the things most vital in times of war. According to some intelligence documents, Switzerland's industries engaged in direct production for the Axis and helped protect the enemy's investments: "Swiss shipping lines furnished Germany with a large number of boats for the transport of goods [and] allowed an unprecedented use of its railways to link Germany and Italy for the transport of coal and other goods.

"Switzerland provided Germany with arms, ammunition, aluminum, machines, and precision tools, as well as agricultural products. Swiss convoys [with immunity from aerial attack by Allied forces because of its neutrality status] carried products from Spain across France through Switzerland to Germany."

Switzerland did not restrict this conduct to the European continent alone. In fact, Swiss banks conducted business in Nazi markets in Latin America.

These activities and business dealings were maintained by the Swiss even after the Germans were pushed back and the threat of their power was diminished. Furthermore, trade continued after an agreement was reached with the United States to freeze German assets and to restrict purchases of gold from Germany.

This ongoing "business as usual" attitude that continued through postwar negotiations was found to be unbelievable by historian William Slany.

The State Department found the Swiss to be stubbornly persistent in their wrongdoing and in their attitude about their activities. In postwar negotiations, the Swiss continued to use legalistic positions to defend their every interest, regardless of the moral or ethical issues at stake. The report states, "Initially, for instance, they opposed returning any Nazi gold to those from whom it was stolen, and they denied having received any looted gold. The Swiss contended that they had purchased it in good faith, that it was war booty obtained in accordance with international legal principles by the Third Reich during its victorious campaigns, and that there was no international legal principle which would entitle the Allies to recover and redistribute Nazi assets."

The Swiss took a position that defied honesty and reality as the amount of Germany's gold reserves both before and after the war were well known. In fact, the Swiss National Bank and private Swiss bankers knew, as the war progressed, that the Reichsbank's own coffers had been depleted and that the Swiss were handling vast sums of looted gold. Furthermore, the Swiss were totally aware of the Nazi gold heists from France of Belgian gold, as well as from other countries.

Evidence that Switzerland was boldly mendacious in their claims of innocence during and after postwar negotiations is eminently clear and incontrovertible.

In 1946 an agreement was hammered out between the war Allies and the Swiss at a gathering in Washington, D.C.

The accord obligated Switzerland to transfer 250 million Swiss francs ($58.1 million) in gold to the Allies for the reconstruction of war-torn Europe, of which a portion was to be redirected to the assistance of stateless victims, for the most part Jews.

In addition, the Swiss were required to commit themselves to the enormous task of identifying dormant accounts which were heirless and could be used for the benefit of Nazi victims.

Even though the accord was a step in the right direction, the $58.1 million in German-looted gold to be turned over to the Allies was far less than the $185 to $289 million in stolen funds the State and Treasury Departments estimated was stashed at the end of the war in the Swiss National Bank vaults.

Another $120 million of German-looted gold was also estimated to be on deposit for other countries at that time. However, as they had been before, the Swiss were not forthcoming about those funds for the "humanitarian" purposes they consented to participate in.

The $58.1 million was promptly paid to the Tripartite Gold Commission for redistribution to claimant countries.

However, another requirement of the accord, the liquidation of hundreds of millions of dollars in German assets, was not carried out. "The Swiss raised one objection after another, arguing over exchange rates, insisting that German debt settlements be included, and demanding that the United States unblock assets from German companies seized during the war, but which the Bern government claimed were actually Swiss-owned."

"They refused to make an exemption for the assets of surviving Jews from Germany and heirless German Jewish assets, and continued to make them subject to liquidation," Stuart Eizenstat's study scolded.

"They refused to recognize any moral obligation to

return looted Dutch gold when evidence became available after the conclusion of the 1946 negotiations."

Four years passed and in 1950, United States mediators grimly concluded that the Swiss "had no intention of ever implementing the 1946 Washington Accord."

Action was also taken in September 1946 to carry out a mandate of the past January's Paris Reparations Agreement reached by representatives of the United States, Britain, and France. The Tripartite Gold Commission (TGC), headquartered in Brussels, Belgium, set out to review and adjudicate claims from governments (not individuals) for the restitution of looted monetary gold recovered in Germany or acquired from the "neutrals" in their negotiations with the Allies.

The TGC was to ensure that each claimant country would receive restitution from the gold pool assembled by the Allies for the Commission in proportion to its loss of monetary gold at the hands of the Germans during the war.

Immediately after the TGC's establishment, ten nations made claims for the looted Nazi gold: Albania, Austria, Belgium, Czechoslovakia, Greece, Luxembourg, the Netherlands, Poland, Yugoslavia, and ironically, Italy.

The Commission made its first distribution of $143 million from the gold pool in October 1947. Allocations went to Belgium, the Netherlands, Poland, and Yugoslavia. Between 1945 and 1948, the Foreign Exchange Depository collected, guarded, inventoried, and distributed to various countries nearly $300 million in gold bullion and gold coins ($2.9 billion today).

A second round of allocations was made by the TGC between 1958 and 1966. The allocations have been ongoing since. In fact, a payment went out to Albania as recently as October 1996.

Overall, payments of 329 metric tons of gold, initially worth $380 million (today $4 billion) have been made to the claimant nations. Of that amount, $264 million came from the FED that was formed in 1945 as a section of the Office of Military Government United States (OMGUS) by the American occupation force in Germany.

The FED was given supervision over the Reichsbank building in Frankfurt and made custodian of some 400 million reichsmarks in gold that the bank had hidden in the Merkers salt mines and which was discovered by American armies who overran Germany in 1945.

The FED worked with Allied governments, occupation authorities, and the Tripartite Gold Commission in inventorying collections that it made (consistent with official definitions of monetary and non-monetary gold), and making disbursements as agreed.

According to Swiss parliamentarian Jean Zigler, author of *The Swiss, the Gold, and the Dead*, the revelations about his government have become "an earthquake, a deep trauma in the Swiss national consciousness. In the past, Switzerland strangled its memories and denied its crimes. Now, with the revelations from abroad, we can no longer deny them."

In contrast to this openness is the report by Reuters that "Switzerland's economics minister... repeated his view that it was not the right time to set up a compensation fund for Jews who might be entitled to money left in Swiss banks after World War II. Delamuras repeated Berne's stance that any compensation should await the findings of a nine-member panel named two weeks ago to investigate the Swiss financial role in World War Two."

The release of one set of documents through the offices of Senator D'Amato and the World Jewish Congress that include a report in January 1997, show that during World War II the Swiss National Bank shipped 280 truckloads of looted Nazi gold to Spain and Portugal. Among the revelations still coming out are:

- The fact that Christopher Meili, a young guard in one of Switzerland's largest banks, saw evidence of the attempt to destroy archive material about bank transactions during the war, in direct violation of a government ban (see United States chapter).

- An October 1943 letter from Admiral William Leahy, one of the joint chiefs of staff, showing that Washington was ready to impose a total economic blockade of Switzerland because of their selling huge supplies of munitions to the Nazis.

- Poignant stories such as the one told in *Time* magazine on February 24, 1997 of Bert Linder who is eighty-five and a survivor of Auschwitz, unlike his wife, ten-month-old son and four others from his family. The Swiss press has labeled him David against Goliath for filing suit against the Swiss bankers who added tragedy to tragedy. "My friends tell me enough is enough. But enough is not enough. The Swiss have the audacity to keep this money that does not belong to them and to make money with it. It should go back to the Jewish people."

On March 27, 1998, the *New York Times* reported that Switzerland's three major banks, the Union Bank of Switzerland, the Swiss Bank Corporation and Credit Suisse had changed their stated views and were negotiating a global settlement for Holocaust victims. They announced a compensation fund would be set up for the victims and their heirs who had been deprived of the money for fifty some odd years. They offered several months later to settle claims against them for $600 million.

However, the Swiss National Bank, which acknowledges it was Nazi Germany's major recipient of gold, refused to join the settlement, although it had contributed 100 million Swiss francs to a humanitarian fund in 1997. And there are others still in denial as well.

The most authoritative voice to speak out in support of Switzerland's widely-condemned role as banker for Nazi Germany and collaborator in the acquisition of gold looted from Europe's Jewry belongs to Hans Schaffner, head of the Swiss Federal Office of War Economy from 1939 to 1946.

Schaffner, who also served as an elected member of the Swiss Federal Council from 1961 to 1970 and was President of Switzerland in 1965, was impelled to sound the strongest protest yet heard against his country's growing

legion of detractors. He dispatched a lengthy pronouncement to the op-ed page of the *New York Times* titled "The
Truth About Switzerland."

"Once again debate has arisen concerning the measures that should be taken by Switzerland to settle the
claims of Holocaust victims whose stolen property made
its way into Swiss banks," wrote Schaffner in his article,
published on April 6, 1998.

"The compensations provided by my country to
date have been widely portrayed not as an honorable act of
compassion but as evidence of a guilty national conscience."

Schaffner then adds, "This confusion comes after
two years of accusations that Switzerland collaborated with
Nazi Germany in World War II by stealing Jewish property
and mistreating refugees. These charges were not based on
any new information. All the relevant details have been
available since 1946.

"But what is new is the surge of resentment against
Switzerland, and the ignorance that underlies it.

"Since I directed the Swiss war economy during the
menacing years of World War II, when we had to prepare
against Nazi aggression, I'm appalled to see Swiss wartime
actions misrepresented so consistently. It is time to set the
record straight."

Schaffner claimed Swiss neutrality wasn't an oppor-
tunistic subterfuge but a "continuation of our policy, maintained over centuries of achieving permanent neutrality."

While Schaffner argued the neutrality was based on
"explicit provisions of international law recognized by the

Allies and it includes the obligation not to take sides with any belligerent nation, [it] never implied moral indifference."

Schaffner claimed that during World War II, most Swiss sympathized with the Allies "and our shared democratic traditions."

The former Swiss head of state then suggested that was why Hitler "continually expressed contempt for us."

Yet there's no evidence anywhere on the record that Hitler ever mouthed a bad word against the Swiss.

Schaffner then has the unmitigated gall to go on and declare that "many who now criticize Switzerland's neutrality overlook the contributions it enabled us to make. Our International Red Cross was permitted into Germany and Japan, where it saved the lives of many Allied prisoners of war."

But how then can anyone reconcile the fact that the Red Cross offered a blanket apology in 1998 for having failed to give Jewish emigrants the proper treatment they demanded to enter sanctuaries such as Switzerland during World War II?

Schaffner went on discussing the twists and turns the Swiss took part in to bring about a negotiation for "an early settlement" to reduce "bloodshed and destruction in the final days of the war."

With one of his comments there's no argument, "Despite these constraints, we defied Germany by sending the Allies precision instruments from our watch industry. We also smuggled plans and know-how to the Allies so they could start up their own production of these items.

"And while the Germans forced us to expand our

credit lines so they could import more Swiss goods, we used German coal, oil, steel, cement, and food to build our mountain fortifications and the guns that held off the threat of Nazi invasion."

Schaffner suggested that sources argued Switzerland should have been tougher with the Germans after the fall of Stalingrad in 1943, which reduced Nazi power in Europe and slightly eased Switzerland's long-term military concerns.

"But that turn of events also made Hitler desperate and multiplied the risk of his making unpredictable moves against Switzerland," Schaffner commented.

"The issue of Jewish property has also been mis-understood," he continued. "First, Switzerland was not the preferred destination for those trying to get their holdings out of Europe. The United States was. Even Switzerland kept the bulk of its gold reserves in Fort Knox. As far as I know, aside from a few isolated incidents, Swiss banks did not pocket unclaimed deposits."

Schaffner claimed, "These accounts continue to exist and are still available to legitimate claimants and their heirs."

However, the facts argue with his claims. Legitimate claimants and their heirs were asked to produce death cer-tificates of their relatives before they could recover their deposits in Swiss banks.

Herr Schaffner continued, "I'm confident that cur-rent investigations will show that only a tiny fraction of those accounts are associated directly with the Holocaust. In any case, those records are available for inspection."

Unfortunately, Swiss bank records had ironclad legal protection, and no depositor's dealings with those banks could ever be revealed under Swiss laws of that time!

Then Schaffner stated, "In 1946, the Allies and Switzerland signed the Washington Agreement, which settled the postwar claims of various European banks."

However Switzerland was left to feast on nearly $6 billion of Nazi gold, without having to be responsive or responsible for even the minutest portion of that illicit loot.

"Initially," Schaffner continued, "the United States still held six billion francs in frozen Swiss assets as well as gold payments owed to the Swiss National Bank. Because international law supported the Swiss position, the United States released the assets."

In truth, the Allied-Swiss Agreement on Liquidation of German Property assured the release of German assets blocked by Switzerland in 1945 at the behest of the Allies. Switzerland agreed to pay the Allies the lump sum of 121.5 million Swiss francs ($28.3 million), less its advance of twenty million francs ($4.7 million) to the International Relief Organization in July 1948. The Allies actually received 101.5 million francs ($23.6 million) from which they were committed to make an additional payment of thirteen million Swiss francs ($3 million) to the IRO. The Allies were entitled to receive the 121.5 million francs in lieu of Switzerland's liquidation of German assets in its country.

"Switzerland, like the United States, made a contribution to the recovery of Europe at that time because she had suffered less than most," claimed Schaffner.

The amount that Switzerland surrendered was a mere pittance, as later disclosures make clear.

"The attempt to reopen this settlement a half-century later is scandalous," Schaffner blustered. "Of all the allegations that have been made against Switzerland nothing disturbs me more than the charge that my country was insensitive to the plight of wartime refugees.

"In 1938, when it became clear that substantial numbers of people would soon be fleeing German control, an international conference was held in Evian, France.

"The Swiss offered to take an unlimited number of refugees on a temporary basis. Despite our tiny populations (about half that of New York City), we accepted more than 300,000 people.

"It is true that we turned away 30,000 Jews. But we sheltered 25,000 other Jews at a time when other countries, including the United States, shut their doors firmly against Jewish refugees.

"Some have pointed out that many refugees were housed in temporary camps, along with the thousands of Allied soldiers and pilots who sought interment in Switzerland rather than be sent to Nazi prisons or face death.

"Yet how else could a small mountainous country deal with a sudden population increase of nearly ten percent—In wartime?"

Switzerland's gesture was commendable and indeed it performed a great service to the Allied cause. But there is every reason to take issue with Herr Schaffner's next argument: "Today, a generation that knows nothing about

World War II is being misled about my country. To compare a diplomat like Walter Stucki with an SS executioner, as some have done, is untrue and shows bad faith. The same holds for those who have referred to the defensive strategy of General Henri Guisan as a 'submissive gesture,' when in fact the Germans hated Guisan because of his visceral distaste for Nazism."

Hans Schaffner's last words sought to win over sympathy and understanding from American readers of the *New York Times*. "It is time for these falsehoods and half-truths to stop. All my life I have done my best to foster good relations with America, Switzerland's great sister republic.

"But good relations must rest on truth."

Indeed they must.

On April 4, 1998, the Swiss National Bank announced it would vigorously fight a planned class action lawsuit (see chapter on the United States) by Holocaust victims and their heirs trying to recover their looted funds.

Meanwhile, other disclosures tumbled out.

On May 25, 1998, the long-awaited report about World War II dealings as early as 1941 in Nazi gold concluded that Swiss National Bank officials were aware that gold sent to their "neutral" Alpine republic had been looted from Axis occupied territories in Europe. The report confirmed allegations that both the precious metal currency and other of its forms—such as gold from Holocaust victims' teeth, wedding bands, and other jewelry—had made its way to the vaults of Switzerland's largest bank whose head offices are still in Zurich.

Among other findings, the most shuddering conclusion of the report was that the looted wealth snatched
from Jewish victims in lands Hitler conquered had made
their way to Switzerland—and helped to pay for services
rendered to Germany that prolonged World War II indefi-
nitely.

Commissioned by the Swiss Government, the
report is viewed by many as the country's ultimate concession to the pangs of conscience it had lived with since the
practice of "aiding and abetting the Third Reich's robber
barons" in stealing Jewish wealth, a practice that had begun
as long ago as 1938, if not earlier.

The panel's director, Jean-Francois Bergier, was
highly critical of officials of the Swiss National Bank
(SNB) during World War II "for pursuing an ethic of the
least effort to trace the source of the gold they were receiving in their account even though, starting in 1941, they
became increasingly aware that Jews and other persecuted
groups were being taken for all they were worth.

"And in 1943, at the latest, the SNB had knowledge
of the systematic extermination of victims of the Nazi
regime. Yet nonetheless those officials neglected taking
measures to distinguish looted gold from other gold holdings of the Reichsbank."

Even before the whole report had been transmitted
to the United States over the news service lines of the
Associated Press, United Press International, and Reuters,
the findings were hailed as "a significant breakthrough" by
perennial critics of Switzerland banks' secretive and
unforthcoming informational policies.

Even some members of Jewish communities expressed satisfaction over the issuance of the report—but that euphoria was quickly stifled when the details of the document were released and the bottom line of all that was stated in the name of *apologia* was aired. It clearly came to light that neither SNB, nor the Swiss Government, had any intention of joining their nation's commercial banks, which earlier had entered into a compact with American Jewish groups to set up a "global settlement fund" to atone for the wartime trade the banks engaged in, and principally to compensate survivors and heirs of the Holocaust.

The figure reached by the study group as the amount of gold Switzerland's central bank had bought from the Nazis and their satellites was worth $280 million in wartime dollars. That amounts to $2.5 billion at today's prices.

And, as Senator D'Amato was to later observe: "As of today, the only response to the Bergier report from the Swiss is the expression of 'profound regret.'"

The *U.S. and Allied Wartime and Postwar Negotiations with Argentina, Spain, Sweden, and Turkey on Looted Gold and German External Assets*, is at great variance in its estimate with the Swiss figures. It states that the worth amounts to a two-to-one ratio—very much in favor of the Swiss.

The *U.S. and Allied Wartime and Postwar Negotiations...* report, issued on June 2, 1998, also doubled the American estimate of how much gold was in a Nazi account that received deposits of wedding rings, teeth fillings, and other personal possessions of Holocaust victims.

The report concludes through continued and far-reaching investigation that much of the looted wealth by the Nazis was routed through Switzerland to pay other neutral nations for vital supplies that sustained Hitler's army in the last year of World War II. Apparently, however, it took the officials preparing the report some time before they became fully aware of the activities of the Swiss.

"Drafts of the report suggest that as State Department officials fine-tuned their conclusions there was considerable internal debate over how to deal with Switzerland," the report states. In an early draft of the report's introduction [prepared by Eizenstat] there was a referral to the Swiss as 'courageous' for conducting a 'searching national debate' about their country's wartime role."

The final version of the report no longer contained the word "courageous."

In a totally defiant voice, the central bank let it be known that they had, "absolutely no intention to join negotiations to compensate Holocaust survivors for stolen gold deposited in our vaults—even if another Swiss agency [issued only the previous week] has concluded that the Swiss National Bank knowingly accepted stolen gold from the Nazis worth billions in today's dollars."

The Swiss government task force's spokesperson, Marie-Marcelline Kurmann, gave a pointed response on June 26, 1998 to the world's criticism of Switzerland's profiteering from the war and not settling with Holocaust victims. "It remains the position of the Federal Council that there is no question of the federal government taking part in the negotiation on a settlement. It also rules out any government participation in a so-called 'global solution' with public money."

The stance of the Swiss banks and government brought reprisals. With the negotiations between the banks and claimants at an impasse, on July 2, 1998, government officials in New Jersey, California, and New York announced sanctions against the Swiss banks which have kept Holocaust victims' assets. Governor Christine Todd Whitman of New Jersey was among the first to act. She ordered the New Jersey Division of Investment to stop buying Swiss bank stocks and "refrain from expanding state investments in Swiss banking institutions."

According to New York State Comptroller H. Carl McCall, New York would bar short-term investments and stop the Swiss banks from handling state and city debt unless a settlement could be reached by September 1, 1998. New York State deposits $150 million short-term per day in Swiss banks.

In California, which has $32 billion tied to Swiss banks, Treasurer Matt Fong told Associated Press his state "would not seek new contracts with U.S. subsidiaries of Swiss banks."

The Swiss government had continued to state that it saw no reason for reopening the 1946 Washington Agreement with France, England and the United States. The Swiss position was that the 1946 pact settled all Allied claims and that international law governs their not being reopened.

But there were those who felt very strongly that

things must change. New York's Senator D'Amato chaired a meeting of the Senate Banking, Housing and Urban Affairs Committee on July 22, 1998. At these hearings, Michael D. Hausfeld, the attorney representing the Holocaust victims, observed that Switzerland was Germany's foremost agent for financial operations and in many instances made available Portuguese, South American, United States, and other foreign monetary units for German use.

One scheme, described by Hausfeld, was especially heinous. "Jews and others in neutral countries received authentic notices that their friends and relations in concentration camps were in great need. Money sent to them in a certain way, it was written, could aid them. Dollars in the form of blank checks were the currency of choice. The blank checks were received by the camp and then gathered together and sent to a neutral country, often to Switzerland. The Swiss banks put their stamp as a payee and the checks were then sent to New York, without there being any trace that they were sent to Germany, and duly paid."

On July 27, 1998, *Business Week's* article titled "Swiss Banks: The Noose Tightens" revealed that not only New Jersey and New York but a number of other state and city finance officials in the United States were ready to escalate sanctions against the Swiss commercial banks.

Although commercial Swiss banks had offered $600 million in settlement of the Holocaust victims' claims, the World Jewish Congress wanted $1.5 billion, "insisting that the Swiss government and central bank contribute a portion."

The timetable for sanctions by participating states and eight hundred local governments was calculated. It was recommended that September 1998 would mark the end of overnight deposits in Swiss banks. November would hopefully find state and city pension funds not making any new money management contracts. Money managers would then stop trading with the Swiss. As the new year dawned, existing fund-management contracts would be ended and legislators would prohibit the Swiss from buying. This momentum would culminate in 1999 when United States pension funds would get rid of their Swiss holdings.

Explaining the severity of this plan, New York State Comptroller McCall stated, "The diplomatic efforts that have gone forward haven't produced results so far."

What would produce results?

In his *Time* magazine article titled, "The Justice of the Calculator," Lance Morrow invoked the words of Elie Wiesel: "If all the money in all the Swiss banks were turned over, it would not bring back the life of one Jewish child. But the money is a symbol. It is part of the story. If you suppress any part of the story, it comes back later with force and violence."

And, Morrow concluded, "The Swiss bankers need to consider that there are many forms of bankruptcy. The moral one is worst of all."

CHAPTER 10

Sweden's Gold Fingers

While Sweden claimed a neutral status during World War II, the country's actions throughout the war were based more on a determination to remain out of hostilities at any cost than on strict neutrality. Its geographical location, bordered on the east by Finland, which was invaded by the Soviets in 1939 but whose territories were used by German troops, placed Sweden in a critical position, jeopardizing its safety. With the Baltic Sea to the south, Sweden was also in danger of invasion through Denmark, which fell under German occupation in 1940. On the west was Norway, which by 1941 fell under martial law after being invaded by Germany. The Swedish government compromised its nonpartisan position, making significant concessions to the Axis powers and minor ones to the Allied governments.

When, in 1940, Denmark and Norway fell to German occupation, King Gustav V of Sweden began correspondence with Adolf Hitler to confirm Sweden's supposed neutral stance. However, Sweden's dealings with Germany, its export of materials for the war, and its allowance of troops and materials to traverse through Norway into Sweden uninhibited, substantially strengthened Nazi Germany's position in the war. Perhaps the most unsettling practice occurred between Germany and Swedish firms that produced and supplied lethal gas to Hitler's Germany. In *Unmasking National Myths*, Avi Beker reveals that, aside from raw materials, Swedish firms also provided Zyklon-B to concentration camps.

A major business partner to the Third Reich, Sweden supplied the Nazi war effort with high-quality iron ore for use in the manufacturing of steel. According to the report, *U.S. and Allied Wartime and Postwar Negotiations with Argentina, Portugal, Spain, Sweden and Turkey on Looted Gold and German External Assets*, "British experts during and after the war were convinced that Sweden's provision of iron ore was the most valuable of all of the contributions of neutral countries to the German war effort." Throughout the war, Sweden provided Germany with over thirty-five million tons of iron ore integral to the Nazi war machine.

Sweden also furnished Germany with ball bearings

for use in aircraft production. The Svenska Kullagerfabriken (SKF), owned by the Enskilda Bank in Stockholm, was responsible for production of 70 percent of the total amount of ball bearings imported into Germany, and nearly 60 percent of the ball bearings produced in Germany were manufactured by a subsidiary company of SKF, also owned by the Enskilda bank of Stockholm.

Until December 1941, payments for materials between Sweden and Germany were made through a clearing committee. German importers purchasing Swedish materials made payments in reichsmarks to the Reichsbank. A Swedish clearing committee, in turn, paid the Swedish exporters in kroner. Likewise, Swedish importers made payments in kroner to the clearing committee, and the committee would deposit the payment to the Reichsbank in reichsmarks. However, because Germany purchased far more materials from Sweden to advance the war effort, the amount of exports and imports between the two countries did not balance.

By the end of 1943, Germany owed Sweden an amount equivalent to 40 percent of its total export value for that year. Because the value of the reichsmark was rapidly depreciating, Sweden requested that this deficit be compensated through gold purchases.

The only Scandinavian country not under Nazi occupation, Sweden was eager to maintain political and financial ties with Germany. Once Germany exhausted its own reserves, payments for iron ore, ball bearings and wood products were made to the Swedish Central Bank—

the Riksbank—by gold looted from German-conquered countries. Having already exhausted their own gold reserves, Germany paid Sweden with gold looted mainly from the central banks in the Netherlands and Belgium.

Recent investigations show that the Sveriges Riksbank was aware of the origin of the gold, but ignored evidence that payment for materials was being made in looted Nazi gold. In a January 1997 article in Sweden's national newspaper, *Dagens Nyheter*, the then governor of the Riksbank, Ivar Rooth, wrote a memo addressing his serious misgivings about the gold transactions from Germany.

According to a newly discovered confidential document, the Central Bank accepted 20,000 kilograms of gold from the Nazis, knowing it could be looted. Despite his reluctance to accept gold that may have been looted from occupied territories, and ignoring Allied reports that it was, Rooth did not pursue the matter of looted gold. While the Riksbank continued to purchase gold from Germany, trade minister Herman Eriksson replied to Rooth's memo, informing him that the Swedish coalition government found "insufficient grounds for raising the matter" to Emil Puhl, deputy governor of the German Reichsbank, and counseled Sweden to continue trade. Anxious to pay off the German trade deficit in the clearing committee, Sweden continued to accept the gold deliveries.

Shortly thereafter, the German Reichsbank tried to palm off gold worth another SK thirty-five million to the Swedes. Once again, Rooth brought the problem to Eriksson and the finance minister, Ernst Wigforss: "I pointed out that a matter of this nature was not something I alone could take responsibility for and said I would bring it before a meeting of the [Central Bank] executive board. The trade minister then authorized me to record in the minutes of the meeting that the government wished the central bank to agree to the Reichsbank request for further gold transactions but that the central bank should not make this conditional on a declaration from the Reichsbank regarding the nature of the affair. He did, however, repeat what he had previously told me—that there was nothing to stop me raising the question with Puhl in private."

In a memo dated February 19, 1943, to Eriksson, Rooth stated, "In view of the declaration from the British and other Allied governments that claims may be forthcoming on property deriving from the occupied countries, the Central Bank faced the risk that gold it had bought or might buy in the future from the Reichsbank could be placed in this category."

Four days later, Gunnar Hägglöf of the foreign ministry told Rooth in a memo he had talked with Emil Puhl himself and was assured that the gold Germany sold Sweden was from the period before the war. This was the memo which Rooth and Dag Hammarskjöld, secretary of state in the finance ministry [and destined to be the first Secretary General of the United Nations], used many times to justify Sweden's gold dealings with Germany.

Even if this was true of past dealing, more gold was taken in with no further reassurances: 10,000 kilograms during the remainder of 1943 and another shipment consisting of 1.5 tons early the next year.

Sweden allowed German troops and materials access
between Norway and Finland. According to the *U.S. and
Allied Wartime and Postwar* reports, the United States estimates
that the German military crossed Sweden in excess of
250,000 times. In exchange for cooperating with the Nazi
war effort in trade and transportation, Germany selectively
lifted the blockade on trade in the Baltic Sea to allow Sweden
to receive much needed supplies such as fuel.

Second only to Switzerland, Sweden was one of the
largest trading partners to Nazi Germany. Along with looted
gold that passed through Sweden on its way to other national
banks, Germany sent looted art and treasures through
Sweden where, according to *Dagens Nyheter*, Swedish contacts
would sell them on the international market.

Sweden's most prominent business leaders before
and during the war, the Wallenberg family were considered
pro-Nazi by United States Treasury Secretary Henry
Morgenthau, Jr. Owners of the Enskilda Bank and numerous other businesses, the Wallenbergs were believed to have
actively funded Hitler's regime and to have hidden Nazi
investments. Along with many other Swedish financial
institutions, the Wallenbergs' Enskilda Bank was used to
hide looted gold from the Allies.

According to the *Boston Globe*, World War II documents prove that while Raoul Wallenberg was helping thousands of Hungarian Jews, "Jacob and Marcus Wallenberg
used their Enskilda Bank to help the Nazis dispose of
assets seized from Dutch Jews who died in the Holocaust."
The Wallenbergs purchased gold looted by the Nazis and
laundered it through Swiss banks to finance major German
companies, including Bosch and IG Farben.

Adolf Hitler and Hermann Goering, the two most powerful leaders of Nazi Germany

Lighted sign reading, "Heil Hitler" hanging above crates of SS loot, gold, and paintings found at the Merkers salt mines

A trunk containing silver-ware in front of dozens of suitcases filled with posses-sions looted from civilians by SS troops

Bags of gold bullion and boxes of looted treasures lining the vault at Merkers

A pile of gold dental fillings found at the concentration camp at Dachau

Some of the thousands of wedding rings removed by German soldiers from victims at Buchenwald concentration camp

Crates of tableware taken from prisoners later killed at Buchenwald concentration camp

Piles of looted treasures stored in the church at Ellingen

NATIONAL ARCHIVES

NATIONAL ARCHIVES

Watches, jewelry, solid gold bars and currency secreted in a manure pile by a French collaborator

CARROLL/A/P WIDE WORLD

Suitcases filled with looted jewelry, currency and other valuables including a box of pearls

NATIONAL ARCHIVES

Trays of ornaments, snuff boxes and antique jewelry looted by the Germans, discovered at the Neuschwanstein Castle

NATIONAL ARCHIVES

Ninety-eight million dollars in French currency recovered and stored in a vault at the Banque de France

NATIONAL ARCHIVES

Seven million dollars worth of gold bullion stolen from Rome by the Germans, recovered and stored in a fort near Fortezza

One-half million dollars worth of gold bars found at the Reichsbank being checked and weighed

As early as March 20, 1940, three weeks before the Nazis invaded Denmark and Norway, the Swedish Security Police received a record of the bugged phone conversation between an aide of Hermann Goering in Berlin and a good friend of Goering's in Sweden:

Berlin: Field Marshall Goering says he would like Engineer D to present himself in Berlin as soon as possible. He has important matters to discuss.

D: I'll try and catch the night train via Malmö. I'll find out if it can be done and let you know.

Berlin: The Field Marshall would like Jacob Wallenberg to accompany you.

D: I'll do what I can.

The extensive corporate empire of the Wallenberg family made substantial loans to German industry. An article by Rob Gowland in the *Guardian* states that the family did not require any collateral in exchange for the loan. According to sources, the Wallenberg brothers also made surreptitious investments for German capitalists in American companies and were also involved in black market operations. *Dagens Nyheter* on November 28, 1996 stated that between 1940 and 1941, the Wallenberg family alone received over $4.5 million from the German central bank, the Reichsbank.

In addition to the prominent Wallenberg family, declassified records implicate the Swedish Red Cross for smuggling stolen art works and jewelry into Sweden for Nazis who were evacuating Germany after the war turned in favor of the Allies.

Aside from financial transactions, trade of war supplies and hiding of German assets, Swedish companies willingly complied with German statutes requiring any corporation that wished to maintain German dealings to also maintain Aryan status. According to an article in *Dagens Nyheter*, the Swedish-German Chamber of Commerce was used to oversee and reinforce the Aryanization of Swedish companies. They willingly reported the status of Swedish companies—Aryan, quarter-Jewish, half-Jewish—to Berlin. Because Germany and German companies were opposed to trading and doing business with companies in which leaders, managers, or stockholders were Jewish, it became lucrative for non-Jewish executives to dismiss their Jewish workers.

Swedish companies, desirous of maintaining business with Germany, eagerly dismissed Jewish workers to comply with the Aryanization laws. Although Germany requested only high-ranking Jews be fired, some Swedish companies went so far as to fire all Jewish employees, regardless of their position within the company.

The Swedish-German Chamber of Commerce, which was composed mainly of Swedish executives but included one Nazi party representative, kept track of the status of companies with warning cards that designated whether a company was Aryan or non-Aryan. Germans who collaborated with Jewish companies would be punished for committing high treason.

Declassified intelligence reports in the United States National Archives suggest that Hermann Goering and other Nazis considered Sweden a postwar refuge. The wartime United States intelligence operation code-named Safehaven was implemented in Sweden in 1943 as an effort to safeguard against Nazi property being stockpiled in that country. As the outcome of the war became clear, the Allies increased their efforts to prevent the enemy from moving resources outside Germany, to preclude a revival of Nazism at a later time.

The new findings about the Nazi gold deposited by Germany in Sweden's banks call up the role that country played in the Safehaven program.

The aim of Safehaven was to deny any safe haven for Nazi-looted assets. The program was designed to block Germany from transferring assets to Switzerland and other "neutral" nations by restricting the financial capabilities and accessibility of assets in those countries.

This move was intended as well to make certain that German wealth would be available for the reconstruction of Europe, as well as pay out reparations to the Allies, enable return of properties looted by the Nazis in occupied Europe to their owners, prevent the escape of key German personnel to neutral havens, and above all, deny Germany the capacity to start another war.

There was general agreement by the United States and its Allies regarding those overall objectives. But internal differences among United States agencies meant the president never received consistent advice about how strenuously to push the Safehaven measures and how far to use wartime economic power to force the so-called "neutral" countries—Switzerland, Sweden, Spain, Portugal, Turkey, and Argentina—to adhere to the program.

Moreover, and most troubling, splits between the Allies exacerbated the problem.

The United States and British efforts to enlist the Swedes in the laudable activity of restitution began in 1944. But the two Allies weren't united in their goals.

Britain favored using a more restrictive program, limited to having control over the gold within the Swedish borders. The United States advocated using all of the enemy assets in Sweden's possession. To coerce Sweden into compliance with Safehaven efforts, the United States proposed that the prospect of renewing trade, which had been suspended during the war because of the close alliance the Scandinavian country had with the Third Reich be broached with Sweden.

Despite the divisions, the Allies' entreaties to Stockholm appeared to have some effect, even as the war raged on in September 1944. The Swedish Parliament (Riksdag) voiced its support for the Safehaven program by conceding that Sweden "felt a responsibility to assist in the postwar recovery of Europe."

Consequently, in February 1945—with the Wehrmacht in full retreat before Allied advances—Sweden began taking a census of its gold and foreign exchange holdings to determine how much might be linked to Axis investors. By that spring, the British agreed to the broader United States objectives, which were quickly followed by a joint Safehaven proposal tailored to accommodate Sweden.

The United States missions in Portugal and Spain, where they were functioning with complete freedom in the capitals of Lisbon and Madrid, were advised by Washington and London to use the proffered joint proposal as the basis for talks they were instructed to carry on in Stockholm.

No United States or British mission operated in Sweden's capital during World War II because of that country's proximity to the combat zones.

The Office of Strategic Services discovered covert dealings between Germany and Sweden. The OSS reported that, as late as August, 1944, major Swedish companies were continuing to aid Germany in laundering and investing looted gold and other personal valuables taken from Hitler's victims.

Informal talks had hardly gotten under way before the Swedes all at once balked over the terms placed on the table. While they expressed desire "not to assist the Germans in hiding assets" in their country, they indicated "some confusion" over the details of the resolution.

The Allied negotiators pressed on, stressing that the implications and importance of the resolution placed before the Swedes was to "thwart German plans for postwar resistance."

The talks dragged on to summer, when a breakthrough appeared to have been reached. Sweden's Riksdag passed a series of decrees to control German property by restricting its sale or dispersal, and expanded the range of their census to include all types of German property.

According to the Eizenstat report, "In November 1945, Sweden provided United States Treasury Department officials with reports concerning Swedish gold transactions during the war. In comparing those records with data on German gold holdings at the time of the Swedish purchase, the Treasury Department believed that Sweden had acquired $23.7 million of looted Belgian gold..." The total amount of Swedish purchases is not mentioned. The report then goes on, "For negotiation purposes, the Allies reduced the claims to about $17 million."

Despite that concession and their beneficent grant that Sweden keep an unwarranted $6.7 million worth of Nazi gold, the Swedish Foreign Office advised the American Embassy that the Scandinavian nation would have to put the issue to the Riksdag, where it would probably be defeated based on belief that Allied claims "weren't valid in international law and assets in the United States, frozen from the start of the war, were to be released before any further negotiations could be continued."

Moreover, Sweden further demanded to be allowed "to inspect Swedish property in Germany." The Allies refused, claiming that both issues needed to be addressed in formal exchanges.

To that end, negotiations were arranged and began in Washington on May 29, 1946. The United States delegation was headed by Seymour Rubin, deputy director of the State Department's Office of Economic Security Policy and included representatives from the State and Treasury departments.

Negotiations continued, and on July 18 the two sides reached an accord. Of some $90.7 million in German assets finally determined to have been stowed in its banks, Sweden agreed to divide the proceeds from their liquidation in the following fashion:

- $12.5 million to go to the Intergovernmental Committee on Refugees for the rehabilitation and resettlement of non-repatriable victims of Nazism.

- $18 million for the Inter-Allied Reparations Agency (IARA), excluding the amounts the United States, Britain, and France would receive.
- $36 million in liquidated German assets for assisting British and United States occupation forces in prevention of disease and unrest in Germany. It would be placed in an account in the Riksbank to be used to purchase essential materials for the German economy from Sweden and other European countries.
- Also, claims were made in a "Gold Declaration" for $15 million in gold that was tentatively identified as having been looted by Germany from the Central Banks of Belgium and the Netherlands.

At last, a solid bottom line had been reached in the negotiations. It seemed that Sweden had yielded the true amount of Nazi gold holdings it had acquired during the war. Many setbacks occurred en route to the payback that the Swedes agreed to honor, but in the end there was a settlement of claims, and negotiations with the Allies came to a close.

In 1949, Sweden returned seven tons of gold to Banque Nationale de Belgique in Belgium. Because of the precise records detailing gold transactions, kept by German authorities and the Prussian Mint and attained by officials of the Belgian National Bank, Sweden could not refute the claim.

Sweden received a dunning request in 1954 from the Dutch, who had first tried to collect their claims in 1946. Ambassador Erik Boheman wrote Osker Undén, the Swedish Foreign Minister, on May 21, 1954. "Dear Brother—The negotiations on the so-called Dutch gold have now been in progress for three days and I want to take this opportunity of letting you know that they seem to have taken an unfavorable turn from a Swedish point of view, partly because of the evidence the Americans apparently have showing that 505 ingots were indeed produced from Dutch gold coins that had been melted down, and partly because, as far as we can see, it appears possible to prove that these gold coins can be defined as 'looted gold.'"

This resulted in Sweden paying back six thousand kilograms of gold to the Netherlands but there remains a sizable difference between this amount and the 20,000 kilograms, which even Sweden admits was in the Swedish Central Bank in 1944. Also, in 1955 six tons of gold was returned to De Nederlandsche Bank in the Netherlands. And more facts about stolen gold continue to come out.

Also, personal belongings, art and other valuables were sent through Swedish dealers into the world art market. In addition, when the Germans closed diamond shops of Jews in Amsterdam, the plunder was transported into Sweden. For instance, Count von Schwerin, a German official, went to Stockholm several times a month carrying stolen diamonds in his diplomatic pouch. Swedish businessmen serving as agents for the Nazis bought the diamonds through the German legation, according to United States intelligence reports and sold them abroad.

The year when the curtain was finally lowered on the Allied tussling with Sweden was 1955—ten years of unremitting squabbling went on before the matter was finally brought to a satisfactory conclusion.

At that point, Sweden began exploring unclaimed bank accounts that had been inactive since 1945. More information is also coming out on the economic links between Germany and Sweden as the United States releases classified documents from the United States Treasury archives. The World Jewish Congress has found documents intimating that gold worth approximately $18.5 million (ten times that amount today) was sent from Germany into Sweden.

In 1996, delegates from many countries gathered in Oslo to discuss the gold and other valuables looted during World War II. At the center of the discussion was how Switzerland, Spain, Portugal, and Sweden disguised and administered Nazi plunder.

How much stolen gold did Sweden receive?

Although the amount under consideration is much smaller than the Swiss transaction, there is no doubt the Wallenbergs as well as the other institutions involved must open their archives and deal with this painful but necessary catharsis in order to clear Sweden's history of the tawdry practice of accepting stolen gold and other valuables from Nazi Germany.

Walter V. Robertson of the *Boston Globe* raises the question: "Were Sweden's pro-Nazi activities more excusable if its collaboration gave Swedish diplomats leverage to save Jewish lives when even the Allies chose to look the other way?"

Late in the war, Sweden used its leverage with Germany to help save the lives of tens of thousands of Jews, most of them in occupied Hungary, by issuing them Swedish visas and passports. According to American Holocaust scholar Paul A. Levine, author of *From Indifference to Activism: Swedish Diplomacy and the Holocaust 1938-1944*, "Until 1942, Sweden's policy was anti-Semitic: They didn't let Jews in because they were Jews. But after 1942, when they learned what was happening, they let Jews in because they were Jews."

A January 1997 article by the Associated Press indicates that previous estimates about the amount of looted gold that Sweden received were low. According to the Swedish newspaper, *Dagens Nyheter*, investigations show that the amount exceeded thirty-eight tons. A new investigation into the Riksbank has found that 59.7 tons of gold were purchased from Germany from 1939 to 1945.

Sweden's Commission on Jewish Assets estimated that nearly half of the gold Nazis sold or traded to Sweden may have been taken from Holocaust victims. In March 1998, the Swedish government, in cooperation with the Jewish community in Stockholm, set up this commission to investigate all possible Jewish assets that are currently unaccounted for.

CHAPTER 11

Spain's Gold Trafficking

As World War II and the Holocaust raged, Spain engaged in an active trading program with the Nazis while Germany, in turn, invested heavily in Spain. Along with open trade and an accessible supply route, Spain provided both military and intelligence support to Germany.

Allied efforts to end Spain's trade association with Germany became an intricate balancing act. On one side was the strategic significance of Gibraltar and Allied concern, particularly in London, that pressing Spain too hard by limiting petroleum exports would in turn provoke the Spanish to seize Gibraltar for Germany. On the other side

lay the Allies' equally serious concerns that Spanish goods
as well as their own oil might make its way into the Nazi
war machine.

Fueled by the propinquity of Spanish dictator
Francisco Franco for Hitler's Germany and a history of
collaboration between the regimes during the Spanish Civil
War, Spain was more than sympathetic to the Nazi cause.
According to Norman J.W. Goda's review of Collado
Seidel's *Zufluchtsstatte fur Nationalsozialisten*, "Franco held, if
not a strong trust for Berlin, then definite territorial and
political aims that he hoped to realize should the Germans
win the war." Franco permitted German representatives to
stay in Spain and provided asylum to Nazi party members
after the war. Goda concludes that by the end of the war
there were, "at least 12,000 [Germans in Spanish territory],
many of whom performed covert activities for the German
government."

"Neutral" Spain favored the Axis powers in matters of trade as well. According to files at the embassy in
Madrid, the two countries established a secret protocol in
which Spain agreed to serve as a link in transporting supplies from South America to Italy. Because of its strategic
location at the entrance to the Mediterranean, Spain
became increasingly important to Germany in trade.

At the center of trade between Spain and Germany
was the large commercial conglomerate, Sociedad
Financeria Industrial (SOFINDUS). Consisting of subsidiary mining, transportation and agriculture companies,
SOFINDUS developed Spain's mining and agriculture
industries to provide Nazi Germany with the materials it

needed to advance in the war. In the article, "Spanish Foreign Trade," it is concluded that more than two million tons of iron ore and pyrites were exported from Spain to Germany between January 1941 and April 1944, along with zinc, lead, mercury, mica, amlygonite, fluorspar and celestite. As Allied efforts to restrict trade between the neutrals and Germany increased, Spain began entering into secret trade agreements with Germany as a means of circumventing the restrictions. Through the SOFINDUS conglomerate, Germany developed a vast system of companies to purchase and export wolfram [used in the manufacture of heavy-duty, high voltage wiring] to Germany and Italy.

Along with SOFINDUS, numerous government industries also aided Nazi Germany in concealing assets in Spain. Spanish-based HISMA (Sociedad Hispano-Marroqui de Transportes) and German-based ROWAK (Rohstoff Waren-Kompensation Handelsgesellschaft) were both German-controlled. Staffed by Hermann Goering, HISMA and ROWAK monopolized Spanish economy, trade and shipments of military equipment. In the article "Hermann Goering and Nazi Germany's Economic Exploitation of Nationalist Spain," Christian Leitz states Goering's aim was "to mold the Spanish economy into a useful dependent of Nazi Germany." Founded to simultaneously exert influence over the Spanish government and secure iron from Spain for the war effort, the companies also functioned to mask dealings between German companies and Spanish customers.

Instituto Española de Moneda (Foreign Exchange Institute) and Instituto Nacional de Industria actively coordinated transactions between Germany and Spanish companies in which Germany could invest.

From the beginning of 1942, the Reichsbank, using the Swiss National Bank, sold $12.7 million in gold to Spain and $20.4 million in gold to the Spanish National Bank. According to the report of the London Gold Conference, the Spanish Foreign Exchange acquired 38.594 tons of gold from the Swiss National Bank and 2.507 tons from the Banco Aleman Transatlantico amidst other massive Nazi gold infusions into the Spanish economy.

During the same time period, the Allies also endeavored to purchase wolfram from Spain as a means of stemming Germany's supply. Along with preclusive buying agreements, the United States implemented trade agreements with Spain to restrict the amount of materials available to the Nazi war machine. Spain again circumvented Allied efforts to restrict trade to Axis countries by increasing the amount of goods being illegally transported into those countries. Via ports in Spain and Portugal, materials essential to the war effort were smuggled into Italy and Germany from South and Central America.

The report titled, *History of the Blockade Division, Enforcement Section*, documents sixty-two Spanish vessels which smuggled materials into Germany. The majority of the contraband consisted of industrial diamonds and platinum. To hamper Allied attempts to regulate smuggling of goods into Germany, rather than being shipped as cargo, smaller, easily hidden materials were illegally carried into the country by individuals on the ships.

Toward the end of the war, Spain's geographic accessibility was used to send German assets out of Europe to ports in Argentina, where holding companies were being established. According to an Associated Press article, "Spain was the 'gold line' used to channel the metal to escaped Nazis in Latin America after the war."

Ignoring Allied pressure to maintain nonbelligerence and deport Nazi agents, Spain allowed numerous German agents to disappear, thus avoiding repatriation. Francisco Franco refused to relinquish the over one hundred Nazi agents living in Spain being sought by the Allies after the war. Spanish authorities also helped former SS and Gestapo members to travel safely to South America. In Seidel's *Zufluchtssatte*, it is cited that a mere one hundred German war criminals were deported on United States repatriate ships.

In the spring of 1944, the United States began to implement the Safehaven program in Spain. Samuel Klaus of the Foreign Economic Administration and Herbert Cummings of the State Department were assigned to investigate Spain's dealings with the Axis countries. In "Memorandum from Klaus to Currie, Coe, and Cox," Samuel Klaus referred to Spain as, "the most discouraging and the most difficult" neutral country. Unwilling to cooperate with Safehaven principles, the United States Embassy in Madrid engaged in concerted efforts to hinder the State Departments investigations.

Early Allied estimates of German non-gold assets in Spain totaled 650 million pesetas (about $39 million), but exact calculations were hampered by the fact that the United States withdrew Office of Strategic Services operatives in the area in November 1945. This, coupled with the common Spanish practice of keeping two sets of financial records, one of which did not reveal outside investments in the companies, hindered Safehaven efforts. To prevent the dissipation of those assets, the Allies began negotiations for the return of the holdings with Madrid in April 1945, just as German armies were being put to their final rout.

The United States had previously presented two notes to Spain requesting a settlement of its obligation of Nazi gold holdings, but Madrid had neglected to respond.

Finally, the United States sent a third, more detailed, note of its Safehaven operatives on April 22, 1945, requesting Spain:

- Announce publicly its intention to adhere fully to the terms of the agreements proposed earlier.
- Immediately freeze all assets of persons of Axis or Axis-controlled countries.
- Immobilize and facilitate the return of any looted assets.
- Conduct a detailed census of all assets.
- Provide the United Nations full information concerning all persons in Spain with the nationality of Axis or Axis-controlled countries and all nationals who entered Spain since January 1, 1939.
- Establish effective controls with respect to any transactions with the Axis or Axis-controlled countries.

On May 5, 1945, under mounting pressure from the United States and Great Britain, Madrid issued a decree freezing all German assets in Spain, arranged for an inventory of those assets, and established administrative bodies to control their disbursement.

A year later, the Spaniards were exposed for their deceptions. By the beginning of 1946, the Department of State reported that Spanish implementation of the Decree Law had "not been altogether satisfactory and the census [inventory of their Nazi gold holdings] has proved to be a complete farce."

The State Department's *U.S. and Allied Efforts to Recover and Restore Gold* study's findings went on to declare, "The United States issued an official declaration charging Spain with failure to implement Bretton Woods Resolution VI and the Gold Declaration and stating that Spain's assets in the United States would continue to be blocked. Spain argued that this criticism was unwarranted and cited the 'lack of appreciation abroad for its efforts.'"

Because there'd been problems resolving Nazi gold issues on how to prevent the flow of German assets to "neutral" countries under the loosely-formulated rules of the Safehaven program, the Allied governments had convened a conference to help arrive at a stronger resolution of that problem. That had evolved into the United Nations Monetary and Financial Conference, which got under way in July 1994 in Bretton Woods, New Hampshire.

In its final draft form, neutral countries had been called on to take immediate measures to prevent any disposition or transfer within their jurisdiction of assets belonging to governments, individuals, or institutions in occupied countries, as well as looted gold or other assets.

The neutrals had also been called upon to prevent the concealment of such assets. The scope of this edict applied to Nazi-appropriated valuables located in enemy-occupied territories.

New and vigorous United States-British action resulted from that Bretton Woods agreement. From that time on, the Allies forced each and every "neutral" and "non-belligerent" nation that had storehoused Nazi gold to adhere to the terms laid down not only by Safehaven but by Bretton Woods as well.

After having accused Madrid of failing to implement the tenets of Bretton Woods Resolution VI and the Gold Declaration and stating that Spain's assets in the United States would continue to be blocked, Allied negotiations with Spain remained stalled.

Spanish reluctance to recognize the Allied Control Council as the German government and its authority to take title to "official and parastatal assets," only served to keep negotiations at a standoff.

The months dragged on and still no resolution could be reached with Spain about its holdings of Nazi gold. An August 1946 State Department report indicated that Spain had acquired at least 122,852 tons of gold between February 1942 and May 1945. The Eizenstat report told that "published figures showed that 'Spanish domestic gold holdings' increased from $42 million in 1941 to $110 million in 1945." The report of the Spanish Comisión de Investigación of April 8, 1998 said that between 1940 and 1945 gold grew from $49 million to $124.2 million.

In September 1946 the principal unresolved issues in the negotiations with Spain were summarized in a resumé the United States drew up. The pertinent issues as the United States viewed them were:

1) Representation of German private financial interests.
2) Disposition of German private financial interests.
3) Distribution of proceeds from the liquidation of German private interests.
4) Return of all of Spain's looted gold holdings, based on a report in May 1946 from the embassy in Madrid that authorities had identified wartime shipments of gold from Switzerland and directly from Germany totaling eighty-five tons worth 414 million Swiss francs (about $100 million).
5) Loot other than gold is to be made available as well.
6) Patents and trademarks taken out by Jews must be revealed.
7) Consular functions for Germans must be defined.
8) Repatriation of persons uprooted from their homelands, are in limbo at present.

Allied negotiators also requested more detailed information on Spain's gold holdings. That prompted this bravura response from Madrid: "Such information is normally treated as confidential and Spain cannot answer the

Allied request without receiving assistance from the Allies
in locating gold possibly looted by Germany after the
Spanish Civil War.... Moreover we believe we settled your
gold claims upon us when we turned over two vessels to
the Allies after the war."

In early 1947, a series of draft accords were
exchanged. Discussions centered on a British proposal for
distribution of Spain's Nazi holdings on a percentage basis.
But the United States was amenable to a lump sum settlement of the German assets, believing that method would
avoid further delays than liquidation on a case-by-case
basis.

On May 16, 1947, Spain submitted a proposed
accord that seemed to favor the lump sum method of
repayment. The Allies' willingness to accept such terms had
a proviso: "Our interests could be limited to the identification of German property and to the protection of our
security objectives."

Spain's reaction to that form of settlement was
"lukewarm."

Madrid's negotiator was concerned that the formula wouldn't adequately compensate Spain for claims
against Germany and complained that the Allies' estimate
of the value of German assets (in the proposal they listed
700 million pesetas, about $43 million—as a maximum
value, but privately they projected 500 to 600 million—
about $30 to $36 million) were too high.

In addition, the negotiator wanted some assurance
that the Allies would abide by Spanish laws governing foreign holdings, a provision that Spain receive a fair share of

any foreign exchange realized during liquidation and a revision of the draft so that permanent German residents of Spain could still be purchasers. In the United States negotiator's estimation, there was still "a wide gulf which must be bridged before a satisfactory accord can be reached."

There could be no doubt that behind the Spanish position against all of the Allied efforts to obtain restitution from that country was a stance dictated by the country's president, Francisco Franco.

Negotiations came to still another impasse in July 1947 when both sides became bogged down in haggling over whether to base the lump sum settlement on the appraised value of German assets, which was the method of settlement favored by Spain, or the liquidation value, favored by the Allies.

Additionally, Spain claimed 330 million reichsmarks (about $33 million) in damages against Germany, but the Allied negotiators only considered 116 million reichsmarks (about $11.6 million) to be legitimate.

In December 1947, the United States Embassy in Madrid was buoyed by "substantial progress in the negotiations" after Spain proposed a method of identifying and recovering German property, which was deemed by the American side to be "practical and acceptable."

Two U.S. officials were allowed to review the gold transaction records of the Foreign Exchange Institute. However, further negotiations were deemed necessary to resolve issues related to "the machinery of indemnification" and "the method of adjudication of properties" from a security standpoint. The Allies made some further progress in the Nazi gold negotiations, but that progress did not signify a target date for a settlement. According to *U.S. and Allied Efforts to Recover and Restore Gold,* "After two years of stalling and excuses, Spain finally provided records of its gold holdings from the Foreign Exchange Institute. The documents, supposedly, were riddled with discrepancies, but by the end of January 1948 the investigators determined that Spain had acquired at least 26.8 tons of fine weight gold (about $30.3 million) through the Swiss National Bank, Bank of Portugal, and Banco Aleman Transatlantico."

The talks continued almost ad infinitum and persisted with little ground gained by the Allies and the United States, which desired "a strong Spanish economy and, once the question of gold was settled, allowed private investors to extend very substantial credits to Spanish industry." There were also potential indirect strategic military benefits in allowing United States private investments in Spain.

In March 1948, the Department of Defense came to the Department of State and discussed the feasibility of equipping three airfields in Spain to handle heavy bombers in emergency situations. The State Department advised against direct United States funding, noting that anti-Franco sentiments in the United States were high enough to compel the government to recommend "once a gold settlement was reached, the United States could permit a privately financed civil aviation program" that could make the necessary improvements in those fields without political risk.

One month earlier, the United States Embassy had

reported that the draft accord, as it stood, was "the best we can expect from the Spanish and that we should attempt to wind this up as soon as possible."

However, another three months of negotiations ensued before the final agreement was reached on March 10, 1948. In the final accord, Spain was to receive proceeds from the liquidation of German assets according to the following formula:

- 20 percent of the first 100 million pesetas (about $9 million) realized.
- 22-$1/2$ percent of the next 100 million (about $9.3 million).
- 25 percent of the next ($10 million).
- 27 percent of the amount following ($10.5 million).
- 30 percent of any amount exceeding 400 million (about $36 million).
- The remaining proceeds to be divided among the eighteen members of the Inter-Allied Reparations Agency (IARA), with the United States and United Kingdom to receive 28 percent each and France to collect 16 percent.

In April 1948 an agreement was reached on the German assets to be distributed to IARA nations. The victims did not receive any. The Allies then went on to arrive at a settlement with the country on looted gold through an exchange of notes on May 3, 1948. Spain agreed to turn over 101.6 kilograms of fine gold ($114,129), identified as having been looted from the

Netherlands, and any other looted gold identified before
April 30, 1949.

In exchange, Spain demanded that the Allies note
and that all public pronouncements acknowledge that Spain
"had not been aware... [at] acquisition or subsequently" that
the gold had been looted.

On November 3, 1948, the embassy in Madrid
reported that the gold had been delivered and deposited in
the Foreign Exchange Institute, freeing Spain from the
restrictions imposed by the Gold Declaration of February
22, 1944.

A year later, in November 1949, the Allies registered a protest over Spain's implementation of the accord.
The Allies objected strongly to the use of competitive bidding for the acquisition of assets expropriated instead of
the agreed upon practice of setting a "justiprecio," a just
price.

They reminded Spain that during the course of the
negotiations they had consistently argued against competitive bidding. The Allies further objected that Spain had
retained a portion of the proceeds, a direct violation of the
terms and intent of the accord.

On November 30, 1950, Spain threatened to sus-
pend the 1948 accord unless Germany ratified it. Then,
with the Allies' concurrence, Germany responded in
February 1951 that since the occupying powers were the
supreme authority in Germany, German ratification was
unnecessary. Distribution of proceeds from the liquidation
of German assets was halted a mere five months later, at
which point only seventy-seven of the 122 German-owned

companies had been liquidated. Spain also terminated any efforts to explore the possibility that German investments may have been concealed in other forms, such as real estate, patents and securities.

After four years—by January 1952—roughly 400 million pesetas (about $36 million) had been distributed to IARA nations.

None of the proceeds, however, were slated for non-repatriable victims, largely because the Allies believed at the time that they would be able to satisfy the $25 million stipulated in the Paris Reparations Agreement from Swiss, Swedish, and Portuguese liquidations, and they didn't believe that pesetas would prove of much value to the International Refugee Organization (IRO).

The debate continued into 1953, when it was addressed during negotiations between the Allies and Germany on German external assets. Not until five years later—In 1958—was the accord with Spain officially terminated with an exchange of notes and the signing of a protocol in Madrid on August 9, which entered into force on July 2, 1959.

Fifteen long years had been squandered in trying to get Spain, finally and at last, to own up to its obligation to return looted gold and other assets that it had zealously held onto as though they were their very own God-given possessions.

Revelations about Spain's role in hiding Nazi gold are still coming out.

In 1997, the Associated Press reported a bizarre story told by the eighty-year-old wife of a senior official in Spain, Emilio de Navasques, Chief of Economic Policy under dictator Francisco Franco.

The woman recalled asking her husband what he was doing carrying five blankets out of their apartment in Madrid in 1945 in the middle of the night. Unbeknownst to her at the time, under the blankets was gold stolen by the Nazis. In 1955, when a German diplomat arrived in Madrid to talk about Germany's wartime assets, the Spanish minister wrote to the Spanish ambassador in Bonn about the two tons of gold. It was then at the German Embassy. Fifty-two kilograms of the gold was later sent to England. The rest, according to the Spanish newspaper *El Pais*, was never accounted for.

Another story has to do with the insistence of many that Martin Bormann did not die in Germany but made his home after the war in Madrid.

Still another tale has Trenton Parker, an ex-Marine colonel with CIA connections, describing his journey to Madrid in March of 1975 "to negotiate the liquidation of various tons of gold which were turned into perfect kruggerands." According to Parker, the gold had remained in the custody of Francisco Franco until that year, after which it was sold to America.

In April of 1998 the Spanish Commission of Investigation announced that the diverse ingots Spain acquired from the Swiss National Bank, the Bank of England, and the Bank of Portugal were stored in the Bank of Spain in Madrid. It was further revealed that during the war Spain made three direct purchases of German gold, one in 1942 of 4.5 tons from the Banco Aleman Transatlantico, one in 1944 of 7.3 tons, and another that year of 1.4 tons from the Banco Exterior de España.

But that wasn't all. Intelligence documents revealed more German gold entered Spain smuggled in diplomatic pouches, and the real extent of Spanish Nazi gold dealings would probably never be known.

CHAPTER 12

Portugal's Auric Stance

Although it adopted the posture of a "neutral" and "nonbelligerent" nation during World War II, Portugal was anything but that in the role Lisbon played in stockpiling Nazi Germany with vital war materials—despite pleas from the Allies not to engage in such blatant partisanship with the enemy.

From the war's inception in 1939 and all during the six years of the conflict, Lisbon, more than Madrid, was Berlin's primary source of wolfram. Besides this metal's use in the manufacture of electric wire, it used to harden steel and in the production of tin, manganese, mica, chrome, and antimony, essential raw materials for Hitler's war machine.

Of those ores, wolfram was the most coveted by the Nazis. Though the Allies pleaded with Portugal not to feed the maw of the Third Reich's armaments arsenals, Hitler's negotiators proposed a lucrative pact with the Iberian nation's hierarchy to obtain fully 100 percent of its German-owned wolfram mines, as well as an additional 50 percent of all other mines. The onset of war produced a competition between the Axis and Allied forces for Portugal's production and drove up prices. By 1943, prices rose 775 percent and production rose from 2,419 tons in 1938 to 6,500 tons in 1942. Wolfram had become a one-hundred-million-dollar-a-year industry even at war prices.

The Germans let on that they weren't "trying to prevent the Allied interests from obtaining wolfram from mines those countries owned and operated in Portugal." However, the Nazis also wanted Lisbon to sell to them only that prized ore from all of other its mines within Portugal's boundaries.

Portugal's government was amenable to such an arrangement.

Second only to Great Britain, Germany was one of Portugal's largest trading partners. Because of Portugal's weakened economy, valuable resources, and strategic location, neutrality provided Portugal with the opportunity to continue trade with both countries.

Portugal was reluctant to accept payment for resources it supplied to Germany in German reichsmarks. Payment for goods exchanged between the two countries was instead governed by the 1935 Luso-German Clearing Agreement. Transactions took place between the German Deutsche Verrechnungskasse and the Bank of Portugal, wherein each country's imports and exports would ostensibly balance.

In January 1942, despite its neutral trade agreements, Portugal entered into a secret agreement with Germany, granting export licenses for up to 2,800 tons of wolfram in exchange for much needed coal, steel and fertilizer. One magazine report in 1996 claimed that Portugal eventually received Nazi gold valued at 1.35 billion dollars, possibly through Swiss middlemen, and tried to use the gold to buy coal from Poland.

Despite Portugal's trade with the Axis, in the November 1942 Trade Agreement, the Allies consented to provide Portugal with much needed wheat, ammonium sulphate, coal, and petroleum in exchange for rubber, sisal, copra, and palm oil. In return, the Portuguese agreed to restrict the export of certain minerals, skins, and wool to Germany, as well as the import of goods from other countries that it could, in turn, export to Germany.

Although trade with Portugal provided the Allies with some essential goods, more importantly, procurement of these materials from Portugal restricted Germany's imports of these materials. However, it was the supply of wolfram the Allies most wanted to stop or at least restrict since wolfram was absolutely necessary for Germany's machine-tool industry, as well as to its production of armor-piercing shells. Although the Allies could more easily secure wolfram from Central America, they purchased wolfram from Portugal in efforts to impede German imports. They also attempted to limit German purchases by fulfilling Portugal's export demands.

Portugal's supply of wolfram to Nazi Germany was

one of the most integral to the war. According to *Ferro-Alloys and their Effect on Steel in the German War Economy, 1943 and 1944*, because German tools were designed for tungsten-carbide tips, they could not be modified without paralyzing German machine-tool industry production, either shortening the war or seriously crippling Germany's capacity.

Another aspect of German trade with the neutrals was important to the Allied cause. Germany imported more materials than it exported, resulting in a deficit. The United States Embassy in Lisbon noted that Portuguese firms and government ministries advanced Germany escudos to purchase materials in an amount equivalent to 30 percent of its total trade.

According to the report, *German Economic Interests in Portugal*, between 1943 and 1944 Germany incurred a debt of between thirteen and 23.5 million reichsmarks ($5.12 to $9.26 million) as a result of its trade with Portugal. The Portuguese asked for payment in Portuguese escudos, Swiss francs, or gold. Though it increased their need for plunder, the Germans agreed and more wolfram began to flow into Germany aboard an endless procession of freight trains.

One postwar document received in code and labeled top secret conveyed the following telling message: "Have contacted high-level Swiss who uncovered [a] trail [of] 280 truckloads of German gold bars sent from Suisse to Spain and Portugal between May '43 and February '44. The total value estimated between 1,000,000,000 and 2,000,000,000 Swiss francs."

During 1944, intelligence reports recorded that other influential officials such as Vichy French officials, the Spanish Ambassador to Portugal (the brother of General

Francisco Franco of Spain), the Uruguayan Minister, and Portuguese diplomats in Germany were implicated in smuggling, many using their diplomatic pouches, to carry diamonds, bonds, banknotes, and, of course, gold into Portugal. Once again the Banco Espirito Santo was singled out as a major repository—and there some looted bars and ingots were building up "postwar credit for the Germans."

By this time there was no doubt the Portuguese Metal Commission clearly favored Germany over the Allies in its trade dealings. The report *Preclusive Operations in the Neutral Countries in World War II* concludes that the Portuguese Metal Commission knowingly included lower-grade wolfram in the Allied portion of wolfram from the independently-owned mines. They also intentionally delayed deliveries to America.

Aside from materials Portugal exported to Germany, Portuguese merchants also smuggled valuable goods and raw materials into Germany from its colonies in South America and Africa. The contraband smugglers provided Germany with included platinum, industrial diamonds, electrodes, and x-ray and radio tubes. And, most importantly, there was large-scale smuggling of wolfram from Portugal into Spain. Despite Allied efforts to stem trafficking into Germany, smuggling continued. Blockade violations revealed in, *History of the Blockade Division, Enforcement Section*, conveyed that twenty-two Portuguese vessels were involved in transporting smuggled goods from Africa and South America into Portugal for delivery to Germany.

In the same period, arrangements were made between the Allies and Portugal to acquire the air and naval base located in the Azores, a group of islands in the Atlantic Ocean about 800 miles off of Portugal's coast. According to the report, *U.S. and Allied War and Postwar Negotiations,* the need for Allied anti-submarine air bases in the Azores was crucial to the Allies in patrolling the Atlantic convoy route which was the site of the "battle between the Allied convoys and a growing German submarine fleet."

Safehaven investigations into the dealings between Portugal and Germany were begun by the United States Embassy in Lisbon in August 1944. Believing Portugal could be a financial center for postwar Germany, head of Safehaven investigations Samuel Klaus in the "Memorandum from Klaus to Currie, Coe, and Cox," disclosed to members of the Foreign Economic Administration that Portugal's five largest banks were actively and knowingly engaging in transactions with Germany.

On June 5, 1944, with the war having turned by then against Germany, the United States and Great Britain compelled Portugal to halt shipments of wolfram to Germany. This came one month after Premier António de Oliveira Salazar announced that Portugal would not stop exports of wolfram to Germany out of fear of invasion. Recognizing the importance of wolfram to Nazi Germany, Salazar defended the reason for continuing trade by stating that the embargo on wolfram would be perceived by Germany as a hostile act. Although it was well known that the Axis were near defeat and Germany did in fact surrender two days after the Allies put forth the demand that the wolfram trade stop, Salazar still insisted that the embargo would provoke retaliation from Germany.

Ironically, one month later, Portugal imposed a complete embargo on wolfram exports to both German and Allied forces.

Nevertheless, despite the embargo, Germany still was able to get about 900 tons of wolfram from Portugal though thereafter the supply to them dwindled.

Because Portugal had ignored requests to refuse any gold as payment from Germany and based on Allied suspicion that any gold used by Germany for purchases after 1943 was looted, the Foreign Economic Administration, along with the United States Treasury, enjoined Portugal to freeze all German assets and carry out a census of Axis holdings within the country. Though the Allies had tried to get concrete data on German external assets in Portugal without a census, the reports varied greatly. At one point they were put at $45 million but later these figures fell and did not include looted items such as gold or diamonds. Moreover, both Germany and Portugal used Swiss banks for trade purposes. Later, much of this gold was brought back to Portugal. The bank most involved in this trading was the Banco Espirito Santo which served as the "German financial agent for wolfram operation." Later accounts were opened in the Banco Lisboa e Accores.

With Hitler and the Third Reich having been disposed of barely a week, on May 14, 1945, Lisbon enacted Decree Law 34,600 to "freeze all German assets in Portugal, and create a licensing system to unlock those assets, provide a census of those assets, prohibit trade of foreign currency notes, and establish a penalty regime to enforce those provisions."

With that much ground gained in their quest to recover Nazi gold plundered from Jews and other victims of Storm Trooper seizures during the war years, the Allies pressed for more concessions by Portugal.

On May 23, the decree was extended to all Portuguese colonies—Guinea-Bissau, Mozambique, Cape Verde Islands, Angola, Sao Tome and Principe, Banks, the Azores, the Madeira Islands off the northwest coast of Africa, and the peninsula enclave of Macau at the mouth of the Xi (Pearl) River in China.

Included in the Nazi holdings were the official state properties of the German government in Portugal.

With Lisbon's seeming total willingness to meet Allied terms in the seizure of Nazi property, the United States and Britain, joined by the French government that was in exile in London, further sought the seizure of German government buildings and their contents throughout Portugal and its colonies.

A month later, Lisbon surrendered those properties to a tripartite representative, the Joint Allied Committee on German Affairs in Portugal, to oversee their liquidation.

Included in those seized assets were 5,000 gold sovereign coins found at the German legation in Lisbon.

However, the Allies were uncomfortable about Portugal's failure to make the Allies aware of two aspects of its just-enacted law—the census and, more importantly, a proviso that permitted transfer of blocked assets to individuals for their "subsistence" and "the normal exercise of commercial and industrial activity." Those exclusions prompted the Division of Economic Security Controls (ESC) to file a protest in Lisbon that Portugal was allowing itself a troublesome "loophole" through which the country could grant excessive living allowances to Germans and also enable that country's renegades to engage in further transfer of their assets at will.

Salazar, Portugal's "strong man," who'd been in office since 1932 and had conducted a repressive government in the years of his rule, showed little flexibility on the issue of looted gold, claiming it wasn't his country's responsibility to return the gold that they had exchanged with Germany during the war for tangible assets.

Incredibly, in at least one instance, Salazar claimed that "no gold whatsoever was shipped from Germany to Portugal between April 1938 and May 1945."

Despite that blatant denial, the Allies had determined through reviews of wartime intelligence and investigations of German and Swiss government and banking institutions that Portugal had indeed acquired a total of 123,827 kilograms of gold (roughly 121.87 tons, valued at the time at $143.8 million) from the Swiss National Bank. Of that amount, 20,117 kilograms ($22.6 million) was definitely deemed to have been looted Belgian gold from the Reichsbank's deposit at the Swiss National Bank.

For the remaining approximately 103,709 kilograms ($116.7 million) the Allies had substantial, but less conclusive proof that approximately 72 percent was looted.

Consequently, the report recommended that the Allies request from Portugal the full 20,117 kilograms of looted Belgian gold as well as 94,787 kilograms (about $106.6 million) of the suspected looted gold.

By June 1946 when the Allies finally added up the figures, they found approximately fifty million escudos (about $2 million) had been liquidated by Germany and plowed into Portuguese hotels, cinemas, and factories.

Premier Salazar was caught in a deep bind and was compelled to seal his lips as his emissaries bowed to Allied pressure. A meeting was held between "technical-level" negotiators in Lisbon on September 3, 1946, to hammer out a program on ways to assess, liquidate, and distribute the stolen German assets that Portugal now had no alternative but to admit it possessed.

At the talks, the Allies proposed that the Portuguese turn over 44,864 kilograms of gold (about $50.5 million), the amount they contended was the gold Lisbon acquired from Germany after 1942, when it had become common knowledge throughout the world that Germany had run out of its own gold reserves and was trading with looted gold.

The Portuguese countered that they were not aware that Germany had resorted to dealing with stolen gold. What they wanted for the time being was assurance that "if we do discover some looted gold in the future, we will turn it over to the Allies—but only after we are compensated from any liquidated German assets."

Yet another phase in the bargaining process began—the establishment of a Joint Subcommittee on Gold to review anew the Portuguese holdings and records. The settlement dragged on for months, then into years.

Nevertheless, Portugal's war dealings with Germany continued to be revealed. In 1946, the former German commercial attaché in Madrid confessed that almost $1 million in English gold sovereigns had gone from

Berlin to the German Embassy in Lisbon, another diplomatic pouch achievement.

Soon it was also revealed that more gold had arrived in June and July 1944 and was speeded away by German Legation cars to the Bank of Portugal and deposited in a special account in the name of the German Ambassador.

In the same period as these negotiations, the United States entered into delicate negotiations with Portugal for a pact that permitted the stationing of American military aircraft at Lagens (Lajes) Air Base in the Azores off the coast of Portugal. Uncle Sam viewed such a base as an important strategic asset, and on February 2, 1948, Portugal and the United States signed a five-year-agreement that allowed American forces to station military aircraft in the Azores.

Meanwhile, the United States had been holding an ace in the hole—it had $63.3 million of Portuguese gold and other assets locked up in its vaults which continued to be blocked, as they had been since the war. Premier Salazar now demanded that, in view of Lisbon's pact with Washington on the Azores, the United States should "loosen up and in a quid pro quo unblock the Portuguese funds" held in its coffers. However, he made no offer to give up the stolen Nazi gold that his country was hoarding.

United States Ambassador to Portugal John C. Wiley was deeply disturbed over what he termed was "a serious problem in our relations and the situation has the most unhappy significance regarding present and future problems in the Azores. If there ever was a moment when we should be seeking a gesture of appreciation to

Portugal... in view of what we have received in the Azores agreement, certainly this is it," he went on.

Wiley recommended "immediate" unblocking of all assets that had no readily apparent German interests.

The State Department concurred with Wiley's logic, inasmuch as United States policy was to "maintain and improve the existing cordial relations with Portugal and to encourage... [its] cooperation in the economic and political rehabilitation of Western Europe."

Additionally, the five-year Azores deal was merely an interim arrangement and the United States was very determined to obtain long-term base rights.

Yet the other critical considerations remained unsolved—the United States and its Allies' moral commitments to the victims of Nazi Germany.

Although the State Department also felt it was best for overall bilateral relations with Portugal to unblock the assets, it recommended caution about the timing of such a move. It wanted to "avert any suggestion that Portugal's intransigence... had earned her the premium of unblocking her assets."

The State Department's willingness to settle with Portugal on the gold issue wasn't shared throughout Washington. The Treasury Department was dissatisfied with the Portuguese offer to settle the issue by surrendering a mere 3.9 tons (328 gold bars valued at $4.4 million) and sought to refer the matter to the Inter-Allied Reparations Agency. That agency then could invite the various claimant countries to make their demands directly to Portugal.

However, after more give-and-take over the summer,

State and Treasury Department officials struck upon a solution on October 11, 1951, when the Treasury agreed to "go along" with the State Department under these conditions:

- The Treasury Department must receive a letter "signed at the Assistant Secretary level, stating... that there are political considerations which warrant a settlement... at this time... and that any agreement... would not result in claims against the United States."
- The United States must receive permission from the Netherlands for such an agreement.
- The State Department must be assured that the Portuguese offer continues in force.

The terms were set forth in a communiqué from Acting Assistant Secretary for European Affairs James Bonbright to Treasury Secretary John Snyder.

The State Department began talks with the British and French in November 1951, but nothing was resolved. Efforts to reach a settlement dragged on through seven excruciating years.

At the end of October, the divided West Germany had agreed to pay Portugal $132.5 million for the gold it would turn over to the Tripartite Gold Commission and 250 million escudos for its claims.

"With this assurance," according to the State Department inquiry that William Slany supervised, "the Portuguese finally decided to settle its Safehaven obligations.

"On October 27, 1958, they signed an agreement on 'German Assets in Portugal and on Certain Claims

Regarding Monetary Gold,' agreeing to turn over a total of
144.5 million escudos (about $4.3 million) to the Allies.

"Of this amount, twelve million escudos (about
$360,000) was to come from the blocked account estab-
lished under the terms of the 1949 agreement. The remaining 132 million escudos (about $4 million) was to be paid
by the Portuguese in either escudos or the equivalent in
gold up to 3,998.74 kilograms. . . ."

The treaty came into force in October 1959. The
Portuguese finally turned over the gold to fulfill its
Safehaven obligations. The Allies had negotiated with
Portugal over a decade and a half merely to extract $4.3
million for restitution.

The investigations into the full story of the looted
gold to be found in Portugal are still ongoing.

In January of 1997, Portugal's central bank finally
opened its archives to historians investigating the looted
gold. Joaquinda Costa Leite, an economic history professor
at Lisbon New University, was appointed by the bank's
board of governors to look into the records of the Bank of
Portugal.

In July of the same year, several newly declassified
United States intelligence documents revealed that the
Bank of Portugal and the Swiss National Bank swapped
tons of gold looted by the Nazis for gold held in the Bank
of Canada and the Federal Reserve Bank in New York.

Still another formerly secret document revealed
that Canada's central bank was holding gold for the Swiss
deposited before the war. However, in a sleight of hand

swap the Bank of Portugal, which had been buying looted
gold from Nazi Germany, deposited four tons into the
Swiss bank. The Swiss then went to the Canadian bank and
asked them to transfer the same amount of gold to
Portugal.

In fact, two wartime figures, Albert Speer, Hitler's
armaments minister, and António Salazar, Portugal's prime
minister, said that Germany might not have been able to
maintain its war effort so long without the raw materials
and industrial goods it received from Sweden, Spain,
Turkey, Switzerland, Argentina, and Portugal.

Setting aside Switzerland, the prime culprit in these
dealings, the other five countries handled approximately
$500 million in assets for the German government. In addi-
tion, an estimated $300 million in looted gold, now worth
about $2.7 billion, came into the coffers of these so-called
"neutral" nations. This was the gold Hitler's troops plundered from banks in overrun countries as well as valuables
seized from Holocaust victims, and which was often sent to
other countries for safekeeping or to pay for essential war
materials.

Elan Steinberg of the World Jewish Congress, told
ABC News in June 1998 that every nation in Europe benefited from the Third Reich's plunder of its Jewish victims'
assets. And Portugal was no exception—Bank of Portugal
statistics show that its gold reserves quintupled from 1939
to 1944.

CHAPTER 13

The Argentine Connection

World War II created a dilemma of no mean proportions for Argentina's then-repressive government, which had done a number of flip-flops in trying to make up its mind on whether to side with the democratic administration of President Franklin D. Roosevelt or ally itself with the fascist regime of dictator Adolf Hitler.

When war broke out in September 1939, Argentina assumed the position of "prudent neutrality" toward all players involved in the fray for several reasons regarding the best interest of the nation. Argentina's foreign policy was based upon the notion of freedom of action. In addition, its neutrality during World War I had been immensely popular at home and helped feed a hungry economy. At the outbreak of World War II, the economy of Argentina was again struggling, as a result of the Great Depression.

However, Argentina had agreed, at the Havana Conference in 1940, that any attack on an American state would be considered an attack against all American states and responded to accordingly. Argentina's view, however, was that the response after any attack was to be carried out according to each country's separate interpretation. After the United States was thrust into the war by the Japanese bombing of Pearl Harbor in December 1941, the leaders of the Western Hemispheric nations met concerning relations with the Axis powers. Two conclusions were decided upon at the Rio Conference of Foreign Ministers of the American Republics and the Final Act of the Inter-American Conference on Economic and Financial Controls, respectively. Both outcomes dictated the severance of all commercial and financial ties to the Axis. Argentina, however, did not adhere to either, citing that it would be damaging, economically and literally, to be involved in an inter-hemispheric war.

Germany's ties to Argentina had grown over the years. Before the choosing of sides for war, the two countries had dealt with each other militarily and financially. The Germans had already established a large network of businesses in Argentina, including import-export firms and banks. In addition to these, more than a quarter of a million Germans had come to reside in Argentina by the time the war began.

After war broke out in September 1939, German agents moved easily through Argentina handing out bribes to ensure the country's continued neutrality. Only two and one-half years later, the Nazis successfully established their neutral "ally" as an intelligence and covert warfare operation center in the West. The Germans ran enough programs in Argentina for it to have been considered an Axis power. It was used as a center for smuggling platinum used for electrical, chemical and dental purposes; for industrial diamonds, used in precision instruments and high speed drills; and for liver extract. Nearly 6 percent of the world's supply of platinum originated in Colombia. It would be purchased there, illegally, for only one-tenth of its black market value in Europe, and then smuggled to Argentina. There it would be sold to German agents, transported on Spanish vessels to Spanish ports and finally shipped into Axis territories throughout Europe. Argentine Nazis also facilitated the production of pro-Axis newspapers, ran espionage against Allied commercial and military operations and supported pro-Axis military officers.

Among other things, Germany had established two banks in Argentina: Banco Aleman Transatlantico and Banco Germanico. As was the case for other German businesses in Argentina, the banks were easily able to communicate with the mother country. Germany used these Argentine banks to help extort money from Jewish people residing in Europe. According to evidence compiled by the State Department in late 1942, "selected Jews could have a sum of Argentine pesos transferred to one of the two German banks in Buenos Aires as ransom for permission to emigrate from Germany."

In mid 1943, an almost-bloodless coup elevated

General Pedro Pablo Ramirez to the presidency and projected army Colonel Juan Domingo Perón as the dominant figure behind the scenes. Early domestic criticism in the press about the new government led to a crackdown on some seventy newspapers, whose publications were halted and editors jailed. The government also suspended many pro-Allied organizations for being "communistic."

However, in January 1944 as Nazi Germany's fortunes grew bleak, Argentina's position as "neutral but leaning toward the Axis" shifted. The United States State Department protested that Buenos Aires was surreptitiously engaging in pro-Axis activity. In a conversation between the United States Ambassador to Argentina, Norman Armour, and the Argentine Foreign Minister, Armour disclosed that the United States was ready to freeze Argentine assets in the United States. The Foreign Minister responded by informing Armour that Argentina was prepared to sever relations with the Axis. A few days later, Argentina broke off diplomatic relations with Germany and Japan, as well as with Axis satellites.

Less than a month later, in late February, Argentine President Ramirez stepped aside from his post in favor of General Edelmiro Farrell with Colonel Juan D. Perón assuming the vice presidency. The timing of these events led United States officials to believe this may have been orchestrated by pro-Axis forces operating inside Argentina. The United States responded by refusing to recognize the new regime, recalling Ambassador Armour from Buenos Aires in June and urging other American nations to do the same. Between August and November, Secretary of State Cordell Hull instituted sanctions against Argentina affecting gold stocks and exports. Farrell responded by withdrawing from the Montevideo Committee (formed at the Rio Conference in 1942 for the political defense of the continent). After this move, the Argentine Central Bank did little to help the American investigators find German assets.

In fact, the wartime records of the Argentine Central Bank indicate that Argentina received Nazi assets, according to documents found in 1997 in Buenos Aires and reported in the Buenos Aires daily, *La Nacion*, from a number of banks in Sweden, Portugal and Switzerland and that Argentina had extensive trade with these countries which accepted Nazi gold. These records support Treasury Secretary Henry Morgenthau's 1945 stated belief that Argentina "was the focal point of Nazi financial and economic activity in this hemisphere."

According to these records, a number of other neutral countries with dubious gold engaged in transactions with Argentina. Portugal, for instance, had ninety-seven bars early on but by mid 1944, 486 bars were accounted for. The Sveriges Riksbank of Stockholm shipped as many as 170 bars. Less significant amounts came from the Credit Suisse of Zurich, the Lausanne and Geneva branches of the Societe de Banque Suisse, and others.

Sixteen foreign firms and individuals from Amsterdam, Madrid, Zurich, Panama, Montevideo, Tangier, Germany, Geneva, and Zurich had gold bars transferred from their countries to Buenos Aires during the war.

Not surprisingly, after the moneys were deposited and the war ended, many Nazi war criminals found their way to Argentina. Among them: Adolf Eichmann, Auschwitz doctor Josef Mengele, and former SS Captain Erich Priebke.

Others said to have put substantial funds into German banks in Buenos Aires are Nazi Field Marshal Hermann Goering and Foreign Minister Joachim von Ribbentrop.

Another interesting bit of evidence linking Germany to Argentina surfaced in 1998 in *Integrantes de la Comision* by Marcos Aquinas where it was exposed that during the war Germany made an unusual proposal to buy Argentine grains. This was to be paid for in gold which the Third Reich was planning on confiscating from the central banks of countries they had taken over. Though this deal was not finalized, evidence is surfacing that others were.

During January 1945, the implementation of the Safehaven program in Argentina was being lead by Samuel Klaus, of the Foreign Economic Administration (FEA). By January of the following year, Klaus had gathered evidence, along with information from other departments, that implicated Argentina to be, in some respects, "the most critical Safehaven country."

During the next two months, Argentina's role in the political dance took another turn. Between February 21 and March 8, 1945, the nations of the Americas gathered for the Inter-American Conference on War and Peace (also known as the Chapultepec Conference). There they drafted a resolution that instructed neutral nations to work against any transfer or disposition of assets in Axis-occupied countries, called the Act of Chapultepec. Due to its dealings with the Axis and its isolation from the rest of the Americas after Farrell's rise to power, Argentina was not invited to Mexico City for the conference. By the end of March, the pressure of being the outsider of the Western Hemisphere caused the Farrell government to cave in. On March 27, Argentina declared war on the Axis powers as well as agreeing to the provisions of the Act of Chapultepec, merely one month before Turkey joined the Allies.

The initial months of the Safehaven program in Argentina were handled by the United States Embassy in Buenos Aires. There it ran its Argentine Replacement Program, which was to eliminate Axis firms through liquidation, expropriations and forced sales. The Argentine program was slow, however, compared to those in other Latin American countries. In June 1945, the two German banks in Argentina were still operating because liquidation measures applied by the Central Bank were lax. Displeased with the apparent lack of progress, the Treasury Department favoring treatment of Argentina as if it were a European neutral instead of a Latin American country. This would mean placing its German assets under the control of the Allied Control Council (ACC). The State Department, however, claimed that ACC control over Argentina would be extremely difficult without the permission of the other Latin American states.

Also in 1945, the State Department began work on the "Blue Book," delineating Argentina's cooperation with Germany. At about this time, an FEA preliminary report fingered Hermann Goering, the top-ranking Nazi official to survive the war, as having millions of dollars, in the form of paintings and sculptures, invested in Argentina. However, investigations failed to find evidence that he had interests or any assets there.

The Blue Book was delivered to Latin American countries in February of 1946. It focused on Argentina's potential to become a base for a Nazi resurgence. It also

stated that Argentina had not asserted control over
German firms prior to its declaration of war against the
Axis. The major finding was that the German Embassy in
Argentina received large sums of money from Nazi
Germany with no serious obstacles during transmission.
Later, another Safehaven investigation revealed that the
Embassy actually received 13.9 million pesos, the equiva-
lent of $4.1 million, from 1939 to January 1944. While a
large bulk of the money went towards a fixed monthly
expense, some also went to the upkeep of prisoners and
toward German espionage programs.

By May of 1946, the Safehaven program had found
680 million pesos, or $200 million, of German assets in
Argentina, sixty-six million of which was found at the two
German banks. Most assets uncovered by the Safehaven
investigation, however, came as bank balances, currency,
merchandise, and real estate. "No caches of gems or art
treasures looted by the Germans had been officially uncovered in Argentina," as had been in other countries.

Negotiations with the Argentine government over
German external assets were never pursued. The occurrence of such exchanges were at first contemplated, at least
as a possibility, at the time of the appointment of negotiator Seymour J. Rubin, the Department of State's chief of
the Division of Financial and Monetary Affairs, and later
the chief United States negotiator in Swedish, Spanish, and
Portuguese bargaining. However, Rubin's appointment as
negotiator between the United States and Argentina in May
1946 was mainly to determine the South American country's relationship with Germany and its involvement in gold
transactions with European neutral nations.

Treasury officials believed that Argentina was one of the countries that remained subject to the February 1944 Gold Declaration. Nevertheless, though it had accepted the principles of the declaration, Buenos Aires delayed its official adherence to that manifesto until the following year. A deferment of such duration aroused suspicions among Treasury and State Department officials that the pro-Axis Farrell-Peron government might have acquired looted gold from either Germany or the European neutral countries during the one-year hiatus.

Back in 1945, Treasury officials had become pessimistic about the success of a Safehaven program in Argentina and had lost faith in the likelihood that its government would come forward with information about gold acquisitions, owing in part to the strained relations between Washington and Buenos Aires during the war years, which seemed to linger even after Argentina officially joined the Allied camp. America's new ambassador in Buenos Aires, George S. Messersmith, had undertaken to turn United States policy toward Argentina. In a series of top-secret dispatches, Messersmith had urged Secretary of State James F. Byrnes that the United States should foster a relationship with Argentina on a "completely friendly, collaborative, and constructive" basis by 1946. He had also contended that Argentine leaders were actively and concretely handling the problem of enemy property and aliens, and that there was no doubt about the determination of the Argentine government to proceed with liquidation of this property.

In February 1947, the Embassy reported that all identified enemy assets had been taken over by the Argentine

Government. The State Department's initial response to Ambassador Messersmith's recommendation to turn toward Argentina was positive, but cautious. The State Department wanted to see compliance based on specific measures against certain prominent individuals of enemy-controlled enterprises, rather than on hypothetical grounds. By that time, Washington officials dealing with Safehaven matters had apparently turned their attention away from concentration on German assets in Argentina, assuming that there was nothing further to gain by continuing to monitor that country for any traces of Nazi gold. Then came a most shocking turn.

By May of that year, Argentina was ready to send about $170 million in gold bullion to the Federal Reserve Bank of New York, and would attempt to sell it to the United States. Concerned that Argentina might have accepted looted assets after the Gold Declaration of February 22, 1944, newly-installed Secretary of State George C. Marshall, the Army Chief-of-Staff during World War II, admonished the State Department for not approaching the Argentine government. He insisted they have Argentina come clean and be aboveboard about its gold acquisitions from Germany as a precondition to authorizing any transfer of its gold to the United States, but the Treasury Department planned to accept only gold with United States assay marks, and officials felt this was protection enough.

The Treasury and State Departments were locked in two diametrically opposite positions. The Department of State was willing to accept any and all gold that Argentina shipped to New York for sale—with no further questions asked. The Treasury insisted that all gold sent to the Empire State for conversion to dollars must clearly bear United States assay marks—proof that the precious metal offered for sale contained no elements of tainted, illicit Nazi gold. Despite the Treasury's stubborn insistence that Argentina must verify the gold hadn't been looted, the country's government stood its ground, trumpeting that Buenos Aires' acceptance of the Gold Declaration in 1945 should be sufficient grounds to accept the bullion into the Treasury's Federal Reserve vaults in lower Manhattan.

Argentine plans to ship gold in excess of its registered United States assay-marked gold gave urgency to the matter. In early October 1947, the State Department asked Argentina for a statement of wartime gold acquisitions at an interdepartmental meeting on looted gold, held on October 3. A cable sent a few days later asked only for Argentina's certification that it had not acquired gold from Axis or "neutral" countries. The Argentine Central Bank then made verbal assurances (later confirmed in writing) that the bullion complied with the Gold Declaration. On October 11, 1947, the Treasury Department reached the conclusion, based on reports from the embassy in Buenos Aires on the discussions with Central Bank officials, that Argentina had not acquired gold looted by Germany. That sufficed to clear the sale of the Argentine gold through the Federal Reserve on October 23, 1947. Despite the fact that the sale was cleared, markers on the gold requested by Under Secretary of State Bob Lovett for investigative purposes were not included. While Lovett attempted to follow up on the missing information, Ambassador Messersmith felt that an interrogation into Argentina's Swiss gold could have adverse effects on the United States-Argentine relationship and opposed Lovett's itinerary. The matter was dropped after that but that didn't close out the issue of looted gold South of the Border.

In the 1990s, after decades of dormancy, the issue of Argentina's ties to Nazi Germany in the forties reawakened. The main player responsible for the new influx of information was the latest in the line of Argentine presidents, Carlos Saúl Menem. When Menem began his term in 1990, his stated aim was to change Argentina's image created in the last half century, that is, the view that Argentina had been sympathetic to the Nazi cause dating back to World War II. In doing so, he announced that Argentina was "paying its debt to humanity." Trying to reestablish a kinder image of Argentina in the world's eyes by repudiating past errors, despite acts of violence which have set that stance back, has sometimes been difficult.

Two years after he entered office, Menem released secret files on Nazis who had escaped to Argentina after the war. Those files contained the names of more than a thousand suspected war criminals who resided there. Three years later, in 1995, his government facilitated the extradition of Erich Priebke to Italy, where the former SS officer went on trial for his part in the deaths of 335 Italian citizens, many of whom were Jews. The following year saw the Menem administration provide bank records that would aid Jewish investigators in locating gold shipments that made their way to Argentina through Nazi agents. In 1996, Argentina provided Jewish investigators with bank records that may help them track down not only gold but artworks smuggled into Argentina by Nazi agents.

The government bank records have led investigators to believe that Argentina was a "transit route" for Nazi treasures sent through Spain and Portugal. The reason for this type of relationship was that, "Argentina didn't offer the kind of political and economic stability that would have made it attractive for this money to stay," but it could facilitate laundering, according to Ruben Beraja, the vice president of the World Jewish Congress. A testament to the close ties between Germany and Argentina can be seen in the bank records showing that German companies such as Thyssen and Krupp moved approximately $150 million to Argentine companies in 1943.

The Central Bank publicized archives that contained records of the gold transfers from neutral European nations to Argentina. The archives contained five volumes totaling 400 transactions during the decade between 1939 and 1949. Despite the fact that President Menem had ordered the state archives to be opened in 1992, for four years nothing was produced save seven folders that contained no pertinent information. One interesting point about the folders was that they had no information on Adolf Eichmann, who had been overseer of the deportation and extermination of millions of Jews during the war.

Many local Jewish leaders reacted with skepticism toward the independent commission assigned to investigate further into the Nazi gold controversy. At the request of Sergio Widder, the Latin American representative of the Simon Wiesenthal Center, Argentine officials were to investigate 334 Nazi officials and businessmen involved in the transfer of gold to local banks after the war. The lack of specific information can be attributed to the fact that

Argentine records were poorly kept and files aren't divided into categories, so they must be searched file by file. This situation led a large contingent of Jewish leaders to believe that the only way to find the truth of the matter was to investigate private banks. "It cannot be ignored that major war criminals," according to Rabbi Hier of the Simon Wiesenthal Center, "ended up in Argentina because they knew they could expect a good welcome and security there."

By 1997, records from the Argentine Central Bank had confirmed the theory that Argentina was a passageway for Nazi wealth. The records showed that, "the Banque Nationale Suisse, the Bank of Portugal and the Sveriges Riksbank of Stockholm deposited gold in Argentina between 1942 and 1944, together with thirty-two other banks, firms and private individuals who safeguarded their gold in Buenos Aires." The books that contained this valuable information were found in a museum showing how records were kept in that period.

The account books found in Argentina's Central Bank show that twenty gold bars from the Banque Nationale Suisse were deposited in Buenos Aires in November 1944. Two years later, the Suisse Bank had 470 bars in the Argentine bank. About half were taken out two years after that. The last portion was airlifted out between 1951 and 1952.

In addition to the neutral states of Europe that did business with Argentine banks, the books also implicate "sixteen foreign firms and individuals" who took part in the movement of gold in and out of Buenos Aires. One of the most infamous of these is the Austrian munitions magnate, Fritz Mandl, who deposited forty gold bars there after fleeing Europe in 1939. Mandl was considered by the United States State Department as a Nazi agent and was tracked accordingly. After he was arrested by the Argentine government at the end of the war, he escaped extradition to the United States by contributing heavily to Juan Perón's 1946 presidential campaign. Mandl remained in Argentina and eventually recovered his gold in the 1950s, according to the records.

The foreign accounts recorded in the Central Bank's books were unique to the bank only around the time of the war. There had been no record of such accounts before. To help facilitate the entrance of Nazi criminals into his country without incident, Perón established a "team" of SS officials and other escapees like Adolf Eichmann, Josef Mengele and Erich Priebke.

Later in 1997, evidence arose implicating Juan Perón's second wife, Eva, in the transfer of Nazi loot to Swiss bank accounts. Eva toured Europe in 1947 in an attempt to boost her husband's image there. While traveling, she made a stop in Switzerland, where, it is believed, she opened at least one account to store funds paid to her by Nazis in return for Argentine visas and passports. After her death in 1952 and Juan's subsequent fall from power three years later, he traveled to Spain and attempted to locate his wife's stash. Neither Perón, nor anyone else, was ever able to locate the account. According to Argentine businessman Jorge Antonio in an unpublished memoir, "All we could get was a handful of gold coins deposited in a safe box belonging to Evita's brother, Juan Duarte."

In mid May of 1997, the government of Argentina established a national committee to trace the influx of Nazi officials who streamed there after the war. The probe would go on to research the amount of safeguard offered these officers by local governments and track the movement of Nazi plunder into the region. This committee, consisting of both high-ranking government officials and non-government figures with an international board of trustees, came to being in reaction to the revelation by a commission funded by the Argentine-Israeli Mutual Aid Association (AMIA) that Argentine officials aided Nazis to settle there.

A report released in May 1947 described the roles of Peron and other administrations that protected Nazi officials after the war. It detailed that in the half century since the war, Argentina deported only Gerhard Bohne, Joseph Schwammberger, and Erich Priebke, while protecting others. In previous years, documents were released confirming that Nazis had sent their looted treasures to Argentina for safekeeping. The documents, uncovered by the World Jewish Congress and the Senate Banking Committee, revealed that the Swiss may have assisted in the transport of Nazis and their loot to Buenos Aires. Another document cited a confidential informer who stated that Nazi capital made its way to South America, unbeknownst to the Swiss government, through Swiss pouches obtained by Hermann Goering and Joseph Goebbels. The document suggested that KLM Royal Dutch Airlines, Swissair, Air France and Air Sweden all played roles in facilitating Nazi movement between Germany and Argentina.

When, in November of 1997, a bank vault in Sao Paulo, Brazil yielded more than four million dollars worth of property including gold bars, jewelry and cash allegedly stolen from victims of World War II, hope was revived that more property of Holocaust victims would be found and returned.

This particular vault was in the name of Albert Blume, a German who came to Brazil before the war and was purported to be a banker for other Nazis who fled to South America and, in particular, Argentina during and after World War II. Among the many fugitives from the Third Reich who either found refuge or passed briefly through Argentina are the following: Ivan Asancaic, Klaus Barbie, Branco Benzon, Gerhardt Bohne, Herbert Cuckurs, Milo de Bogetic, Pierre Daye, Jacques de Mahieu, Jan Durcansky, Adolf Eichmann, Hans Fishboeck, Carlos Fuldner, Vojteh Hora, Jan Olij Hottentot, Abraham Kipp, Walter Kutschmann, Joseph Mengele, Wilhelm Mohnke, Oliverio Mondrelle, Ante Pavelic, Erich Priebke, Walter Rauff, Franz Röstel, Auguste Ricord, Andreas Riphagen, Eduard Roschmann, Hans Ulrich Rudel, Wilhelm Sassen, Joseph Schwamberger, Friedrich Schwend, Otto Skorzeny, Franz Stangl, Vlado Svencen, Ludolf von Alvensleben, Constantin von Gromann, Vkekoslav Vrancic, and Gustav Wagner. Blume's family denied that Blume was active in the Nazi Party after he went to South America, but his early ties to the party seem undeniable.

One of the most infamous of the Fuhrer's Nazi leaders, Martin Bormann, is said to have escaped Germany and fled to the Argentine side of Patagonia. A passport now held by an aged German man living in the so-called "Nazi Triangle" where many ex-German officers resided after the war shows a birth date and physical description which match Bormann's. One journalist, Abel Basti, of the newspaper *La Manana del Sur* spoke to people who remember the ex-Nazi.

"They say that Bormann lived in southern Chile until 1973, the year General Perón returned to power in Argentina after eighteen years of exile prompting his move to the Argentine side of the border to enjoy Peron's protection."

Ruben Beraja, who is a member of the Volcker Committee and a prominent Argentine Jew, declared in an interview appearing in the *New York Times* on April 18, 1997, "This government wants to make a clean break with the Argentina of the past which is seen as having been pro-Nazi or a haven to Nazism. Mr. Menem has assured me of his personal support and that of his administration that we investigate this issue to the very end and to let him know if we have any problems."

To this end, President Menem has created an international truth committee to insure that investigators have access to needed information on Argentina and Nazi gold transactions.

Nevertheless, though Argentina is making some strides in confronting its pro-Nazi past, a number of attacks on local Jewish targets undermine these efforts.

However, the more open disclosure of the Argentine government was seen again in early 1998, when a Swiss state prosecutor, Carla de Ponte, was assisting a Spanish court investigation into the disappearance of 600 Spaniards in Argentina during the dictatorship of the junta between 1976 and 1983.

It was common practice during the dictatorship for

the militia to loot the homes of people detained on suspicion of subversion, confiscate their motor vehicles and real
estate, and then resell them, as well as extort money from
businessmen and family members of the detainees.

Prosecutors learned the identities of four former
military men who engaged in the practice of looting valuables from Argentine victims and were found to be holders
of Swiss bank accounts, which, human rights groups
revealed, contained millions of dollars pillaged from political prisoners during the junta's torturous seven-year regime.

Although Argentine amnesty laws protected former
members of the military from prosecution for abuses during
the dictatorship, the prosecutors said they were trying to determine if those who held Swiss accounts could be charged with
tax evasion, illicit enrichment, or other financial misconduct.

Saying "the time is ripe to jail officers who have
escaped responsibility for their crimes," Ricardo Quintela, a
congressman from the governing party which seized power
from the junta, called for Argentine prosecutors to model
their cases after the United States government's successful
prosecution of Al Capone in the 1930s for income tax evasion that broke his grip as "boss of all bosses" over United
States gangland's most powerful underworld organization.

"Though the mere fact of holding an account in
Switzerland does not constitute a crime," said Emilio
Martinez Garbino, also a Peronist congressman, "it's clear
that it raises suspicions that call for an investigation into the
possible criminal origins of the funds."

Based on the testimony of survivors and relatives
of victims, human rights groups estimate that the armed
forces stole $70 million in assets—including cash, cars, real

estate, and jewelry—from those detained. At least 9,000 people were killed or disappeared, and tens of thousands more were tortured, a government inquiry concluded.

Human rights groups put the death toll at 30,000.

The four Army officials who secreted huge amounts of cash that was converted to gold by Swiss banks were:

- Antonio Bussi, a former general and most recently governor of the northern province of Tucman, who faced impeachment proceedings by the provincial legislature after he admitted under pressure that he had failed to declare the Swiss account on his tax return.

- Former Sergeant Carlos Vega, who worked at a torture camp in Cordoba Province, where 3,000 detainees disappeared.

- Ex-Lieutenant Alfredo Astiz, who was recently forced out of the military because of his actions during the dictatorship and was wanted in France for the killing of two French nuns in Argentina during the dictatorship.

- Colonel Roberto Rouaides, who died in 1995, a leading figure in a military strike against leftists in Cordoba.

While Argentine prosecutors had not been told by the Swiss exactly how much money the four bank accounts contained, they said they had reason to believe that the total was at least three million dollars.

Legal experts said they were convinced prosecutors could build a strong case against the three surviving Army strongmen if it could be proved that they failed to declare their bank accounts as personal assets or failed to pay taxes on the interest. Moreover, they could also be prosecuted for illicit enrichment.

Until late February 1998, when the details of Argentina's ex-soldiers' involvement with Swiss bank holdings came to light, Buenos Aires had refused to cooperate with the Spanish inquiry, contending that Spain had no jurisdiction and that the amnesty laws prevented the government from taking the accused to court.

But in releasing the names of the holders of the Swiss accounts to Argentine prosecutors, Spanish investigators had taken the case directly to the Argentine public. That put Argentine officials in a bind and they eased their adamancy against acting with more severity against the army rip-offs.

At that time, terrorists slaughtered eighty-six people in the bombing of a Jewish community center in Buenos Aires. It happened on July 18 when a van loaded with explosives was driven to the Argentine-Israeli Mutual Association and parked alongside the building, where it blew up.

Despite efforts by the so-called "democratic government" of President Menem, if the Argentine government took the slightest interest in getting to the bottom of this heinous massacre and went in pursuit of those responsible for it, there was virtually no indication of it.

According to politicians and Jewish leaders interviewed in Buenos Aires, the case remained "dormant for all the years since it occurred—until President Clinton visited Argentina on a goodwill mission in October 1997.

"Clinton met with relatives of the victims, listened

to their pleas for justice, and made his moves," according to the *Los Angeles Times* South American correspondent Sebastian Rotella. "He promised to apply pressure on the Argentine government, an infusion of political will, and old-fashioned police work."

Those moves led to a start-up of unexpected momentum on the part of government officials, with President Menem taking the lead in calling for a "full inquiry into this senseless slaughter."

In the United States, President Clinton ordered the FBI to comb the domestic front for clues and evidence about the bombing. That step was generated by Havier Astigarraga, a lawyer for the survivors of those killed in the blast, who passed on a report about one of several newly-targeted suspects, Juan Jose Ribelli.

Labeled the chief suspect, Ribelli had been commander of the Buenos Aires provincial police at the time of the bombing. The investigation went into overdrive only after it developed that Ribelli himself had acquired the van on July 13, 1994—seven days before its deadly cargo was detonated. The probe determined that the van, which had been stolen, then recovered by the police and stored in its motor vehicle compound until the owner could reclaim it, was instead driven off by the provincial police commander, Ribelli.

Marcelo Stubrin, a member of the Chamber of Deputies and its commission investigating the bombing, revealed that Ribelli received $2.5 million in cash the day after he appropriated the van. The payment is now believed to have come from terrorists—not, as Ribelli claimed, from his father, a retired railroad worker who was collecting a small monthly pension from his former employer.

Adding to the finger-pointing at Ribelli was the revelation that he spent days after the bombing holed up in a hotel that housed an Israeli rescue and forensic team. Argentine probers suspected from the start that Ribelli spied on the Israelis and severely obstructed the investigation with the aid of higher-ranking police officials—an effort that effectively scuttled efforts that Argentine government officials exerted in the beginning to solve the community center bombing.

Not until Argentina picked up the tempo of inquiry after Clinton's visit did it become public knowledge that former provisional police officials had been rounded up and charged with involvement in providing the van used in the bombing. But the case had lain in limbo because there was no incentive in Argentina to continue a full-scale adjudication of the case.

At the same time, the probers were said to believe the attack also involved Iranian terrorists and members of Modin, a rightist political party of former military officers known for coup attempts and anti-Semitic violence. The most recent and politically prominent investigative target was congressional deputy Emilio Morello, a pony-tailed former army captain and a member of Modin. Under questioning at the end of December 1997, Morello denied allegations that he met with Iranian diplomats and traveled secretly to the Middle East.

Police were looking into Morello because of his known ties to accused arms traffickers connected to Modin, including a military explosives expert who was yards away from the scene at the time of the bombing. Other Modin activists showed up at the bombing site in a

phony ambulance. All of those arrivals at the scene of ter-
rorist activity intrigued Argentinean investigators, lately
bent on getting to the bottom of the Jewish center bombing and bringing those responsible for it to justice.

While the puzzle about the bombing continued to
move toward a possible solution, Argentine Judge Juan Jose
Galeano sought to find other still-missing pieces of that
puzzle—now with a suspected Iranian connection. After
gathering information in France and Germany on Iranian
terrorism, Galeano flew to Los Angeles to interview a new
witness, Manouchehr Moatamer, an Iranian defector who
was living in California.

Moatamer had fled Iran in 1994 and gone to
California, after having provided a brief statement about
his awareness of the Argentine bombing to an operative for
Judge Galeano. With interest now strongly aroused and
with a determination to bring the long-delayed investigation to fruition, Galeano decided to do his own inquiry
with the Iranian who claimed he had "all the inside knowledge about the bombing that Argentina would ever want to
hear."

More and more it was beginning to appear the solution to the bombing rested in large part on the credibility
of Manouchehr Moatamer, and his claim to have vital
information. He told Judge Galeano that, as a former well-
placed Iranian operative with powerful family connections,
he had access to meetings where intelligence officials plot-
ted the Buenos Aires bombing.

During his deposition in Los Angeles in December
1997, Moatamer backed up his claims by providing what he
described as official Iranian documents on the plot.

Moatamer first told his story to Galeano's probers in 1994 in Venezuela, where he said he had eluded a kidnap attempt by Iranian spies. That testimony led Galeano to issue arrest warrants for three Iranian diplomats in Argentina, but the effort hit a standstill for lack of evidence. Meanwhile, in California, Moatamer was appearing on Iranian-language television and radio and being questioned about his allegations by United States intelligence agents.

Iranian officials, who repeatedly denied any role in the bombing that killed the eighty-six Jews, called Moatamer a con man. Nevertheless, investigators still believed he could help them—and they based part of that belief on what he had told them during his interrogation in 1994: that the Israeli Embassy in London was to be bombed, and a few days later it was.

In early 1998, as the investigation of the Buenos Aires bombing appeared to be winding down to resolution, Argentine prosecutor Jose Barbaccia came out with a telling assessment about Moatamer: "What we have found out during these past three years has made him more credible. If his information is authentic, it is important."

Another voice out of Argentina, that of Marcelo Stubrin, member of the commission investigating the bombing, voiced an even more heartening message about closing in on the renegade police and right-wing extremists who apparently were responsible for the atrocity perpetrated on the Jewish community center. "We have to cleanse this society of all this garbage that has survived despite years of democracy," declared Stubrin.

A labyrinthine trail led authorities through the Middle

East, Europe, Los Angeles, and Florida where the deadliest anti-Semitic attack since the Holocaust would finally be resolved.

More encouraging was the news from Buenos Aires on February 10, 1998, reported by Reuters News Service: "The widow of Oskar Schindler, the German industrialist who rescued more than 1,000 Jews from the Nazi Holocaust, has been granted a pension by the Argentine government to save her from poverty.

"A government spokesman said yesterday Emilie Schindler would receive $1,000 a month. In interviews, the ninety-year-old had complained of poverty. She lived in Argentina in anonymity for fifty years before Steven Spielberg told her husband's story in the memorable, prizewinning film *Schindler's List*," from which she received nothing.

Perhaps finally and at last, Argentina, which during World War II and thereafter had dealt extensively and unconscionably in Nazi gold, has begun to expiate its past by building a more humane future.

CHAPTER 14

Turkey's Gilded Espionage

Postwar Safehaven negotiations with Turkey took a somewhat different direction than did those with Sweden, Switzerland, Spain, Portugal and Italy.

Turkey, a country that lies between the Black Sea to the north and the Mediterranean Sea to the south, found itself sandwiched between the Axis and Allies when the threat of brutal defeat and subjugation loomed close enough to force them into neutrality.

Until February 1945—three months before the Third Reich's cataclysmic collapse in World War II—Turkey had alleged it practiced "strict neutrality." But as a noncombatant nation, this crossroads of European and

Asian peoples, speaking Turkish languages and living in the
region from the Adriatic to the Okhotsk, played an insidi-
ous role of incomparable double-cross virtually the entire
duration of the war.

When the conflict was underway and Hitler's
Panzer divisions were running rampant over the European
landscape, fear of its likely enslavement by Hitler's far-
reaching Nazi military juggernaut gripped Turkey. Because
of the looming threat, it expeditiously declared itself a
"neutral" nation and escaped the almost-certain subjugation it would have endured had the Wehrmacht's armies
crossed its borders. With that reprieve gained, Turkey
entered into a game of cross-and-double-cross to an extent
which no other nation ever resorted in order to immunize
itself against Der Fuhrer's wrath.

Although Turkey was officially "neutral," it was still
an important trading partner for Germany because it supplied one of the most coveted resources that the Nazis
could demand—chromite. Chromium derived from the
chromite ore was used extensively by Germany to produce
stainless steel for use in its war industry.

Hitler had made Turkey his next target for conquest
after the Soviet Union. He saw it as a useful asset and valuable trading partner. To help sustain its economy, Turkey
agreed with Germany to export raw materials, such as
chromite. Through the initial memo of understanding,
known as the Clodius agreement, and supplemental pacts,
Turkey supplied Germany with 45,000 tons of chromite in
1941 through 1942 and 90,000 tons in each of the next two
years. With this blaring aid to the Germans visible to the
Allies, Turkey attempted to downplay its significance by

stating that they did not expect the Germans to live up to their side of the deal and in addition, they were purposely slowing the process of shipment through the use of lengthy negotiations. Despite these measures, however, the Germans made every effort to expedite delivery of the chromite by freeing more than a hundred trains for transport and penetrating the Black Sea with merchant ships due to lax enforcement of the 1936 Montreux Convention by the Turks.

Since the import of chromite was so vital to the Germans, the United States and Great Britain sought to cripple them by cutting that supply. This had to be achieved, however, while keeping Turkey appeased. The Allied strategy in this case was to embark on a program of "preclusive purchases," in which the United States and Great Britain would obtain Turkish chromite and other materials in return for a ban on their exports to Germany. As the war continued, the preclusive purchase program worked effectively and as the German stockpile of chromite eroded, the war between the Allies and Germany for Turkey's precious commodity grew. Britain, France, and the United States banned together to impede the entry of chromite into Germany. However, in 1943, as part of the Clodius agreement, quantities in excess of 45,700 made their way into Germany. Allied estimates of Germany's annual necessity for chromite fell between forty and forty-five thousand tons, meaning that Turkey was supplying the Nazis with most, if not all, of the important substance.

With the increase in chromite shipments to Germany, the American and British roles in the preclusive purchasing program increased. Between 1942 and 1944, the

Allies bought most products that Turkey exported to Germany through trade agreements. These items included "mohair, antimony, copper, flax, hemp, textile fibers, and molybdenum." American purchases in this program during the time period came to $125 million, according to the *Preclusive Operations in the Neutral Countries in World War II* report published in 1947.

Again, however, in October of 1943, Turkey signed another pact with Germany that would see 135,000 tons of chromite change hands. It was later learned that in some years, Turkey provided 100 percent of Germany's chromite, necessary for steel producton, which was used to make armor. This action prompted President Roosevelt to have a strong letter transmitted to Turkish President Ismet Inönü indicating that Turkish trade with the Axis was a major factor in keeping the Reich running and showed a disregard for the good of the world. Through the eyes of German Minister for Armaments and Munitions Albert Speer, the Nazi regime depended even more than Roosevelt thought on Turkish chromite. As was detailed in Speer's *Inside the Third Reich: Memoirs*, a memo sent from Speer to Hitler gravely pointed out that if Turkish chromite imports ceased, the current German stockpile would last less than half a year.

Roosevelt's message was never seen by Inönü because it was construed by British Prime Minister Winston Churchill as too soft, showing the Turks that the tough Allied stance on Turkey was crumbling.

According to the Eizenstat report, in diplomatic and intelligence circles, reports circulated about Turkey's receiving looted gold. Turkey purchased three tons of gold worth about four million dollars from the Swiss National Bank. In May of 1943 the Reichsbank supplied Turkey with 249 bars and the Swiss bank transferred 3,048 kilograms to the Reichsbank. Turkey's foreign trade surplus for 1939-1946 totaled $341.5 million.

By the end of 1943, Turkey was upset with the lack of support extended by the Allies and denied them access to bases there to prevent inciting the Germans to attack. As Sir Llewellyn Woodward describes in his book, *British Foreign Policy in the Second World War*, when the Allies asked President Inönü to enter the war by mid February of the next year, he showed the desire to join them, but requested an increase in the amount of military assistance which would ease his concerns about any German attack. In response to this, the British informed the Turkish government that their delay would mean the rescinding of aid to and isolation of their country for the remainder of the war. The British then added that there would be the supplemental possibility that they would not lend support in the case that the Soviet Union applied pressure to the Turks regarding the status of the Dardanelles after the war. After the Turks failed to act in February, the British withdrew their aid without warning. A short time later the Americans took the same course of action.

In April of 1944, when German agents entered Ankara seeking to renew the German-Turkish trade pact, the American and British joint response stated that "any renewal of agreements or the conclusion of fresh agreements on the same lines will entail the application to Turkey of blockade measures such as the two Governments have throughout the war applied to neutral countries." Less than a week thereafter, Turkey ceased the trade of chromite to Germany altogether and, within two months, all other exports to Germany were reduced by 50 percent.

With the German Empire's collapse after the Allies opened their Second Front in Western Europe in 1944, their Turkish "allies" made moves to abandon the fascist sinking ship. On July 25, the Turkish Government requested the Turkish Grand National Assembly to end all relations, diplomatic and economic, with Germany. By the next week, on August 2, the ties between the two had been severed. Without Turkey as a crutch, Germany's limp became more obvious. Finally, the Allies offered Turkey an invitation to the San Francisco conference which would initiate the United Nations as long as they became belligerents toward Germany by March 1, 1945. Again, the Turkish hesitancy to harm the Nazis showed itself when Turkey held out until finally declaring war on February 23, three months before the end of the war in Europe.

Allied intelligence, however, discovered that gold flowed through the Turkish free market at a resounding rate, especially from 1943 through 1944. Through this system, the two major German banks in Turkey, Deutsche Bank and the Dresdner Bank, received looted gold from the Reichsbank, in return for Swiss francs or other foreign currencies from Axis diplomats. The diplomats would then receive Turkish currency at almost double the official exchange rates in return. After the gold was brought to Turkey, the banks could sell it on the free market for a greatly increased price in comparison to the fee they paid. One confirmed instance of Turkish purchase of looted gold was recorded in the Office of International Finance, valued at $3.4 million worth of Belgian gold in March of 1943. Records given to Stuart Eizenstat by Turkish Minister of State Sukru S. Gurel in 1997 revealed that the Swiss National Bank (SNB) purchased "3,048 kilograms of gold for fifteen million Swiss francs," on behalf of the Central Bank of the Republic of Turkey (CBRT). However, due to hardships faced while transporting gold during the war, the CBRT turned to the Reichsbank, which offered 249 gold bars measuring a total of one kilogram less than the original amount bought by the Swiss National Bank. This, in turn, meant that the SNB sent its gold to the Reichsbank. The gold bars from the Reichsbank came into Turkish possession on June 3, 1943.

Safehaven files in the Ankara Embassy showed that Turkey continued to receive looted gold after the war concluded. In September 1945, Turkey received "12,800 assorted gold coins, 140 kilograms of gold ingots and 250,000 Turkish pounds" from the Swiss Legation in Ankara. With other assets that entered the Dresdner Bank from Switzerland, the total gain for Turkey was more than $400,000. It was later learned that the gold supplied for these transactions actually came from a Reichsbank account belonging to German Foreign Minister Joachim von Ribbentrop which contained assets looted from Nazi occupied territories during the war.

A wartime study, conducted by the United States, of gold bars transferred from the Reichsbank to the Deutsche

Bank measuring 1.582 metric tons concluded that 339 kilograms originated in "specific conquered areas," especially
Belgium, while 904 kilograms were traced to "other questionable sources." The former of the sources included gold
from the Prussian Mint and the Degussa smelting company. The gold smelted included the SS stash of "gold bars,
coins, jewelry, and dental fillings," that were taken from the
victims, Jewish and non-Jewish alike, of the concentration
and death camps. The study, conducted by the United
States, calculated that 42.5 percent of the more than one
and one-half tons of gold ingots had come from "individual victims of Nazi persecution." A separate postwar investigation of the Reichsbank conducted by Albert Thoms,
head of the Precious Metals Department of Reichsbank,
revealed that the bank also sold gold bars to the Dresdner
Bank. With gold from the Dresdner Bank being turned
over to the Turkish government by the Swiss Legation, the
gold obtained by the Turks may have included that
obtained by Nazis from Holocaust victims.

Meanwhile, the government in Ankara, not aware
that agents from America's Office of Strategic Services
were operating in their midst, began to deal with Berlin and
engaged in the rampant practice of storing and safeguarding
German looted gold. More disturbingly, however, Turkey
also allowed itself to become a center for espionage by the
Axis. It neither put up resistance nor sounded any alarm
when Nazi Ambassador to Turkey, the dread "fraudulent
deceiver" Franz von Papen, sent shipments of "gold pieces,
other valuables and documents" there, as his term came to

a close. The likes of which could have served as significant and damaging enough evidence at the postwar Nuremberg trials to send him before a firing squad. But Turkey declined to cooperate in that endeavor—just as its government had allowed von Papen to conduct German espionage operations out of Ankara without complaint. In short, Turkey was not a friend of the Allies—despite her pose as such when the Allies sought to open a dialogue with the Turkish government.

After November 1944, the United States pressed Turkey through diplomatic notes not to acquire or store any additional German gold than it had during the course of the war. Washington cited that its grounds were based on the February 1944 Gold Declaration and Bretton Woods Resolution VI. Then, on January 25, 1945, the State Department sent word to the United States Embassy in Ankara to alert Turkey that they must retain German holdings "for disposition in accordance with Allied policy." The Turks failed to reply and did not act on controlling German property within their borders through March of 1945.

As the end of the war edged closer, the Allies began to appraise enemy holdings in Turkey. "By April 1945, they estimated there was ten million dollars in private and $25.5 million in state assets in the country." However, Turkey—posing then as an "Ally" based on its three-month tenure in that guise—set its ultimatum at "five million dollars from private funds and twelve to thirteen million dollars from the state funds" as restitution for its own case against the Nazi regime. The State Department ignored that "bogus" attempt to enrich its already-bulging coffers with the blood money it had dealt with throughout the war. In fact, Washington stepped forth, fourteen months after it issued its initial estimate, and reassessed Turkey's obligation to the Allies with updated figures: "Twenty-eight to forty-four million dollars in private and twenty-three million dollars in state assets." Turkey, however, argued that it now had a compensatory $15.5 million due its government.

After lengthy talks and several amendments to the accord, on March 28, 1946, the Allies proposed Safehaven to Ankara. Turkey responded half a year later, and, "while claiming that it had already taken necessary measures to protect German assets and was happy to cooperate further, Turkey demanded that it receive most of the proceeds from the liquidation of the assets and retain full sovereignty over the enforcement and control of these assets and enemy personnel."

Although this response fell short of the State Department's expectations, it did not want to continue to pressure the Turks and have to deal with their hard-nosed adamancy against all reasonable proposals that were tailored to fit Ankara's always-changing stance in every successive round of negotiations. The State Department advised the United States Embassy to persuade Turkey to keep the proffered terms private for the time being lest they complicate further discussions.

A series of probes begun in April 1947 led to official negotiations by both sides on June 2. Those resulted in Turkey's announcement that it was "willing to adhere to the January 1943 Declaration and the February 1944 Gold Declaration, as well as Bretton Woods Resolution VI."

However, Ankara continued to argue that because Turkey "had joined the Allies in the last months of the war," they were not bound by the Paris Reparations Agreement and, therefore, that the bulk of liquidated German assets within the country must go to satisfy Turkey's claims against Germany. Despite another month of negotiations, the issue remained unsettled.

According to the Eizenstat report, "By September 1947, Allied investigators confirmed that Turkey had purchased the 3,047 kilograms of looted Belgian gold from Switzerland in 1943. (The Allies suspected that Turkey also had eight tons in gold ingots of low fineness and three tons of looted European gold coins [totaling about $12.43 million], most of which came from the Latin Union)." Although the reference points principally to Argentina, it conceivably included other South American countries that did business with the Nazis on a more modest scale while insisting they were neutrals. "The Allies considered pressing this claim. Turkey argued, however, that it had purchased the gold in good faith, that it was not looted and therefore they were not obligated to return it."

What was left unsaid in the report was that the OSS had determined the German Foreign Office likely had secreted almost another ton of gold from their own collection, known as the *Ribbentrop Gold Fund in Ankara* (named after Foreign Minister Joachim von Ribbentrop, who was glomming loot from under Hitler's nose in the event the Third Reich lost the war and he'd have to go on the lam.)

The Eizenstat Report findings continue: "On August 12, 1947, the Allies presented their terms to Ankara. In addition to professing adherence to the three agreements noted above, they asked Turkey to agree to return the property of Germany's victims, [the vast majority being Jews], deliver to the Allies all monetary gold proven to have been looted by the Germans, place controls on German assets, and begin liquidating these assets. In addition, they asked that the Turks not use those assets to settle their own claims against Germany until an agreement on this issue could be negotiated. Turkey responded on December 30, agreeing to most of the Allies' terms, but stipulating that it would only turn over proceeds from the liquidation of German assets once its claims against Germany had been satisfied. Ten days later, the Allies presented similar notes to the Turks, officially requesting that they turn over 249 bars of looted Belgian gold and investigate the origins of 32,000 gold coins and 243 kilograms of gold ingots believed to have been looted by the Germans," [and at that time assumed to be in Turkey's possession].

"After studying the proposal, on March 25, [1948], [the] State [Department] presented an aide-memoire to the British and French Embassies recommending that the Allies accept these terms, but the British convinced the United States to push for additional talks. The Allies made a number of requests for renewed negotiations into 1950, but the Turks would not respond...."

The Turks' refusal to commit themselves to renew negotiations on the issues at hand teetered on their insistence that "they were awaiting passage of a bill in their

National Assembly, which they had submitted in November 1949, proposing to grant them authority to negotiate a Safehaven agreement. However, the Assembly adjourned on March 25, 1950 without passing the Safehaven legislation. Frustrated by the lack of progress and convinced that the Turkish government was using the bill as a means to delay the return of looted gold, the Allies considered separating the gold issue from German assets and pushing for new negotiations."

After another year of fruitless efforts to settle the claims on Turkey, the Allied powers relayed a message to the Turkish Foreign Ministry on May 21, 1952, that offered "to settle the gold issue for a mere one million dollars." In return, the Allies would relinquish their claim to German assets in Turkey, remove Turkey from "HC Law 63 and consider justified Turkey's recompense to itself for proceeds from liquidation of German assets." The bottom line, written and recorded in this narrative forty-six long years later in 1998, is that Turkey never has turned over any monetary gold to the Tripartite Gold Commission.

The German-Turkish protocol of November 3, 1960 called for the return to Turkey's Deutsche Bank and Dresdner Bank of 100 kilograms of gold bars and 20,000 gold coins and from the Federal German government, 123 kilograms of gold bars and 20,000 gold coins.

In early 1998, the Turkish government claimed that it was not among the list of countries that saw profit from looted Nazi gold during World War Two. The statement was issued in response to a United States report that was presented to a forty-one-nation audience the previous

December. The report stated that Turkey, among other
neutral countries, had been evasive in negotiations regarding the return of gold taken from countries which bowed
to Germany during the war. Turkey used its three-month
status as an Allied nation to deny claims for restitution.

Turkey's Minister of State Sukru Sing Gurel retali-
ated against the report that claimed that Turkey's free gold
market was lively between 1941 and 1943 with looted gold.
In defense of his country, Gurel argued that the gold that
came into Turkey in that period was, in fact, theirs and was
returning from Switzerland, where it was stored.

However, it was difficult to explain how Turkey's
gold reserves went from twenty-seven tons before the war
to 216 tons afterward unless it was the result of trading
with Nazi Germany. And there was no doubt that Nazi
Germany purchased badly needed supplies from Turkey,
largely with gold extorted from Jewish victims.

CHAPTER 15

Vermeil Secrets
of the Vatican Archives

President Clinton's press conference on July 22, 1997 heard him deliver a sudden and unexpected blockbuster from the lectern. "I have ordered an inquiry into whether the Vatican conspired with Nazi quislings to hide millions of dollars worth of Swiss coins stolen from victims of The Holocaust...."

In New York, seat of the largest Roman Catholic diocese in America, John Cardinal O'Connor, the Archbishop of New York, declined to comment himself but let a spokesman speak for him.

"There is nothing the cardinal can add to what has already been stated at the Vatican," stated Joseph Zwilling, the Archdiocese's Director of Communications.

What was stated in Rome by Pope John Paul II's spokesman Joaquin Navarro-Valls was a sharp denial that the Vatican conspired in any Nazi gold plot. "The charge has no basis in reality," declared Navarro-Valls. "The allegations have come from an anonymous source and its authoritativeness is more than dubious."

Back in Washington the air remained charged with echoes of Clinton's explosive revelation which, reporters soon learned, was the fallout from a discovery made by investigators from television's Arts & Entertainment cable network. The video sleuths uncovered an October 21, 1946, memo that Treasury agent Emerson Bigelow wrote to his superior, Harold Glasser, the Treasury Department's director of monetary research, and kept secret for fifty years: "Approximately two hundred million Swiss francs were originally held in the Vatican for safe-keeping...."

Bigelow evaluated and turned over to higher ups information from intelligence sources. The Treasury was in the midst of Operation Safehaven which was trying to ascertain what became of the gold the Nazis plundered.

It was later shown through other documents that Bigelow was getting much data from American Overseas Special Services and was investigating the whereabouts of looted gold.

The Treasury Agent's memo reads as follows.

21 October 1946
Mr. Harold Glasser
Director of Monetary Research
Room 5000, U.S. Treasury Building
Washington, D.C.

Dear Harold:

The following report has recently been received from a reliable source in Italy. It is sent to you in the belief that it may be of interest.

The Ustasha organization (a Croatian fascist organization, headed by Ante Pavelic) removed funds from Jugoslavia estimated to total 350 million Swiss francs. The funds were largely in the form of gold coins.

Of the funds brought from the former Independent Croat State where Jews and Serbs were plundered to support the Ustasha organization in exile, an estimated 150 million Swiss Franks [sic] were impounded by British authorities at the Austro-Swiss frontier; the balance of approximately 200 million Swiss Francs was originally held in the Vatican for safe-keeping. According to rumor, a considerable portion of this latter amount has been sent to Spain and Argentina through the Vatican's "pipeline," but it is quite possible this is merely a smokescreen to cover the fact that the treasure remains in its original repository.

Sincerely yours,
Emerson Bigelow

Although the Vatican denied with great vehemence the suggestion that it conspired with Nazi quislings to hide those millions in Swiss coins looted from Holocaust victims, Clinton stood his ground with his insistence that he was obligated to look into the matter.

"All I know is that there was apparently some suggestion that maybe there's a document here somewhere in the government archives which would shed some light on that question," Clinton said at the press conference.

"The Treasury Department has assured me that they have historians combing the records, and we will reveal whatever information we have and let the facts take us where they lead us."

Elan Steinberg, executive director of the World Jewish Congress (WJC), scoffed at the Vatican spokesman's denial. "As somebody told me, he sounds like a Swiss banker."

It is estimated that today the money would be worth approximately 170 million dollars plus hundreds of millions more in accumulated interest.

Steinberg then urged Pope John Paul to open the Vatican's "own archives to an independent commission for a full accounting for the sake of memory and history." He revealed that the WJC's researchers had come across similar documents in United States archives pointing to papal complicity in possessing assets stolen by the Nazi-allied Ustasha regime in Croatia during World War II.

Fashioned by Ante Pavelic, a veteran of many Croat right wing movements, the Ustasha insurrection organization combined mysticism, Croatian nationalism, and

Roman Catholicism, requiring new members to swear their vows before a crucifix framed by a dagger and a revolver. The Vatican maintained ties to the organization which had exterminated hundreds of thousands of Serbs, Jews, and Gypsies and which funneled millions of gold coins from its plunder of Holocaust victims. One hundred fifty million francs were confiscated at the Austrian-Swiss border and the rest was held by the Vatican.

Later rumors thought to be untrue arose that the money was sent to Spain and Argentina.

The link between the Ustasha regime and the Vatican went deeper than just these financial ties. Ustasha political and religious leaders were received at the Vatican. Moreover, according to official records, the Pope was well aware of Croatian affairs because of the hierarchical administrative machinery, the papal legate, which had a personal representative to the Pope, Cardinal Tiscerran, head of the Holy Congregation of Eastern Churches, Ante Pavelic through whose special representative Pope Pius XII sent "special blessings to the leader" (Pavelic) and lastly, the American Archbishop Stepinac who visited the Pope twice.

All lend substance to the reports of the cordial relations which existed, especially from 1940 to 1942, between the Vatican and Hitler.

After the Third Reich was defeated, Pavelic and his Ustasha recruit Artukovic, who had supervised the extermination devices for thousands of Jews and Serbs who were burned alive, went on the run. They moved through Austrian monasteries disguised as Father Benarez and Father Gomez. Pavelic regularly traveled around in official

Vatican cars. Pavelic's eventual passport was issued in the name of Dal Aran Yos.

Dressed as a priest, he left Rome in 1948 for Buenos Aires. Pavelic lived in Argentina for many years but then, after an assassination attempt, emigrated to Spain where he died in a monastery in 1959.

Documents about the Vatican Bank's implication in possibly illegal transactions with Nazi Germany came to light in the summer of 1997. United States intelligence reports revealed that the Institute for Religious Works used the Swiss to obtain funds from the German Reichsbank. For instance, on November 12, 1944 the Credit Suisse wrote the Vatican Bank, "We credit you 6,407.50 francs on order of the Reichsbank Berlin." Another gave the Portuguese bank instructions to "forward 2,500 large dollar notes in a sealed packet to the Vatican through the medium of the papal nuncio in Lisbon." These wire transcripts were described as "hard evidence" linking the Vatican to Nazi Gold, despite the Vatican unwillingness to open its own archives to investigators.

Some additional evidence in the Vatican's possible role in Nazi Gold has come from the International Romani Union which represents Gypsies. Five hundred thousand Gypsies were killed by the Nazis during the war, many at the Croatian camp Jasenovac.

Dr. Donald Kenrick, an official of the International Romani Union, stated, "The particular point about Jasenovac is that it was run by Catholics, including Catholic monks, some of whom were extremely brutal, and we think the money taken off the Gypsies as they came into the camp has, in fact, gone into the Vatican." Jews and Serbs were also exterminated at Jasenovac and their effects intermingled.

The person who linked together the CIA, Masonic Lodge, several South American governments, several international banks, and the Vatican was Licio Gelli, head of the 2400-member secret Masonic Lodge. A double agent of the CIA and KGB, he assisted many former Nazi escapees. It was rumored their passports were supplied by the Vatican. Because the Vatican was more afraid of the Communist threat to Catholicism, it gave help to the fascists. A report by Vincent La Vista, United States diplomat in Rome, says that, "The Vatican was 'the largest single organization involved in the illegal movement of émigrés'" after World War II. Licio Gelli with Klaus Barbie and Heinrich Rupp later met with Ronald R. Rewald in Uruguay to arrange for the Argentine purchase of the French-made Exocet missile used in the Falkland Islands attack to kill British soldiers. Gelli, an ardent Nazi, was the go-between for the CIA and the Vatican through his P2 Lodge. He was even a guest of honor at the 1981 inauguration of President Ronald Reagan.

The treasury minister of Italy, Carlo Ciampi, in 1997 released five crates which had been gathering dust in a Reichsbank vault, and which were then placed in a U.S. Treasury depository. They were found to contain valuables, including pocket watches, precious stones and gold false teeth, which, during the long interval, languished. The valuables were likely confiscated from the many Jews who died in San Sabbia, Italy's only Nazi death camp.

There are reports that convicted Nazis such as Klaus Barbie, the "Butcher of Lyon," and SS Captain Erich Priebke were aided by the Vatican through the so-called "Rat Line" which facilitated the emigration of disguised former Nazis who had been issued fake passports. Some also found refuge in the Pontificat College of San Girolamo in Rome before leaving Europe.

For the December 1997 London Conference on Nazi Gold, the Vatican sent a two-member delegation which made little contribution to the proceedings and did not speak to the press.

Elan Steinberg of the World Jewish Congress expressed the sentiments of many when he said, "The Vatican is a great moral center of this world. For its own sake I think it is of the utmost importance that it cooperate with this international ethical and moral effort to uncover the truth."

Steinberg was referring to the Vatican's unwillingness to open its archives to scholars and researchers, who want to sort out the truth. He urged the Vatican not only to open its records but to appoint a special committee to study the Vatican's role in Nazi gold trade.

Although in February of 1998 there were media reports that Lord Janner of Braunstone in a London meeting with Vatican Undersecretary of State Archbishop Tauran had achieved a breakthrough in getting the Vatican to release its archival files pertaining to Nazi gold, these reports turned out to be premature.

In actuality, according to Avi Beker, director of the World Jewish Congress office in Jerusalem, and reported by

Jay Bushinsky in the *Jerusalem Post*, "Tauran offered to hand over to the Holocaust Education Trust twelve volumes of documents which were published over twenty years ago."

Beker decried that the "Actes et Documents du Saint Siege Relatifala Second Guerre Mondrale" was published under Pope Paul VI between 1967 and 1977 and was even in the library of the Hebrew University.

To understand the notable efforts of the recent past by Pope John Paul II in offering apologies for the role that Christianity played in the rise of anti-Semitism, one need not go much further than to turn attention to David I. Kertzer, professor of anthropology and history at Brown University in Providence, Rhode Island.

Author of *The Kidnapping of Edgardo Mortara*, Kertzer is one of only a handful of scholars to have been granted the privilege to study documents in the Vatican archives, a practice prohibited for hundreds of years—until the late 1990s, when Joseph Cardinal Ratzinger, head of the Sacred Congregation for the Doctrine of the Faith, proclaimed that the historical doctrines bearing on the Roman Inquisition would be open to certified researchers.

The Roman Inquisition—or the Congregation of the Holy Office, as formally known—amassed a vast quantity of heretofore unavailable records dealing, for the most part, with heresy dating back to 1542.

History's most famous "heretic" was the Italian astronomer and physicist Galileo, who unlike other dissenters of that period, was not burned at the stake after being convicted in 1633 for claiming that Earth revolved around the sun.

Scholars who gain access to records of the Inquisition are expected to concentrate in illuminating the Roman Catholic Church's relations with the Jewish people, a practice that had been deeply relegated to the shadows— until Pope John Paul lifted the shroud in early January 1998 when he issued his historic "preliminary apology"—the first ever—to Jews the world over for the mistreatment they received by the Vatican over the centuries.

This treatment was commented upon by David Kertzer who said, "the earliest act of the Inquisition....was the order, in 1553, that all copies of the Talmud be located and burned.

"The office of the Inquisition also forced an order, promulgated later in the sixteenth century, that called for the Jews of the Papal States to be evicted from all but a few towns, where they were restricted to ghettos."

Kertzer went on to stress, "Records of the Inquisition's conduct in the nineteenth century may prove especially revealing, as this was a critical moment in the church's treatment of Jews. Despite the trend elsewhere to give Jews full civil rights, the church held to its principles.

"An edict the Holy Office issued in 1843, for example, called for more vigorous enforcement of age-old restrictions. All social contact between Jew and Christian were forbidden. Jews were not allowed to own homes or land....."

In 1996, Kertzer went to the Vatican to research "one of the Inquisition's most notorious acts of the nineteenth century," which resulted in his book, *The Kidnapping of Edgardo Mortara.*

The professor sums up the plot in this succinct passage that showcases the church's anti-Semitic past as perhaps no other case can do as lucidly, "In 1858, the Inquisitor of Bologna learned that an illiterate Christian servant employed by a Jewish family had sprinkled water on their infant and recited the baptismal formula.

"The case was a simple one for the Inquisition: a baptized child could not be raised by Jewish parents. Therefore the Inquisitor ordered the boy, Edgardo Mortara, taken off to a monastery in Rome.

"The boy's parents naturally objected. Napoleon III, Catholic Emperor of France, protested strenuously, as did Protestants and Jews in Europe and America. The furor contributed to the demise of the Papal States shortly thereafter."

Professor Kertzer applauded the movement that the Roman Catholic Church was pursuing in recent times, yet he was quick to note that the "great change" coming about is "not without resistance from within. More than a few members of the hierarchy strenuously oppose the recent efforts to cast a critical eye on the church's history.

"The most heated debate today revolves around the question of how the Vatican, and Pope Pius XII in particular, acted during and after World War II. What could the Pope have done to save the Jews from the Nazi horror? To what extent did the church aid the escape of Nazi war criminals?

"But while we still await access to the records that will help answer these questions, we can learn much from the newly-opened archives. The explanation of what made the Holocaust possible is to be found in the files of the

Inquisition. Those documents will deepen our knowledge of how for centuries the Roman Catholic Church conditioned the European population to view the Jews as inferiors.

"So scholars can now open the dusty folders that include new information on cases like that of the Jewish boy of Bologna. In allowing this to happen, the Vatican has taken yet another significant step in coming to terms with its past."

Just weeks before Cardinal Ratzinger's historic lifting of restrictions on the Vatican archives, Pope John Paul convened an unprecedented conference on "the Christian roots of anti-Judaism." That was the first time the church had so actively encouraged discussion of that history and, more pointedly, of church actions—or inactions—during the Holocaust.

When Kertzer spoke out about awaiting access to the archives that would answer what Pius could have done to save Jews from Nazi tyranny and the extent to which the church had aided in the escape of Nazi war criminals, he couldn't have known that the answers to the questions he was posing at the time would be addressed no longer than six weeks from then by the highest authority of the Roman Catholic Church.

Nearly a half century after the Vatican had begun examining its conscience about its role in Catholic-Jewish relations during World War II, the seat of the Papal government in Rome issued a document that it described as an "act of repentance" for the failure of Roman Catholics to stem the mass killing of Europe's Jews during World War II.

The entire text of John Paul's cover letter, dated March 12 and issued on March 16, which accompanied the

Vatican's historic statement about the Holocaust was addressed to the president of the Commission for Religious Relations with the Jews:

"To My Venerable Brother Edward Idris Cardinal Cassidy,

"On numerous occasions during my Pontificate I have recalled with a sense of deep sorrow the sufferings of the Jewish people during the Second World War. The crime which has become known as the Shoah [Hebrew for the Holocaust] remains an indelible stain on the history of the century that is coming to a close.

"As we prepare for the beginning of the Third Millennium of Christianity, the Church is aware that the joy of a Jubilee is above all the joy that is based on the forgiveness of sins and reconciliation with God and neighbor. Therefore she encourages her sons and daughters to purify their hearts, through repentance of past errors and infidelities. She calls them to place themselves humbly before the Lord and examine themselves on the responsibility which they too have for the evils of our time.

"It is my fervent hope that the document 'We Remember: A Reflection on the Shoah,' which the Commission for Religious Relations with the Jews has prepared under your direction, will indeed help to heal the wounds of past misunderstandings and injustices. May it enable memory to play its necessary part in the process of shaping a future in which the unspeakable iniquity of the Shoah will never again be possible. May the Lord of history guide the efforts of Catholics and Jews and all men and women of good will as they work together for a world of true respect for the life and dignity of every human being, for all have been created in the image and likeness of God. "From the Vatican, 12 March 1998."

When the Pope referred to the Holocaust in his preface as an "unspeakable iniquity," he was very pointedly recalling his experience as a young man in Poland who witnessed the deportation of Jewish friends, colleagues, and neighbors to concentration camps.

The papal document itself clearly underscored what the Pope's message was referring to when it declared, "In the lands where the Nazis overtook mass deportations, the brutality which surrounded these forced movements of helpless people should have led [us] to suspect the worst.

"Did Christians give every possible assistance to those being persecuted, and in particular to the persecuted Jews? Many did, but others did not."

The eleven-year period it took to produce the Vatican's "repentance" was attributed by many observers to divisions in the Papal ranks over to what extent the Roman Catholic Church, its leaders, and its teachings contributed to the vicious anti-Semitism of the Nazis.

Speakers at the news conference in Rome said the process had required waiting for the church itself to "mature."

Reaction from the Jewish community in the United States was mixed.

Rabbi David Rosen, director of the Israel office of the Anti-Defamation League and its co-liaison with the Vatican, complained, "It is a very important statement, but it is disappointing in certain respects."

He pointed out that Catholic bishops' conferences in France, Germany, Hungary, Poland, and other countries had gone further in acknowledging a deeper responsibility for the moral climate that allowed Nazism to dominate much of Catholic Europe.

While the document examines the "catastrophe" of the Holocaust, when Jews were persecuted and massacred "for the sole reason that they were Jews," it also examines the "tormented" history of Christian-Jewish relations, worsened by "erroneous and unjust interpretations of the New Testament"—a phrase used in 1997 by Pope John Paul in addressing a Vatican-sponsored symposium on the origins of anti-Semitism.

Elan Steinberg found in the Pope's "repentance" "positive elements," yet he concluded, "There are also problems—the defense of Pius XII, who the document says personally or through his representatives saved hundreds of thousands of Jews and the failure to discuss the role of the church as an institution.

"It could have been a lasting legacy; it could have been a great leap forward. Instead it was a holding action."

Despite Steinberg's harsh assessment, it must also be pointed out that since he became the pontiff in 1978, John Paul had been widely credited with having taken the Catholic Church far down the road to reconciliation with the Jewish people. He buttressed the Second Vatican's Council's rejection of the last remnants of anti-Semitism in Catholic teachings and liturgy, and went on to become the first pope in modern history to visit a synagogue, to establish relations between the Vatican and Israel, and to condemn disfavor of Jews repeatedly and forcefully.

In the same week that John Paul passed unprecedented milestones in the church's relations with world Jewry, a little-known Jew, who grew up in Poland with Karol Wojtyla, as the pontiff was known from the 1920s until he was elevated to the pontificate in 1977, was featured in a front page human interest story of the *New York Times*.

"Jerzy Kluger says the first memory he shares with [the Pope] is of being chased around the square in their hometown in Poland by an irate policeman," wrote *Times* reporter Laurie Goodstein. "They were only four or five years old and had tried to pluck the policeman's sword from its sheath while he dozed on a bench.

"That town, Wadowice (pronounced vahd-oh-VEE-cheh), had one policeman, 8,000 Catholics and 2,000 Jews. Young Jerzy and Karol, a Jew and a Catholic, studied together in the same state-run school, played soccer in the fields and cowboys and Indians in the woods, and did their homework in one another's homes."

After Hitler's invasion of Poland in 1939 that started World War II and gave impetus to the Holocaust, the Jewish population of Wadowice was decimated.

With the German invasion, Jerzy and his father joined the Polish Army as it fell behind the Soviet border and joined the retreating Kremlin forces being pursued by the Panzer divisions.

After the USSR rallied and put Hitler's Wehrmacht to rout, it began discharging its soldiers. Jerzy Kluger's father was sent to Palestine, and from there was dispatched to Cairo, then Iraq, and finally the front in Italy to fight.

Jerzy's sister and mother, who refused to leave his

ailing grandmother, were taken away by Nazi soldiers. His grandmother was put on a train to the concentration camp at Belzec, and died there. His sister and mother's lives were taken in the more infamous Nazi center for mass annihilation of Jews, Auschwitz.

During those years, Karol Wojtyla (pronounced Vo-TEE-yah) worked for four years in a limestone quarry. His father died, and priests whom Karol admired were martyred with the Jews after Nazi occupation forces cracked down on the Catholic Church in Poland and simultaneously embarked on rampant anti-Semitism.

Karol Wojtyla then enrolled in an underground seminary in Cracow and studied secretly to become a priest.

"For twenty-seven years, the two childhood friends [Jerzy Kluger and Karol Wojtyla] were out of touch," Ms. Goodstein stated in her *Times* article.

Mr. Kluger married a Catholic woman from Ireland, settled in Rome, and started a business importing heavy equipment.

"One day in 1965, he heard a news report about a Polish Archbishop named Wojtyla giving a speech at the Second Vatican Council. Kluger decided to leave a phone message for him in Rome.

"'I was a bit frightened, embarrassed,' Mr. Kluger said. 'Maybe he won't want to speak to me. An archbishop is an important person.'"

The archbishop phoned back right away, and the two childhood chums were reunited. And from then on, whenever the archbishop visited Rome, Kluger and Wojtyla made it their business to meet.

Then when the archbishop was consecrated as Pope

in 1978, Wojtyla stunned the world by granting his first papal audience, or formal reception, to Kluger and his family.

Three years later, the Pope was wounded in that frightful assassination attempt in Rome and Kluger began a series of visits to the hospitalized pontiff.

During the third visit, Pope John Paul suggested that with the Camp David accord that was struck by Egyptian President Anwar Sadat and Israeli Prime Minister Menachim Begin that pointed the way for peace in the troubled Middle East, it was time for the Vatican to consider opening diplomatic channels to Israel.

"Are you willing to help?" Kluger was asked by the Pope.

"We must proceed cautiously, officially, and unofficially."

Kluger then played the role of "broker and host."

He invited Israeli and Vatican representatives to dine at his tennis club in Rome and played bridge with influential cardinals.

"The steps were often small and symbolic," wrote Ms. Goldstein. "Once [Kluger] relayed an Israeli diplomat's suggestion that the Pope send a telegram with Jewish New Year greetings to the President of Israel. The Pope then sent the telegram."

In 1994, at the ceremony welcoming the first Israeli Ambassador to the Holy See, Kluger stood for a photo op next to the Pope, flanked on either side by Israeli and Vatican dignitaries.

"I was a friend," Kluger said. "And we had friendly conversations and friendly relationships which, one way or another helped these developments. That's all."

Despite the efforts of Pope John Paul, the Vatican's declaration on the Holocaust was lacking in many respects.

While it opened with a rousing declaration that the "unspeakable tragedy" must never be forgotten, it then walked a tightrope by cautioning there was a need for a long, hard look at historic Christian attitudes toward Jews, offered an unmistakable defense for Pope Pius XII, and closed with the call to "repentance."

In an interpretation of what the *New York Times* described "The Meaning" of the Act of Repentance document, its news analyst Gustav Niebuhr came forth with a sequence of succinctly summarized conclusions on the report's value in "combing through history for the truth":

- In its central section, the document acknowledges that hostility toward Jews existed for centuries in "some Christian quarters." But it draws a line between religious "anti-Judaism" and nationalist anti-Semitism, saying it was the latter that produced the genocide practiced by the "neo-pagan" Nazis.

- The document credits many Catholics, including Pope Pius XII, with saving Jews during World War II, but it avoids mention of the long debate over whether Pius XII could have done much more.

- Near its conclusion, the document seeks a "call to penitence" on behalf of the many who were silent in the face of the Holocaust. "We deeply regret the errors and failures of those sons and daughters of the church," it states.

After dispensing with these conclusions in its study of the Papal document, the *Times* analysis observed that there was a very mixed reaction on the part of the Jews and Gentiles who studied the document for its implications. For example, it has been noted by some that the Vatican's report on the Holocaust was not as self-critical as, say, the public declarations of French and German Catholic bishops who have stated that Christians should have vehemently resisted the Holocaust and now have the responsibility of fighting anti-Semitism.

Mixed reactions about the Vatican's historical report were additionally voiced by several of America's more notable Jewish and Christian leaders.

Rabbi Jack Bemporad, director of the Center for Interfaith Understanding at Ramapo College in Mahwah, New Jersey, called the document "spectacular," then observed, "They are repudiating anti-Semitism."

But Abraham Foxman, national director of the Anti-Defamation League of B'nai B'rith, protested, "We expected a lot more under the leadership of this pope. He's been so courageous in reconciling the church with the Jewish people."

The Reverend Richard P. McBrien, a professor of theology at the University of Notre Dame, said he thought the document was "too subtle."

"Even if you analyze it rhetorically, the language is very, very cautious, very restrained, very diplomatic," Father McBrien went on to say.

Rosann Catalano, a Catholic theologian at the Institute for Christian-Jewish Studies in Baltimore, enthused, "I applaud it. It makes me proud."

Prominent Catholics, such as William Cardinal Keeler, Archbishop of Baltimore, observed, "It's a teaching document for the whole church. It will be directed toward colleges and seminaries that haven't dealt with this material in many parts of the world."

The bottom line on the Vatican's pronouncement is that, despite Pope John Paul's message of his own issued with the statement, the document actually was written, according to a number of observers, by a committee rather than an individual.

The Vatican's Statement on the Holocaust was given the defining meaning needed here to end the discussion on the subject by Eugene J. Fisher, director of Catholic-Jewish Relations at the United States Catholic Conference.

"I see a single, consistent argument running through the document," he observed. "What they're building up to is the call to repent. It makes a very strong case that the whole church has to repent and assume not guilt, but a sense of responsibility."

The document was intended to foster a "reconciliation of memory between Catholics and Jews through research into the church in World War II." But the real reconciliation according to Jewish authorities around the world can only come when the Vatican reveals completely its link to Nazi Gold.

It is this sentiment that has been expressed by members of the forty-one-nation conference in London that was formed in an effort to trace the trail of looted Nazi gold. The official report of the December 1997 conference was released by its chairman, Lord Mackay in late

August 1998. According to the Associated Press, although
Mackay lauded the efforts of countries that pledged over
fifty-seven million dollars towards a fund for victims of
Nazi persecution, his report "pointedly noted that the
Vatican has not responded to calls to open its World War II
archives." The two Vatican representatives present at the
conference offered no answers or explanations.

Despite leaps forward in the Vatican's relations with
the Jewish world community, it will only be with full and
open disclosure of the secrets in the Vatican archives that
the truth of that dark period in history can be revealed.

PART III

Allied Gold Maneuvers

CHAPTER 16

British Gold "Fallout"

Much credit must be given to Great Britain and the Allied forces for their efforts in the aftermath of World War II (that history is encapsulated in Part I). However, it is to their failures to compensate Holocaust victims that we now must turn. For it is vital that the Allies as well as the neutrals and belligerents investigate their own financial dealings with, and reception of, the plundered loot of the helpless Holocaust victims so that finally and at last the needs of justice may be served.

Great Britain was the first to see the Nazi menace. Although England and the other Allies had won the war, for the British Empire the price was heavy. Not only was

their casualty list high but, by 1945, England was nearly
bankrupt. Her citizens had suffered great deprivations,
London had endured the Blitz, and now the country faced
a fractured economy.

Moreover, of the little hard currency England did
have in its banks, 350 million pounds were frozen assets.
Partially, these were from Hungary, Bulgaria and
Romania—and this portion England kept as reparation for
Nazi Germany's belligerence and all it had suffered during
the prolonged conflict, even though some of these funds
were not really Axis-related but from Jewish Holocaust victims.

Much of that portion had been put into England's
banks for safekeeping by Jews. These funds had been
placed in the banks, often at peril to their owners. They
smuggled out bank notes in briefcases, had British friends
or family open accounts, or sent securities, life insurance
policies, or artworks (see the chapter, "Pandora's Box").
Some of the money was deposited in the clearing banks:
Barclay's, Lloyds, Midland, Westminster, and National
Provincial. The merchant banks which specialized in the
discount of bills of exchange were also transferred funds
which they then sold to the clearing banks.

London was an important site for foreign banks. It
was here that they opened branches. They were British in that
London was their base, but they operated in Europe and
countries in the Far East and South America. To this can be
added small firms or even individual financiers, many of
Central European background. All figured to greater and
lesser extents in being receivers of funds from those who
would become Holocaust victims.

Most of these funds were not reclaimed at war's end. Many of the Jews who had opened the accounts were dead, and most of the few survivors or their heirs didn't even know the accounts existed. The Romanian, German, Hungarian and Bulgarian Jews' accounts were taken over by British creditors, and, if the dormant accounts were in "allied" countries, British banks retained them for half a century.

Not only was the British economic scene dire at war's end but Britain was fielding debt of 3,500 million pounds. When President Truman cancelled the Lend-Lease assistance, Britain was placed in the position of a creditor with a poor credit history, since after World War I Britain had not paid back all its loans.

According to the report, "Holocaust Gold Credit to the Nation," a September 1997 publication of the Research Department of the Holocaust Educational Trust, the number of people who had placed their savings in accounts and were given them at the end of the war and thereafter was small. In order to reclaim their savings they had to prove they were victims of the Nazis.

The report goes on to say that "The burden of proof on 'victims' was heavy. They had to have left enemy territory (usually impossible under Communism) and prove they had been imprisoned in camps. Heirs had to produce hard evidence of their relatives' deaths (usually unrealistic where death was in a concentration camp)."

The real concern of England at this point was not the victims but their own country. British leaders spent almost a decade rebuilding their war-torn land through a

group of agreements: The Bonn Convention, the Final Act
of London, and the Paris Agreement. At the time, the
claims of victims were not a priority. During this period
Britain dealt with Hungary, Bulgaria, and Romania as belligerents. In fact, the Emergency Laws Bill of 1953 allowed
Britain to label any country an enemy and removed the
right of challenge by creditors. The claims of Holocaust
victims were treated the same way as German victims.

It was not until 1957, and then largely because of
worldwide pleas, that Britain made a token payment to
about 1,000 survivors who could prove that in World War
II they had been "deprived of liberty," no longer lived in
their homelands, had not acted against the Allies, and had
been deprived of their full rights of citizenship by the
Nazis.

Jewish groups noted that a minimal fund of only
250,000 pounds was apportioned for the victims. The highest award paid was 1,500 pounds, and most were only one-
third as much. The recipients had to pay income tax on the
amount and in the case of Germans, double. Although,
unlike the Swiss banks, the British didn't refuse legitimate
claims, they made it difficult for the claimant, who had to
prove the claim by rigid compliance to the law. They made
it most difficult for those who had escaped Communism.

At the end of the agreements in 1956-1957, of the
9.5 million pounds paid out, victims had received only 1.5
million.

In January 1996, an official history written by A.W.
Mackenzie, principal of the Enemy Property Branch, was
released but was marked "confidential." In one of the documents, Arthur Bottomley, the Overseas Trade junior minister

to Prime Minister Harold Wilson, wrote to J.L. Edwards, Economic Secretary of the Treasury in 1950: "The property here of Jews who have died heirless in belligerent enemy countries (except in the case of Italy) will normally come into the hands of one of the Administrators of Enemy Property and will eventually be used along with other assets owned by non-Jews in belligerent enemy territories to satisfy as far as gross value will go, the claims of British creditors on those countries."

Indeed, by the end of 1957 the assets which remained in England were confiscated by the British government to compensate British citizens who themselves had been deprived of their assets during wartime.

Almost forty years later in September of 1996, the United Kingdom's Foreign Secretary, Malcolm Rifkind, revealed that Britain might release to Jewish groups forty million pounds of looted Nazi gold, some made from melted down jewelry and gold teeth of concentration camp victims. The Bank of England had received the looted gold in a postwar agreement with Switzerland. This was an affirmative step for England to come to terms with the increasing evidence that revealed that Great Britain retained money of Holocaust victims, and especially of those victims from Germany, Hungary, and Romania.

Witnesses speaking to the Israeli Knesset (legislature) in July 1997 described the difficulties they had in reclaiming confiscated funds after the war from British banks.

Yochanan Leopold's mother, Susan, came from Romania. She had managed to live through four concentration camps but when she went to reclaim her family's savings from the Midland Bank, she was unable to get them.

Iraman Levin, an Israeli who's been investigating what has become of the assets Britain held, revealed to the committee that he has found evidence of 6,000 files which the British public records office holds.

In response, the British Foreign Office in London said the records were being examined. "We recognize people have genuine concerns about their assets. There was a fallout from the war that assets from it were disposed of on a mutual basis—collectively by the State. Unfortunately, because of the situation after the war it could not always be done equitably."

Three cases highlighted in the *Holocaust Gold Credit* Report are especially significant of the ways claims in the United Kingdom were mishandled. In the first case, a man lost thirteen family members and had all his property seized when he went underground. After the war his property was nationalized, but when he sought compensation he was refused because he hadn't lost his liberty. The rationalization for his turndown was given by Toby Low, later Lord Aldrington. He said that sometimes criminals went into hiding and Jews could still be "enemies" or criminals.

Another man who fled Bulgaria for Israel was also turned down. The reason in his case was he had not been deported.

Still another man, who had been in Bergen-Belsen and with only 1,700 survived and reached Switzerland, had gone back to his native, pre-Communist Hungary and didn't leave it by 1947. He was refused because 1947 was the last cutoff date England had set.

It was these cases and others, which drove the media and the world's Jewish organizations to clamor for the British government to right the monetary wrongs done the victims of the Holocaust.

At the beginning of the December 1997 London Conference on Nazi Gold, Robin Cook, England's Foreign Secretary stated: "This conference is not designed to take decisions or to pass judgement and apportion blame. It will allow everyone included the chance to talk through the issues—whom the gold came from, what the Nazis did with it, what happened to it after the war. Many believe that governments are hiding the facts—I hope this conference will go some way towards assuaging these suspicions."

The aims of the Conference were:

- To pool available knowledge on the historical facts relating to gold looted by the Nazis from both countries and individuals.
- To examine steps taken hitherto to reimburse countries and compensate individual victims.
- To examine the case for further compensation of individuals or reimbursement of countries.

However, many of the facts which were revealed, questioned or alluded to did not allay suspicions but, in fact, did the opposite. For instance, one report which high-lighted England's role identified 134 kilograms of coins, medals, and tokens which TGC told the bank to melt into "good deliverable bars."

Lord Greville Janner, head of the London-based Holocaust Education Trust, observed, "It is not only the Swiss who should be answering questions and paying reparation. The spotlight should fall on the many others who participated in this terrible deed. The world must now address the issue of the profound moral responsibility of those who benefited from the seizures."

At the conference, two of the beneficiaries, Britain and the United States, agreed to contribute $5.4 million to a compensation fund for Holocaust survivors.

Nevertheless, the full story of English involvement is still coming out. In January 1998, still another piece of the puzzle fell into place. A Portuguese historian, Antonio Louka, who has been studying his own country's involvement in the plundered loot, interviewed a retired Portuguese civil servant, Fernando Brito. Brito said he personally viewed Nazi gold bullion coming into Macao in 1969, and that it probably came from the Bank of England. Brito also revealed that earlier other Nazi gold imports coming into Macao were from Hong Kong. They had gotten there in the 1940s during the Japanese occupation of Hong Kong.

In March of 1998 Lord Greville Janner met with a senior government official. A report on the government's investigation of the looted gold deposited in British banks was due out in April and would give the details about 25,000 accounts seized as enemy property as well as any payments made.

However, Janner was discouraged. "I got the impression that the government is not going to give compensation. They are going to say no to the survivors and their heirs."

The funds of which he spoke, estimated to be

worth about five hundred million dollars, are those spoken of earlier, deposited in England by European Jews in Germany, Bulgaria, Romania, and Hungary.

In response, famed Nazi hunter Simon Wiesenthal wrote to the *London Times*: "If Britain turns away these claims now, it will give a painful and damaging message to the few remaining survivors in their final years and will give other countries the signal that Britain doesn't care."

To this day, Britain has yet to give a full, accurate, and unequivocal account of its dubious dealings in Nazi gold during and after World War II. Prime Minister Tony Blair owes it to World Jewry—but especially those residing in Great Britain and its few remaining but yet still far-flung territories—to bare the truth.

CHAPTER 17

French Gold Links

At the beginning of World War II, the French were divided into two factions, the Free French who were part of the Allies and the Vichy government which was sympathetic to the Nazis. Although the French nation endured bloody battles fought on its soil, it also dealt with Nazi gold and was involved with the deportation and maltreatment of French Jews and other French citizens. France's postwar position as one of the three powers of the Tripartite Commission that investigated the whereabouts of looted gold proved that even the so-called "good guys" could not escape the tarnish brought on by the Nazis and their stolen Jewish assets.

After the invasion of France by German forces in 1940, the nation was ripped apart internally by the two factions fighting for control of the seized territory. The pro-Nazi Vichy faction came into power when the Germans arrived. The legitimate French government fled the country and operated remotely. The seeds of anti-Semitism were planted when, on August 27 of that year, the Marchande au Order in Council which prevented anti-Semitism in the press was repealed. Then in October several brutal measures excluding Jews from holding office or from professions in the media were enacted.

The Vichy regime not only aided the Nazis militarily, but also mirrored them when it came to the treatment of European Jews. In 1941, the French police conducted the first Nazi-ordered raids against the Jews. The Vichy French helped hunt down and deport Jews living in France to concentration camps in Italy and Germany. With thousands of Jews being shipped out of France, many valuables belonging to the victims were left behind. According to Reuters, in all, 76,000 of the 320,000 Jews living in France were deported to Nazi camps. Of these thousands, only 2,800 lived through their ordeals. With all of these lives transplanted, the Vichy government was able to benefit by collecting the properties of these unfortunates. "Under its law of July 22, 1941, the pro-Nazi Vichy government," according to the *New York Times* on January 28, 1997, "set as its objective the elimination of 'all Jewish influence in the national economy.'"

A report in the winter 1996-97 edition of the Wiesenthal Center's magazine, *Response*, said French "government files show that thousands of homes were sold under coercion at 10 percent of their value." Shimon Samuels investigated the French files and discovered that, "apartments, land deeds, companies and trusts were consigned to agents for liquidation with huge commissions." He went on to describe that when only a small fraction of the many thousands of Jews who were deported to Germany during the war returned, up to 27,000 properties—just in Paris—were never reclaimed by their owners. This prompted the Wiesenthal Center to push Paris Mayor Jean Tiberi to investigate the charge that the city took control of property which belonged to Jews before their deportation and failed to relinquish it after the war. Motivation for the attention to this controversy came from the publishing of Brigitte Vital-Durand's book, *Private Estate*, which announced that "the municipality owns 150 buildings in the medieval Marais district, some of which had belonged to Jews, and that some property was sold without its history being disclosed." A section of the Marais had long served as the Jewish section of Paris, a fact that led to the demise of thousands who called it home.

The matter of recovering booty stolen from the French Jews caused Prime Minister Alain Juppé to set up a commission in January 1997 to investigate the whereabouts of gold taken from French Jews. The objective of the commission was to identify and track down property and assets that were stolen from Jews during World War Two. The six main objectives of the commission were:

- To assess the scale of the plunder
- To indicate the specific categories of natural and legal persons who or which benefited from it

- To determine the fate of this plundered property from the end of the war to the present day
- To seek to identify its current whereabouts and legal status
- To draw up an inventory of assets seized on French soil which are still in the possession of French or foreign public institutions and authorities
- To make proposals to the government on the future of these assets.

Chairman Jean Matteoli, who also chaired the Economic and Social Council and was a survivor of a Nazi concentration camp and former Resistance fighter, a vice-chairman and six other members from a variety of professional backgrounds, led the commission.

A report from the French Audit Office, commented on by Radio Free Europe/Radio Liberty Inc., claimed "that close to 2,000 works of art taken from Jewish collectors now hang in France's top museums. The confiscated property is also believed to include hundreds of apartments in Paris alone." Reuters described how when the Germans withdrew from France in 1944, the French authorities who assumed control continued to administer the apartments that were left behind when French Jews were sent to die. Another story in the Sunday, July 6, 1997, edition of the *New York Times* confirmed that "buildings now owned by the city of Paris and 1,995 art works in French museums were stolen from Jewish families by the pro-Nazi Vichy government."

Many of the Vichy confiscations came from the Drancy detainment camp, which was located just outside

Paris. Drancy had originally been a camp established for the detainment of Spanish refugees who had fled from the new fascist leader, Franco. When the Germans moved into France in 1940, the French police who guarded the camp handed control over to the Nazis. By the next year, Germans were using the camp to house Jews arrested in raids conducted by French police under the government of Philippe Petain. The camp, along with others like it, was the site of cruelty and maltreatment toward the Jewish victims detained there. "Proof exists that more than 3,000 prisoners died in the French camps from lack of medical care or starvation." After a roundup of Jews at a bicycle racing stadium at Velodrome d'Hiver, thousands of people were transferred to Drancy, where parents were separated from their children before being sent to Auschwitz and killed. The orphaned children were kept there for weeks before being shipped, also to Auschwitz, where they, too, were sent to the gas chambers. "More than 6,000 Jewish children from all regions of France were arrested and transported to their deaths between July 17 and September 30, 1942."

It was here at Drancy that Jews were last allowed to stand on their homeland before being moved to Auschwitz, where most stood for the last time altogether. The release of recent records from Drancy show that French police kept detailed records of property belonging to their Jewish prisoners before sending them to have their lives taken as well. The archives revealed that millions of dollars worth of "jewelry, stock and bond certificates, gold pens and other valuables were systematically deposited into state banks and credit unions." These records were kept behind doors sealed with red tape for decades until Jewish leaders began to accuse the French government of dragging its feet in the investigation to uncover the extent of the Vichy confiscations. *Response* stated that the stopover at Drancy netted twenty million francs from the Jewish victims. The magazine said that twelve million of that was turned over to the French National Bank with the remainder going to Germany. After the war, as restitution to the only 2,800 of the 76,000 Jews who survived the Holocaust and their families, Germany sent 499 million deutsche marks to France. The sum, however, was made available to non-Jewish survivors as well as their Jewish counterparts.

A commission set up by France in 1997 to investigate the whereabouts of Jewish assets came across a 2.2 ton portion of 5.5 tons of looted Nazi bullion that it expressed desire to use as compensation for French Jews who were wronged during the war or their survivors. It urged France to identify the recipients of the repayment before the conclusion of the commission's investigation. However, at the London conference in December 1997 on Nazi gold, France voiced its plan to regain the gold plundered from its citizens in the early 1940s, but keep it in the government instead of putting it into a new fund for its originally intended recipients. A report from the commission given to French Prime Minister Lionel Jospin early the next year, according to ABC News, recorded that "the sum thus recovered could be used to meet national goals, which does not exclude an eventual direct contribution to an international indemnification fund which certain participants at a recent conference in London announced."

The five-and-a-half tons of gold, controlled by France along with the United States and Great Britain, the three countries that make up the Tripartite Gold Commission (TGC), were the final remnants of the 377 tons of looted gold that were recovered by the Allies after the war and redistributed by the TGC. Reuter's Information Service quoted Rabbi Abraham Cooper, an official from the Simon Wiesenthal Center who described the origins of the looted gold. "Some gold came from national banks looted by the Nazis. But much was from victims—privately held gold, jewelry, wedding bands and, yes, gold teeth the Nazis wrenched from the mouths of their victims after gassing them to death." The Wiesenthal Center solicited Paris, London, and Washington in attempts to amend the policy of the TGC that would distribute the gold to states and not to individuals who had lost the treasures in the first place. "This is not a charity," said Cooper, who described the situation realistically. "This is a matter of reassigning property that people really owned." A report from the BBC in December of 1997 said that France was opposed to opening the archives of the TGC, which was an action being pursued by the World Jewish Congress. A French spokesperson stated that "the TGC had long agreed the archives should remain closed until the organization completed its work.... We just want the TGC to finish its work before opening the archives."

ABC News claimed in December of 1997 that France knowingly kept looted gold that had been seized by the Nazis from Jewish citizens and businesses after the conclusion of World War II. The report, which cites the

French magazine, *Le Point* said that "French officials delib-
erately made no effort to identify the rightful owners of the
precious goods so they could use the loot to help finance
reconstruction." The authorities harbored large amounts of
gold, jewels and other precious items that were never
returned to their rightful owners. In 1947, France had
opposed several attempts by the United States to sell some
of the Nazi treasure and distribute returns from the sale to
war refugees or their heirs. Several confidential memos
from the time proved that French authorities vehemently
objected to "turning over spoils to refugees or relatives of
Nazi victims."

One secret 1950 memo of a senior finance minister
pointed out that the policy of non-return was deliberate in
that France didn't want its share of the spoils diluted.

In 1953, France finally caved in and transferred 2.7
tons of gold to 120 firms and individuals. The catch, in this
case, being that gold was only given to people who bran-
dished receipts which proved their belongings had been
confiscated by the German government during the war.
One documented case stated that when a man asked for the
Nazi officer who was taking his valuables to manufacture a
receipt to show his losses, the officer merely produced a
gun and pointed it at him as his offering of proof.

As proof of the Vichy regime's compliance with
Nazi Germany during World War II, a message from
German Foreign Minister Ribbentrop to Vichy officials outlined the powers and duties of the Nazi Ambassador and
former Minister Otto Abetz. These included advising the
secret military police and the Gestapo on the seizure of
politically important documents. Another important duty

was the seizure and securing "of all public art treasures and private art treasures, and particularly art treasures belonging to Jews, on the basis of special instructions relating thereto."

Significantly, the French war crimes went well beyond the comparatively petty example of theft, however. In 1997, when France put an eighty-seven year old man on trial for his role in aiding in the murders of Jews, the world learned how Maurice Papon took part in shipping more than 1,500 Jews to death camps as a Vichy official during World War II. Papon was described as "just an obedient civil servant, like hundreds of others, who sent fellow citizens into the jaws of the Holocaust," in an October 20, 1997 article in *Time* magazine. He was being tried for "complicity in crimes against humanity." In what the *New York Times* called an historic judgment, Papon was convicted by three judges and twelve jurors and sentenced to ten years and $500,000 in court costs plus an additional $266,666 in damages to Holocaust survivors and relatives.

The trial came to fruition after the election of President Jacques Chirac, after a long line of French presidents who looked the other way when it came to facing up to France's actions during the war. "The criminal folly of the occupier was seconded, as everyone knows, by French people and the French state," a post-trial statement declared. This declaration set off a chain reaction that resulted in apologies from many different sources. Just before the Papon trial got underway, the "French Catholic church publicly apologized to the Jewish community for their silence maintained in the face of Vichy's anti-Jewish policies." Later, the largest police union in France "apologized for the active role that French police played in rounding up Jews for the Nazis."

Soon after the conclusion of the war, 15,000 such collaborators were put to death. Despite the overwhelming number of postwar executions that took place in France, many of the participants in the Vichy government were able to escape the swift stroke of French justice and re-enter ordinary lives. One of these was Papon, who eventually entered France's legitimate government and worked his way up to a cabinet position in 1978. Three years later, it was discovered by Michel Slitinsky, a historian and Holocaust survivor, that Papon had been an agent of death decades before, but due to France's state of denial and wishes for quiet on the matter, Papon's date in court did not come for sixteen years. During the trial Papon expressed no regrets. He denounced the "prefabricated" trial as a "masquerade unworthy of a law-abiding state." He used the defense that as a government official working "under foreign military occupation, he had no freedom to disobey orders and was unaware of the fate that awaited the deportees." Lower magistrates, however, did not agree with his defense and stated that Papon "was well aware that their arrest, detention and deportation to the East would ineluctably lead them to their deaths." When his defense failed him, according to the Associated Press, he was sentenced to ten years in prison and ordered to pay a three quarters of a million dollars in court costs and damages to survivors of the Holocaust and their families who filed civil suits.

Like Maurice Papon, President Chirac's predecessor Francois Mitterrand, had also been a Vichy official during

World War II. In a *Time* magazine article, Mitterrand admitted to using his power as president to avert Papon's case from being tried in 1994. Mitterrand had been the last in a line of French presidents who failed to acknowledge the actions of Vichy France during the war. In addition to his refusal to take responsibility, he enraged many with other shows of Vichy affections. According to a story from the *Jewish Bulletin of Northern California*, "He was booed in July 1993 by militant Jews at a ceremony marking the fiftieth anniversary of the notorious roundup at the Velodrome d'Hiver, the cycling stadium where on July 16, 1943, some 13,000 Jews, about 4,000 of them children, were deported from France to Nazi death camps. Only about 2,500 returned." He was also criticized for celebrating Vichy leader Marshal Philippe Pétain's heroism during World War I by sending a wreath to his tomb every year. The pressures subsided after Mitterrand stopped the delivery of the wreaths in 1993. Controversy emerged again for Mitterrand the next year when a book exposed his support of right-wing ideas near the start of World War II and described his tight-knit relationship with Vichy Police Chief Rene Bousquet, the coordinator of the Velodrome d'Hiver incident who was assassinated while awaiting trial for war crimes in 1993. At the same Velodrome gathering three years after Mitterrand's poor showing, new President Chirac used the event "to acknowledge that France shared responsibility for sending Jews to their deaths."

President Chirac, however, could not steer clear of the controversy that seemed inevitable when dealing with France's dark past. A *Le Point* magazine report released in

1997 stated that one of Chirac's former deputies, Michel
Junot, was responsible for sending 1,000 Jews to die at Nazi
camps in 1942. Junot served as deputy to Chirac while he
was the mayor of Paris from 1977 to 1995. Junot confessed
in the interview with the magazine that he was responsible
for maintaining the Pithiviers concentration camp, a stop
forty miles south of Paris from where prisoners were
shipped north to Drancy and eventually to Auschwitz.
Junot's moral crime can be seen in statements documented
in Vichy records. In a request for extra security for the dispatch, Junot was quoted as saying, "I have the honor of letting you know that I have just been advised that a shipment
of 1,000 Israelites . . . will take place tomorrow." He later
wrote that he had feared the chance of a situation arising
which would compromise the departure, but when nothing
happened, he felt a great relief. Like other former Vichy
officials, Junot claimed that he was unaware of the fate
which awaited the Jews after they departed France. "The
rumors said they were sending them to work in the salt
mines in Poland. We imagined they were not going on an
agreeable vacation. But I never learned about the existence
of the extermination camps until 1945." He later went on
to speak on behalf of the Vichy regime, describing its
members as "conscientious" and stating that the recent
exposure of Vichy France's actions during the war was
unnecessary.

One of the worst crimes committed by France is
that of denial. Despite living in a country which has been
proven to have aided Nazi atrocities during the war while
under control of an illegitimate government, it has taken

decades for France to face its past as such. Instead, president after president refused to acknowledge the part France played in fueling the Nazi death machine with its own country's Jews. This does not erase in any way, however, the additional and remorseless crime of stealing their victims' properties and livelihoods, and doing nothing to return them. It seems, though, that France may finally be taking some responsibility in helping to right the wrongs it helped deploy on the Jews a half century ago.

At the end of 1996, the TGC had redistributed 337 tons of gold. Distributions continue today with the October 29 payment of 1.5 tons of gold to Albania. "This leaves five point five tons for distribution before the dissolution of the Commission in early 1997," stated Shimon Samuels, European Director.

In January of 1998, the French commission studying the Nazi gold problem announced that vast amounts had been stolen and that it was going to take years before all the thousands of boxes and dossiers on Jewish valuables in the French archives could be evaluated. "It will be a long and difficult task," said French Finance Minister Dominique Strauss-Kahn.

In March of 1998, the Jewish Telegraphic Agency (JTA) reported that in an attempt to find millions of dollars in bank accounts and elsewhere that were stolen from Jews by the Nazis during their occupation of France, the French will establish a "surveillance committee." The committee will watch banks and other financial institutions as they search their records for proof of the missing loot. The actual search would be conducted by employees of the bank under the watchful eye of the new committee. The committee would then report its findings to the commission which was founded a year before and is in charge of estimating the value of Jewish losses at the hands of the Nazis and Vichy French.

CHAPTER 18

The United States Recasts Nazi Gold

The records are gone. They no longer exist!

So, how are we to learn which United States Treasury Department officials—dead or alive—are to be blamed for another scandalous twist revealed in the official archives? How can we get to the bottom of a critical aspect in the Nazi gold investigations that screams for answers?

The inception of this occurrence in 1950, a time when the Federal Reserve Bank in New York, the historic depository in lower Manhattan where billions of dollars worth of gold is stored in its vaults for the United States, as well as for scores of other nations, accepted hundreds of gold bars bearing Nazi swastika markings and recast them with the pristine stamp imprint: "United States Assay Office."

Today, what woefully meager records remain on file at the Federal Reserve show that the United States Treasury Department in Washington, D.C. was totally aware that much of the gold had been looted from countries overrun by Hitler's Panzer divisions during the six years of World War II. The nations that unquestionably sustained the largest gold thefts—amounting to approximately $23 million at the time (ten times that amount or $230 million by today's values)—were the Netherlands and Belgium.

That gold, like most of the monetary metal stolen by Germany during the war, had been discreetly sold on world markets prior to May 1945 to finance Hitler's war machine. That, of course, was before the establishment of the Tripartite Commission for the Restitution of Monetary Gold. That body of Allied nations, as cited in earlier passages, was formed to ensure that all nations which had suffered looting by the Nazis would be indemnified in proportion to their losses from a pool containing gold recovered from Germany, or obtained from another country to which it was transferred by the Third Reich.

This concept was followed closely after the war by the Allied nations, especially by the United States, as reported extensively throughout Part II of this book (namely the unremitting efforts that led to recovery—or at the very least a well-defined accounting—of Nazi gold in negotiations with Sweden, Portugal, Spain, Italy, Turkey, and Argentina).

In 1950, the Federal Reserve conceded that America's main concern was rebuilding Europe, not asking questions about the origin of gold that moved from Swiss hands to other nations and eventually crossed the Atlantic into the Federal Reserve's deep vaults below the ground populated by the world's leading stock and bond exchanges on Wall Street. Consequently, at the request of National City Bank, which later became Citibank, the Treasury Department authorized the "reissue" of the gold—a polite phrase for purifying it and wiping out the German "Nazi gold" swastika markings—so that it could be used as collateral for a transaction between Spain and the International Telephone and Telegraph Corporation, the documents reveal.

The Federal Reserve's dealings with the Nazi gold actually began when Spain needed to put up collateral to buy a telephone system from ITT in the late 1940s, as Europe was being rebuilt under the American assistance program known as the Marshall Plan. After the United States had settled its grievances with Spain, the Federal Reserve was given clearance to receive $31 million in gold bullion from Spain, worth ten times as much today ($310 million). Now we learn from a piece of interoffice correspondence from the Federal Reserve that "some of the gold in the shipment by Spain was identified as having been part of the gold looted by German authorities during the last war and melted and reissued as 1937 Prussian Mint bars."

The thread of this story was picked up by reporter David E. Sanger of the *New York Times* in November 1997, when he went on to expand on the report about America's involvement in converting Nazi gold into legitimate currency on world markets.

"'The facts seem pretty plain,' said Jack Morris, the spokesman for Citicorps, the parent company of Citibank, after reviewing documents that the Federal Reserve provided to researchers for Swiss television. This all happened in an era when there wasn't as much introspection about this kind of transaction," Sanger reported.

The documents not only provide a stark view of the trafficking that was going on in that period of Nazi gold transactions—first through Swiss banks, then through the central banks of Europe, and finally to the Federal Reserve—they also raise some haunting issues.

Uppermost was the matter of Germany's conversion of gold stolen by its troops of occupation in captive countries and melting it, together with gold from Jewish victims' teeth and jewelry, and converting it to negotiable financial currency on world markets. Among the other objects melted down were: gold plates, buttons, coins, and smoking pipe ornaments.

In New York, the Federal Reserve Bank's primary concern, once it obtained the tainted gold with the telltale swastika markings, which may or may not have contained gold from the teeth of Jewish victims, was to convert it to a condition that met the rigid American Government's gold standard: a "purity" of 99.5 percent or higher. Though some of the gold clearly and unmistakably bore Germany's swastika markings, the bullion was smelted into "pristine" American gold bars and from then on carried the imprint of the Federal Assay Office.

According to Sanger, "Jewish groups and the United States government plan to use the documents to press their case that $54 million in gold remaining in the possession of the Tripartite Commission for the Restitution of Monetary Gold—the panel assembled to return looted assets to central banks—should be given to Holocaust survivors and their heirs."

Because of the Cold War, the stabilization of Europe was the primary American objective, so the need for gold of any kind took precedence over all else.

While Uncle Sam has shied away from revealing too many details about the way America was used by the Swiss to stash an estimated $1.5 billion in Nazi gold at the Federal Reserve Bank in New York, Washington couldn't muzzle the New York State Banking Department (NYSBD) from letting it be known that the Treasury and State Departments had played a troubling role in Bern's dealings with the Wall Street depository. The NYSBD might not have revealed what is on its record about Nazi gold issues were it not for a series of suspicious fires that erupted at Swiss storage depositories in Pennsylvania and New Jersey. Those respective facilities—Diversified Services Inc. in Pittston, Pennsylvania where two separate repositories were rented, and a single one at Iron Mountain Inc. in South Brunswick, New Jersey—were retained by Swiss banks in 1939, just after World War II broke out. Fearing that sooner or later they would be invaded and taken over by the Germans despite their declaration of neutrality, the Swiss took desperate measures to protect some $1.5 billion on deposit in her banks and to preserve their records in a depository that would be beyond the reach of the German Panzer divisions then running roughshod over the European landscape. Ultimately, the Swiss let it be known that they shipped 11,000 boxes of World War II documents for storage in the United States.

What information, it should be asked now, did those boxes contain?

Just when—in mid 1997—the world seemed about to receive an answer as to what secrets the Swiss had stored in the New Jersey and Pennsylvania facilities, a series of mysterious fires erupted in two of the three repositories. That made it appear the truth about Switzerland's motives in retaining those United States sites for safekeeping the records might never be made known. But everything changed after the NYSBD moved in and tried to find out the details of the fires that hampered their recently-launched state banking investigation into the $1.5 billion the Swiss were still keeping in their secret accounts at the Federal Reserve Bank. The State's primary objective was to determine whether it was entitled to levy taxes on those savings accounts. It was estimated that one-third of those funds belonged to Holocaust victims. The rest, according to the NYSBD, included what it believed to be "the concealed accounts of prominent Axis officials—including several million dollars understood to have been placed for safekeeping in Uncle Sam's New York depository for Italian dictator Benito Mussolini."

For six months during early 1997, state banking officials had conducted intense negotiations with Swiss banks, urging them to review their records about that $1.5 billion on deposit in New York. When the NYSBD probers felt the Swiss were trying to stonewall them, they threatened to launch a crippling financial boycott, according to state Insurance Superintendent Neil Levin, who had taken charge of the inquiry. It was when the Swiss appeared prepared to turn over the records of their American bank deposits that a vast number of them were reduced to ashes in the fires of March, May, and finally June 1997.

Even as Levin was bemoaning the loss of the records stored in those facilities, Swiss banking officials, who denied complicity in the fires, allowed that 3,500 boxes of documents "relevant to the New York State investigation had earlier been safely removed from storage before the blazes."

Almost at the same time, this word came from Bern: "On the basis of available information, Credit Suisse [the major dealer in the country's banking activities] does not envisage that our role during the Second World War [in Nazi gold finances] will be affected by the fire at Diversified Services—and we stand ready to cooperate with New York tax officials."

In the early summer of 1997, a shocking turn developed in Bern. A bank guard for the Union Bank of Switzerland, twenty-nine-year-old Christopher Meili, came across bushelsful of records at the bank's shredding machines and carried them out of the room to safety. The documents contained listings of thousands of depositors from World War II days who were Jewish refugees who had fled to Switzerland and deposited their life savings in accounts with, among other thrift institutions, the Union Bank.

After Meili "rescued" the records, he summoned bank officials and pointed to his find.

"What I had done," Meili was to lament later, "saving those documents struck me as a good thing—and I received high praise outside the bank from many Swiss citizens."

But the accolades were of short duration. Back at his place of employment, "All of a sudden the bank's officials reprimanded me for going public with what I'd done—and they began making accusations against me." Suddenly, "Instead of being looked at as a good guy, I was turned into a criminal."

Meili then acted on his own. To make certain Union Bank would never return the records to the shredders, he removed them from the bank premises and handed them over to a Jewish group. This act precipitated a rash of threats against his life and his family. On April 30, 1997, after receiving a number of those warnings, Meili took his wife and their two young children and fled Switzerland. They went to the United States, where they sought asylum.

On May 21, he was summoned to Washington, where he appeared before the Senate Banking Committee to report his plight.

"After I did my duty by salvaging the records that the Swiss bank was trying to destroy, I was subjected to a series of death threats," he testified. "I was also informed that my children would be kidnapped because of the episode, which had suddenly turned into an international embarrassment for the Swiss people and their government." Meili went on, "It was too frightening and I had to flee the country."

The Senate committee listened to his testimony and agreed the next day to grant Meili and his family asylum in the United States.

Before Meili left the committee hearing room, he told the lawmakers, "If we are allowed to stay here, I have many more things that I can and want to say, and much more evidence to provide to help in the search for truth about Switzerland's role in the Holocaust and the bank's actions over the last fifty years."

In Switzerland, the district attorney in the canton of Zurich, Peter Cosandey, said he had no intention of caving in to the Senate's demand to drop their investigation of Meili, who may have violated bank secrecy laws and could face prosecution leading to possible imprisonment. He asserted this position even though Switzerland, in an effort to crack down on criminal financial transactions, has been easing its strict secrecy rules since 1990.

The Swiss banking industry was further rocked into a sense of greater openness after it was stung by accusations that assets seized by the Nazis and deposited in Swiss banks during World War II had not been properly accounted for, and that an estimated $4.7 billion was due to be returned to its rightful owners.

Less than a month later, on June 3, the House Banking Committee affirmed the Senate's action granting Meili and his family asylum in the United States. That action infuriated the Swiss government. They claimed, "there are no existing records in Switzerland containing the names of the depositors whose accounts were transferred to New York at any time in the past."

New York State Banking Department Investigative
Counsel Irwin Nick, highly suspicious about Switzerland's
"evasive role" in the inquiry to determine what funds were
owed to Holocaust victims, was outraged at the Union
Bank spokesman's statement that they did not have any
records of these transactions. Nick quickly reacted.

"We think that claim is absurd," he snapped. "It is
inconceivable the bank didn't keep records of its deposits
in the Federal Reserve Bank in New York.... Moreover, we
believe there is a conspiracy to deny proper accounting,
which the United States set out to establish in 1947—and
is continuing to exert those efforts toward that end to this
day."

Then he added, "The fires in Pennsylvania and
New Jersey only serve to deepen the mystery surrounding
those secret Swiss accounts in New York."

Initially, small amounts of movable wealth were
transferred to New York at the outset of World War II. But
as the demand for a haven for Swiss banks grew while
Hitler's troops marched ever closer to Switzerland, Bern
opened Manhattan offices to serve as "funnels" for the
gold shipped out of the Alpine nation to the United States.

The major players in that operation were revealed
to have been the Swiss Bank Corporation and the Swiss
American Corporation, an investment banking arm of
Credit Suisse. Swiss America's operation in New York was
headed by George Lindsay, father of former Mayor John V.
Lindsay of New York City.

"It was well known at the time that the one and
one-half billion dollars finally deposited in the Federal

Reserve was considerably more than what Switzerland could ever be expected to hold on behalf of itself and its citizens," State Insurance Superintendent Levin declared. "That leads us to believe holdings of individuals living in the German-occupied nations were included in this amount."

The Swiss hid the identities of the account holders from American regulators by using pooled or omnibus accounts and sub-accounts known as rubric accounts.

Levin went on to say, "The overwhelming amount of assets controlled by these institutions were held not in the name of the European owner, but rather in the name of the Swiss branch where the true owner originally deposited the assets."

That allowed the Swiss banks to sidestep United States laws that called for the freezing of all assets in this country controlled by Germany or countries that it occupied.

Before America's entry into the war, the United States Treasury Department—then headed by Henry Morgenthau, father of New York County (Manhattan) District Attorney Robert Morgenthau—was intensely interested in the secret accounts. Morgenthau based his concern on the suspicion that the Swiss were hiding German-owned assets that were possibly helping the Nazis finance their war effort. Treasury agents also obtained evidence that high-ranking Nazi officials were using the secret Swiss account in New York to convert money looted from Holocaust victims into American stocks, bonds, and other securities. Secretary Morgenthau then placed Treasury agents inside the Swiss bank office to monitor their activities.

With the disturbing evidence they unearthed, Morgenthau was moved to take swift action in June 1941. He persuaded President Roosevelt to freeze all Swiss accounts in New York or anywhere else in the United States. FDR ordered the deposits confiscated, and they remained out of reach of the Swiss banks until a year after the end of the war, 1946. At that time Swiss bank officials claimed that all but $500 million of the $1.5 billion frozen by Roosevelt were "certified to be the property of Swiss and European citizens not connected to the Nazis."

Now, so many years later, the war of words about what really happened to the stolen treasure had begun in earnest.

If not for New York State's decision in 1997 to explore the Swiss bank accounts at the Federal Reserve and its investigation of the $1.5 billion the Swiss still had on deposit in the Wall Street gold repository, the truth about the Bern banking industry's hoarding of the looted wealth of Holocaust victims might never have surfaced.

Despite the voluminous information in *United States and Allied Efforts to Recover and Restore Gold and Other Assets,* nowhere in that lengthy State Department study does it show the significant memoranda in Treasury Secretary Morgenthau's files that raised warning flags about the Swiss banking industry's methodology of hiding confiscated Jewish gold holdings in their New York accounts.

From the Treasury Department's trove of documents from Morgenthau's files comes a sobering look at the paper trail that surfaced in the State Banking

Department's probe of the Wall Street connection into missing Holocaust accounts. These documents include:

- A letter written in 1940 by a New York representative of the Swiss Banking Corporation to a London colleague on the origin of gold shipped to New York for sale to the Federal Reserve Bank states:

  "What the origin of the stuff is, I can only surmise, preferring not to ask.

  "I have an uneasy suspicion which makes me think at times of the monument below the Devil's Bridge in the Reuess Valley."

  Then he added:

  "I refer to a legend about a Swiss town that made a deal with the devil to build a bridge...."

- A Treasury Department investigative report prepared in 1942 states:

  "The presence of Swiss-managed refugee capital in the United States raises grave problems since... the Swiss bankers have used every means of concealing its beneficial ownership."

- Also in 1942, a staff memo to Treasury Secretary Henry Morgenthau asked:

  "If you approve, we propose to place a group of Treasury men in the New York agencies of the Swiss Bank Corporation, Swiss American Corporation, and Credit Suisse for the purpose of examining all of the files and records of these agencies.... We have reasons to believe that negotiations and transactions in connection with the transfer of ownership from German and Italian firms to Swiss or American names were, in many cases, conducted through the Swiss agencies."

- In 1947 a secret State Department cable sent to the United States Embassy in Bern, Switzerland states:

  "Treasury Department seriously disturbed by reports of falsification of affidavits attached to American securities...."

One telling consequence growing out of the machinations led to fingers being pointed at the sale of one gold shipment to the Federal Reserve Bank by the New York branch of Swiss Bank Corporation as far back as 1940, which bore on the origin of the gold.

This revelation, it can be said, to use a timeworn but utterly apropos cliche, was the "straw that broke the camel's back."

For no sooner was the New York State Banking Department's inquiry under way than the wheels of the three Swiss banks under investigation began to roll slowly—but irreversibly—toward a capitulation to the demands voiced from across the Atlantic. The three principal Swiss banks involved in the scam called hurried emergency sessions with government officials that were carried on behind closed doors and under total secrecy for the next nine months.

Then on March 26, 1998, Switzerland's three major banks reversed their earlier position that they had no reason to face the charges advanced by the New York State Banking Department. In a stunning announcement, the banks let it be known that they would negotiate a global settlement with Holocaust victims.

They pledged to set up a compensation fund in the United States to make restitution a half century after World War II ended.

The agreement was announced just minutes before a meeting in New York of officials who, after waiting for months for a response to the ultimatum issued on the Swiss banks, were prepared to impose severe sanctions against that country's entire banking industry in all of its operations in the United States. Undersecretary of State Stuart Eizenstat, working tirelessly to head off the boycott in the finest traditions of good old Yankee diplomacy, told a steering committee of New York State and City officials that a "breakthrough" agreement had been reached with the Swiss banks, paving the way for them to seek means of reaching a global settlement with Holocaust victims.

"They have clearly committed themselves to engage in a process with the hope of a settlement," Eizenstat declared.

The steering committee, comprising five public-finance officials, had undertaken to consider whether to recommend a boycott of Swiss banks or to continue a ninety-day moratorium against any punitive action, which was to expire five days hence, on Tuesday, March 31, 1998.

Eizenstat released a letter from the big three Swiss banks asserting that they wanted to reach "an honorable and moral" conclusion through a global resolution of Holocaust issues. However, a consensus on how much money would be involved had not been reached, Eizenstat stressed, and quickly pointed out that those talks could last for months.

"But I have every expectation that a bottom line will evolve," he declared.

Echoing his observation was World Jewish Congress Secretary General Israel Bashevis Singer, who said he hoped the talks would ultimately lead to "completion of a process we began on May 2, 1996... which will transfer every penny of dormant and looted assets" back to Holocaust survivors or their heirs.

Officials of the three banks—Credit Suisse, Union Bank of Switzerland, and Swiss Bank Corporation—felt the agreement, in the words of Robert O'Brien, United States corporate banking head for Credit Suisse, "was a very important step forward."

The deal didn't affect the ends being sought by a separate United States commission, headed by former Federal Reserve Board Chairman Paul Volcker, which had undertaken to audit dormant Holocaust accounts in Swiss banks to determine their rightful owners.

"This will continue as an independent procedure," Volcker was quick to submit.

In all of the aforesaid developments, it appeared that the steps taken by United States officials could be extremely detrimental to recently launched plans by the Swiss to merge the Union Bank of Switzerland and Swiss Bank Corporation, which would create the word's second largest bank. With these proposed sanctions looming, and after grueling negotiations, on August 13, 1998 the Swiss banks settled with Holocaust victims. The *New York Post* headlines on the summer day read: "Nazi Gold Deal." The article, bylined by Devlin Barrett, began, "Swiss Banks reached a historic $1.25 billion deal with Holocaust survivors yesterday—ending a three-year battle over Jewish assets stolen by Nazis and hidden for decades in secret accounts."

The announcement was made by Senator D'Amato from the steps of the courthouse. He further commented that the American threat of boycott had been effective and that now all sides should "turn to the business of healing... to bring this sorry chapter to a close."

Christopher Meili, the young Swiss guard who had saved the key bank records from destruction and brought them to the attention of Jewish organizations, stood close by during the announcement. Although he received threats after doing what he thought was the right thing with those bank records, he had withdrawn his own lawsuit. His lawyer, Ed Fagan said, "He's not getting a penny. He was willing to give up his suit to help the Holocaust victims."

On the courthouse steps, D'Amato called Meili, "a beacon of inspiration." He then embraced the shy, young guard and thanked him saying, "Had you not done the work you did... we wouldn't be here now."

CHAPTER 19

Additional U.S. Gold Diggers

On February 23, 1998 another U.S. element was added to the growing list of suspects who have been alleged to have made illicit profits from World War II. The Ford Motor Company is facing a lawsuit for allegedly making a profit from slave labor. Ford's factory in Cologne, Germany, its largest in Europe, built trucks for the Nazis. According to the BBC, "it is believed to be the first time a legal action has been brought for compensation against an American multi-national for its activities in Nazi Germany." The class action lawsuit was undertaken by thousands of the former slave laborers. Ford says it will vigorously fight the allegations.

One of the former laborers, according to the BBC,

was Ivanova, an elderly woman, who now lives in Antwerp, Belgium. She states, "The foreman was like a wild animal. He pushed us about. He wore a swastika on his uniform."

During the war, Ford in Germany was put under the Reichscommissar Robert Schmidt, a Nazi party member, who according to reports worked for both Ford and the Nazis and became a director at Ford in the post World War II era of the 1950s. Before the war had ended, Ford's managers reportedly had begun taking prisoners from the concentration camps and using them as workers in the factory. It was established that fifty prisoners came from Buchenwald.

Attorney Melvin Weiss is representing the ex-slave laborers and their heirs in the suit against Ford. According to Weiss, Ford America was well aware of what was happening at the German site and when the war was over, re-employed key managers. A *New York Times* article revealed that Weiss's team further argued in the suit that both anti-Semitic remarks made by Henry Ford in the 1920s and the alleged close relationship that Ford and Hitler shared were the reasons that Ford's subsidiaries in Germany were never overrun by the Nazis. Ford spokesman Ian Slater countered that claim, stating that the company did in fact lose control of its subsidiaries and that plants in Germany were badly damaged when Ford eventually regained control of them.

The profits made by Ford in Germany are at stake, since Weiss strongly believes they were reinvested in America. Though Ford's lawyer has denied this, Hans Grundig, Ford Cologne head of production during World War II, has asserted that the Nazis were not in control— Ford was.

PART IV

Tip of the Art-Berg

CHAPTER 20

Pandora's Box:
Art Looted by the Nazis

Adolf Hitler, a failed art student and amateur water colorist, developed, along with his grandiose plan to take over all of Europe, a scheme to build the world's largest art museum in Linz, Austria. The museum building was to have a colonnaded façade which would equal that of the Haus für Deutsche Kunst in Munich. To begin it would have a 250,000 volume library, a theater, and a separate collection of armor in addition to German paintings of the nineteenth century. For this and for his own personal use, Hermann Goering by 1937 began to assemble by threat

and coercion—if not murder—of mostly Jewish citizens
and the museums of overrun countries, 53,000 works, the
most extensive art collection ever known.

In 1939, Dr. Hans Posse, director of the Sonder
Auftrag gave Martin Bormann a list of 182 pieces which he
had selected for Linz from the confiscated collection of the
Rothschild family. Some of the old looted masters' paintings of the Dutch, Flemish, French, Italian and German
schools were kept for the museum. Others were allocated
to Goering's and Hitler's private collections. Still others
such as Renoir, Gauguin, Picasso, and van Gogh, etc. were
labeled "degenerate artists," and their paintings were sold
on the Swiss art markets or smuggled, sometimes in diplomatic pouches, to neutral countries to be sold on the international art market. Much of the art, plundered from the
Netherlands, France (whose auction houses for art flour-
ished under German occupation), Eastern Europe, and
other occupied countries, or confiscated from museums
and private collections of Jewish families, was put in the
Reichsleiter Alfred Rosenberg "Einsatzstab Reichsleiter
Rosenberg," (ERR) which operated in Eastern Europe
sweeping up all the treasures they could find. In the West,
many public museums were allowed to keep their collections. However, the property of Jews, Free Masons, and
other designated enemies of the Nazi state were seized and
"Aryanized."

From the late 1930s on, the ERR was able to con-
fiscate Jewish-owned paintings. Many of them were sent to
German embassies in neutral countries to be sold later. The
British *Daily Telegraph*, on September 21, 1996, writing of

the value of the stolen art funneled through Switzerland, reported it was worth twenty-nine to forty-six million dollars. Swiss citizens and dealers bought a goodly amount. Some of the booty was shipped to South America and so-called "neutrals," as well as other conduits.

Circumstantial evidence, intelligence reports, and the known fact that diplomatic bags were used as smuggling devices during the war for artworks, precious metals, and gems make it logical, along with later or now-known findings, that many of the artworks were safely transported to Sweden, Spain, Portugal, Turkey, Latin America, and, of course, Switzerland.

Unscrupulous art dealers quickly picked up the pace and sought to profit. For instance, in Lucerne, Switzerland, the Fisher Gallery auctioned off 125 "degenerate" art works.

One painting—Claude Monet's *Le Repos dans le Jardin Argenteuil*—which later found its way into New York's prestigious Metropolitan Museum of Art was handled by Alexander Ball, a notorious art dealer who helped the Nazis locate French-Jewish collections which were later looted. Marc Masurousky, an art historian, views Ball as "a major conduit for a lot of paintings that made their way to the United States." Ball, according to intelligence records provided by Masurousky and Jonathan Petropoulos, an art historian at Loyola College in Baltimore, Maryland, aided Hitler's henchman Haberstock in locating the soon to be looted collection of Guy de Rothschild.

Many other instances of Nazi looting of Jewish treasure occurred as the Nazi hold on Europe tightened.

In 1941, Georges Wildenstein who, because he was Jewish, fled Europe, settled in New York and opened a large art gallery. Later, he engineered a scheme in which he asked other prominent art dealers to join. Art of dubious origin would be funneled from the Louvre museum in Paris through neutral Switzerland and sent on to America.

It was estimated in one recently released United States government report dated August 1945, that the Nazis stole approximately one-fifth of the world's greatest art treasures and tried to profit from them by disposing of the looted works, through art dealers in Madrid, Lisbon, and Paris, as well as Argentina.

The way in which artworks came to the Nazis resonates with their evil designs.

In May 1942, Jewish citizens in the Netherlands were coerced by decree 58/42 to turn their art objects over to Lippmann & Rosenthal & Company, an agency created by the Nazis. About 75 percent of Dutch Jews, 107,000 persons, perished in the concentration camps. Without death certificates, returning goods to rightful owners was difficult. Also, large parts of the records of Lippmann & Rosenthal and other looting institutions had been destroyed and in fact Lippmann & Rosenthal since 1943, assuming their clients would never return, had put all private accounts into one.

Another dark plan brought nearly two thousand artworks looted from French Jews during the Nazi occupation of France into state-run museums which, for fifty years, made little or no effort to return them, according to the January 29, 1997 edition of the French daily newspaper

Le Monde. The Louvre had 1,878 paintings while the Musée d'Orsay in Paris had eighty-five. Among the artworks were paintings by Monet, Renoir, and Gauguin and sculptures by Rodin.

With the Nazi occupation of Hungary (March 19, 1944) more looting came. Much of the art belonging to Hungarian Jews was plundered and transported back to Germany. Some works were even stored in what later became the Soviet Zone. Russian troops then took this art back to the Soviet Union. The paintings of artists like Herezog and Hatvary are now in the Pushkin Museum and Grabar Institute in Moscow. Other so-called "trophy art," works of Rembrandt, Matisse, van Gogh, Goya, and Renoir, are in the Pushkin and the Hermitage. The Russians have been reluctant to return them since many citizens feel reparations are due them for the twenty-seven million Russians killed in World War II.

In 1945 and 1946, the United States Office of Strategic Services expressed concern that art stolen by the Nazis was being moved around Europe and through Argentina and Mexico City and then to the United States.

Willie Korte, a noted United States investigator of looted art, says that there is proof of this 'art line' in the United States National Archives. Speaking of recently declassified papers, he said, "These documents clearly show that the chapter yet to be written about Nazi plundering is the one about art dealers and collectors who clearly took advantage of the situation at the expense of Jewish victims of the Holocaust."

One plan which has come to light is that during World War II a program was evolved to deflect art from the

Louvre in Paris through Switzerland and on to New York,
where some works were to be sold by noted dealers.
Though this particular plan failed, confiscated documents
show that other similar contrivances to evade the Allied
naval blockade succeeded and paintings and other artworks
were smuggled into New York through Portugal, Spain,
and Argentina. Some American and European art dealers
opened showrooms and offices in Havana, Mexico City,
and Argentina.

With a largely uninterested United States government distracted by other matters, the looted van Gogh's *The
Man Is At Sea*, which was smuggled out of France, was sent
to a Nazi collaborationist art dealer in New York and later
sold to film actor Errol Flynn for $48,000.

The facts are, despite the long term government
and art world's disinterest, much proof already exists as to
the art looting. This includes: once secret intelligence
reports from United States agents in Europe, FBI and
Treasury Department reports, testimony from many of the
collaborationist dealers, and the reports of art historians.

However, according to art investigator Willie Korte,
"Since the early nineteen sixties, not one government
penny has been spent on the recovery of Jewish art losses."

The wartime documents now available present a
picture not only of indifference by many to the Jewish
plight and the awful truth about the position of European
Jewry but also seem to indicate that many art dealers in
New York and on the continent knew where the paintings
originated and had knowledge of the massive art theft.

It is now apparent that, unfortunately, very few
museums around the world make inquiries about the past

Valuable plundered oil paintings and original texts hidden by the Nazis

Dr. Hans Posse, Hitler's Grand Acquisitor, responsible for selecting pieces from large quantities of confiscated art to be displayed at Hitler's projected Linz Museum

Two of many looted paintings Alfred Rosenberg and the Rosenberg Task Force stored in tunnels under Neuschwanstein Castle

Several million dollars worth of art treasures, including Francesco's *King Louis XIII*, stolen by the Nazis

NATIONAL ARCHIVES

French-owned objects of art, including fine silver, glass sculptures and ceramics looted by the Einsatzstab Reichsleiter Rosenberg

Czech and Polish treasures looted by the Nazis

NATIONAL ARCHIVES

NATIONAL ARCHIVES

Room full of furniture belonging to Maurice Rothschild of Paris, looted by Hitler's Rosenberg Task Force, found in the Neuschwanstein Castle

The Reich Kommissar for occupied Netherlands and SS major (far right) admitted after capture that he had been entrusted with over one million dollars worth of looted securities

NATIONAL ARCHIVES

NATIONAL ARCHIVES

German secret documents and currency found in a safe at police headquarters in Germany

Czech representatives checking looted cultural material stored at Banz

NATIONAL ARCHIVES

NATIONAL ARCHIVES

Looted art found in the possession of Paul Joseph Goebbels, Germany's propaganda minister, including Cuyp's *Moon Landscape* and Gerrick's *Rembrandt's Mother*

One of seventy rooms containing Hermann Goering's looted art collection, some of which adorned his house

A/P WIDE WORLD

Silverware of great antique value looted from all over Europe by Hermann Goering

Twenty-eight tons of looted antique silverware, worth two million dollars recaptured from the Nazis at the salt mines and put on sale at United Nations Galleries

A/P WIDE WORLD

ownership or provenance of master paintings they want to acquire. A case in point, for example, is the background of Claude Monet's *Le Repos dans le Jardin Argenteuil* which found its way into the New York Metropolitan Museum of Art. The growing evidence of this painting's ownership shows that it is looted art of the Nazis.

The Monet was given to the Met by Jayne Wrightsman, widow of Charles B. Wrightsman, a generous benefactor of the museum. The painting had been seized by an agent for Hermann Goering, Hitler's chief hench-man, from the Belgian collection of Emile Redners. Wrightsman purchased it from the infamous Alexander Ball in 1954.

The Met recently became embroiled in a "non-hos-tile dialogue" with Wrightsman's widow who has urged the museum "to do the right thing."

Meanwhile, other questionable art purchases by museums have come to light. Claims have been made for paintings in the Seattle Art Museum and the Museum of Fine Arts in Boston. Even the Impressionist show at Washington's National Gallery in 1990 contained four allegedly looted paintings.

The *Boston Globe* in an in-depth investigation of art looted by the Nazis has reported, among others, one sticky situation which began in 1987 when the Art Institute of Chicago could not afford the $850,000 price tag for an Edgar Degas pastel it coveted. The museum got Daniel Searle, former chairman of Searle Drug Company, to buy it. The museum took no note of the painting's past owner-ship which included Hans Wendland, Goering's chief art buyer. Wendland had, in fact, during World War II moved a railroad car filled with looted artworks from France to Germany.

The Degas was really owned by Dutch Jews, Friedrich and Louise Gutmann. Friedrich was beaten to death at the Resienstadt Concentration Camp, and his wife perished in the gas chambers of Auschwitz. Their descendants have instituted suit against Searle, which still rages in a bitterly fought battle.

Commenting on the museum claiming ignorance of the Degas's checkered past, Thomas Hoving, former director of New York's Metropolitan Museum of Art, stated: "There have been Hollywood movies about the Nazi looting, not to mention substantial literature... They could have gone to Blockbuster and rented one of the movies."

Another murky museum piece's history revolves around French art dealer Cesar Mange de Hauke, who was denied a United States visa because of his Nazi affiliations. Intelligence data suggest de Hauke may have been involved with Haberstock in obtaining paintings for Adolf Hitler, Hermann Goering, and Heinrich Himmler.

In 1949, de Hauke sold Degas's *Singer with a Glove* to Maurice Wertheim, a New York financier, who eventually left it to the Fogg Museum of Harvard College, which he'd attended. Before de Hauke acquired the Degas, it had belonged to a Swiss doctor, Fritz Heer, and before him to Camille Giroult whose collection was "exportized" by Karl Haberstock—a common step before confiscation. Wertheim earlier bought another van Gogh painting, in

1943, from Georges Wildenstein (who dealt with Haber-stock). This painting, *Three Pairs of Shoes*, was owned previously by Marcel Kapferer, a French Jew, who sold his collection one by one for food so his family could survive. Such sales were later deemed invalid.

These and many other instances being revealed provoke agonizing questions as to how many collections and museums around the world now possess looted art treasures.

Artwork and gold were not the only treasures looted from victims in Nazi overrun countries. One instance with a uniquely feminist slant is of particular interest to those studying the approach of the Third Reich to women's issues.

The International Archives for the Women's Movement in Amsterdam which had as its goal the promotion and scientific study of the women's movement was flourishing in 1935. Three Dutch feminists, Rosa Manus, Johanna Naber, and Willemijn Posthumus-van der Goot had founded the archives which, in the next five years, collected four thousand books, pictures and periodicals, including the books and papers of Aletta Jacobs, the first woman medical doctor in the Netherlands and the leader of the Dutch women's suffrage movement.

On July 2, 1940, the Germans, who had been occupying the Netherlands for two months, closed the archives and later transported the contents to Germany. They explained the closure as "Die deutschen Frauen haben es sich gewünscht (the German women wanted it)." Efforts made after the war to find and reclaim the contents of the

archives met with only minor success and were mostly
thwarted.

In January 1992, the Dutch historian Marc Jansen
visiting the Osobyi Archive in Moscow found twenty-five
boxes, some of which contained the women's archive's
stolen materials. Although an agreement was soon signed,
they were not sent back to Holland. So, in 1994, Mineke
Bosch and Myrium Eveard, researchers in women's history,
went to Moscow to study and record the found materials.
Later, the International Institute for Social History in
Amsterdam got permission to microfilm them. Thanks to
a government grant, 35,000 copies were made of the feminist papers. In addition, minutes of the Synagogue in
Amsterdam and documents in French and German were
also found, bringing hope that more of the archives would
someday be recovered.

When *A Dune with Two Figures by a Fence*, one of the
disputed paintings by the foremost seventeenth century
Dutch master of landscape painting, Jacob van Ruisdael,
surfaced in a Sotheby's London auction in November 1997,
the *Boston Globe* raised penetrating questions about its ownership history. Learning of the dispute, the Henles, a
German family which owned the work and had placed it for
sale, were sensitive to the moral issues raised by the *Globe*.
The family asked that the painting be withdrawn until an
inquiry was completed. The name of Guenther Henle, a
major art collector and an industrialist, came to light.
According to Henles's records, the painting had been
acquired by the Nazis in 1941 for the Nazis' Linz Gallery.

Investigating further, the *Boston Globe*, assisted by Sotheby's and other art historians in Holland and Switzerland, traced the painting's lineage to a sale in 1934 to Robert Maas, a German Jew, who fled to the Netherlands during the war. Subsequently, there was a resale in 1938 to an unidentified buyer.

Henle had bought the painting in 1961 from Pieter de Boer, an Amsterdam art dealer, who served the Nazis (Hermann Goering bought paintings from him) by helping them "buy" hundreds of paintings. Henle had sought counsel in his art acquisition during the 1950s from another Nazi sympathizer, Edouard Plietzsch, wartime deputy director of the Dienststelle Muehlmann, which gave advice to the Nazis on art looting in the Netherlands.

Ori Z. Soltes, the director of the National Jewish Museum in Washington, D.C., praised Sotheby's for removing the painting from the sale. "[It] has set a new standard for behavior, rather than succumbing to greed."

Art treasures of Jewish victims of the Holocaust lingering in American museums and collections are increasingly coming under scrutiny.

New York County District Attorney Robert Morgenthau may never have believed he'd have a role to play in the recovery of stolen Jewish treasures. Yet he ended up having to do just that.

It all began in early January 1998 as the Museum of Modern Art in Manhattan concluded its exhibit of two prized paintings by Austrian expressionist Egon Schiele that were on loan to the Big Apple's renowned art museum.

During the showing, a story of seemingly small consequence surfaced when a claim was made that the artworks being shown had been plundered by the Nazis from their rightful Jewish owners.

After the complaints by the owners—New York residents claiming to be heirs of the original owners, who died in concentration camps—were filed with the prosecutor's office, Morgenthau stepped in just as the exhibit closed and sought to intercept the pair of paintings.

The district attorney commanded that the works not be returned to their "current owner"—the Leopold Foundation in Vienna—until "rightful ownership is established."

The Museum of Modern Art (MOMA) objected vehemently.

MOMA went on the offensive, thundering that "works of art lent by one cultural institution to another have a 'diplomatic immunity' under New York State law and are 'legally protected from seizure and detention.'"

That was what the museum's lawyers purported as they filed a motion to quash a grand jury subpoena for the paintings that Morgenthau sought to retrieve.

The cause for the claimants of the paintings' ownership was taken up by *New York Post* columnist Richard Z. Chesnoff, who trumpeted, "Morgenthau has what I believe to be a solid position, legally and morally: Possession of stolen property is a crime. There's an investigation, and until it's over, the paintings stay here."

Chesnoff went on, "MOMA is carrying its frenzy beyond the courts. If the judge doesn't release the paintings, museum spokespersons warn ominously, the entire future of museum loan exhibits is at stake. After all, goes

MOMA's argument, who'd lend a painting if they weren't sure they'd get it back? Probably no one—if they were stolen to begin with."

The hullabaloo brought into scrutiny a conventional practice which appears to prevail in international art markets—especially at museums and auction galleries—there is a universal cover-up that ignores honest dealings. Rather than acting with meticulous conduct in establishing whether paintings are owned legitimately by the providers of works on loan, exhibitors at all too many art locations routinely neglect to ask questions about ownership.

More and more in recent times—especially since the revelations about the Swiss Nazi gold scandals—attention has focused on what the World Jewish Congress claim are "long-hidden truths about stolen art treasures that Hitler and his collaborators snatched from victims of the Holocaust."

MOMA's entanglement with Morgenthau over the ownership of the Egon Schiele paintings and the interest of the World Jewish Congress in recovery of what could turn out to be billions of dollars worth of art stolen by the Third Reich created an ironic twist—if not an embarrassment—for a member of the organization's art committee engaged in the search for the stolen artworks.

He was cosmetics magnate Ronald S. Lauder, chairman of the museum embroiled in the dispute with Morgenthau.

However, that seeming conflict-of-interest was not a deterrent when the WJC scored its first major accomplishment: "A verbal commitment from the directors of four major American museums to conduct self-audits of

their collections to weed out works that may have been
plundered during the war and then found their *legitimate* way
into museums through auction sales and collectors' gifts."

The ultimate goal that the WJC special task force's
Constance Lowenthal was assembling—in conjunction
with the New York-based Association of Art Museum
Directors—was to enlist some 175 other American museums for the same kind of self-search that the French finally
voluntarily instituted in the interest of justice for victims of
the Holocaust and their heirs.

Hardly a month after Morgenthau's crackdown on
the Museum of Modern Art, a groundswell arose on vary-
ing fronts calling for a rigorous effort to resolve "chal-
lenged ownership" of paintings exhibited in the nation's
museums.

No person closer to the source of the sudden flare
up over pirated artworks—nor one of greater prestige—
could have emerged from the shadows to lead the task
force for that purpose than the director of America's most
prestigious exhibition hall for the world's most renowned
artworks, New York's Metropolitan Museum of Art,
Philippe de Montebello.

He agreed to direct the elite thirteen-member committee formed by the Association of Art Museum
Directors, which includes the heads of the 170 largest art
museums in North America.

The group was asked to develop guidelines to
resolve individual ownership claims arising from the illegal
seizure of artworks before, during, and immediately after

World War II. But their major thrust was determining which of those pilfered masterpieces reposed in museums in the United States.

Some experts expressed belief that hundreds, if not thousands, of looted works hang in American museums or in the homes of collectors.

De Montebello stated emphatically that he had no awareness about "how big the problem is." But he expressed willingness to make a thorough search and identify all stolen artworks in the United States. He also agreed to cooperate with the World Jewish Congress's inquiry, as well as with the B'nai B'rith Klutznick National Jewish Museum in Washington, which established a Holocaust Art Restitution Project to create a database of Jewish cultural losses.

Meanwhile in Washington, some members of Congress had grown concerned about the possibility of difficulties that could be posed by Holocaust survivor claimants to artworks hanging in American museums and decided to get involved in the problem.

The House Banking Committee held a hearing on looted art in mid February 1998, but a spokesman made it clear its goal was "strictly informational, merely to give a sense of what the problem looks like from the museum directors' standpoint.... We simply want to know how much artwork is out there, what precautions museums take [to avoid dealing with looted artwork], does the incident at the Museum of Modern Art place a chill on art exchanges, the difficulties in establishing provenance, and the moral-versus-the-legal responsibilities."

To further its mission and to decide whether there is a need for a government role in the matter, the House committee called on a number of museum directors for their testimony.

Appearing at the session on February 12 were Philippe de Montebello and Ronald Lauder; Glenn D. Lowry, the director of MOMA; Earl A. Powell 3d, director of the National Gallery of Art in Washington, D.C.; James N. Wood, director of the Art Institute of Chicago; Gilbert S. Edelson, administrative vice president of the Art Dealers Association of America; and Stephen E. Weil, emeritus senior scholar at the Smithsonian Institution's Center for Museum Studies. Their testimony appeared to satisfy the House committee, but established no indicator of what governmental participation was likely to result in that area.

Some observers suggested that the House committee might influence a government-sponsored study into the matter of the stolen art works, just as the State Department embarked on its study for the recovery and restoration of gold stolen by Germany during World War II.

Meanwhile, the legal action to prevent the Jewish artworks from being returned to their Austrian looters initiated by D.A. Morgenthau was continuing.

Morgenthau had obtained a grand jury subpoena to keep the paintings in limbo until his staff could investigate claims that the pair of masterpieces were stolen more than a half-century ago by the Nazis.

Rita Rief, a New York resident, charged that the paintings were looted from a relative who died in a concentration camp. The Leopold Foundation countered that the Schieles in question were acquired in good faith from legitimate postwar owners.

The appeal by MOMA to quash the subpoena was heard by New York County State Supreme Court Justice Laura Drager. Her ruling stunned Morgenthau and many Jewish organizations that were looking for "justice" in what has been a continuing problem in the exhibition—as well as sales—of artworks that are known to have been pillaged from Nazi Holocaust victims and other tyrannized Jews.

In her twenty-six-page ruling, Judge Drager maintained that state law "protects borrowed art from government seizure," and agreed with MOMA's argument that, "should the prosecutor prevail in preventing the paintings from leaving New York, such action would threaten the city's position in the art world."

Morgenthau disagreed and immediately filed an appeal to the state's second highest court, the five-member Appellate Division of the New York State Supreme Court.

"We remain firmly of the view that New York's Exemption from Seizure statute does not apply to criminal investigations," the prosecutor declared. "In addition, we believe it to be bad public policy to exempt any stolen property from the reach of the law. We do not believe New York should be a safe haven for stolen art.

"The exhibition of stolen paintings, or those of questioned provenance, does not advance the cultural life of our city and state."

Morgenthau had made his move toward seizing the two questioned paintings just five days before the exhibit ended on January 4. Judge Drager then delayed the date that her ruling was to take effect for two weeks so that

Morgenthau could file his appeal. Since he did so at once, the lower court had to succumb to an indefinite stay of the ruling pending the Appellate Division's ruling.

Meanwhile, ten state museums in Austria sifted through their records to try to determine which paintings were originally owned by Jewish citizens and looted during World War II and not returned. Cultural Minister Elizabeth Gehrer declared, "There is now a moral obligation to exactly figure out the origin of every object."

Although Austria embraced Nazi occupation in 1938, it wasn't to happen for sixty years, in 1998, that a leading Austrian newspaper, *Der Standard*, began revealing that thousands of looted art works were bought by museums and collectors during the war. After the conflict ended, the real owners were obstructed by the government from reclaiming them.

Investigative reporters Walter V. Robinson and Elizabeth Neuffer reported in the *Boston Globe* on March 5, 1998 that one letter they were shown was from a Nazi official and concerned a Degas painting which the Oesterreichische Galerie Belvedere wanted. The letter states: "In the possession of Mrs. von Mendelssohn, there is a Degas available which is of great interest to Professor Grimschitz... The price... is not expensive. Heil Hitler."

"This is not only a problem in Austria, but France, the Netherlands, Germany, and the United States," said a representative of the Kunsthistorisches Museum. "It's a Pandora's Box."

The Schiele paintings "are but the tip of a mammoth art-berg that could sink the legitimacy of many collections—

and collectors," according to *New York Daily News* art critic Richard Z. Chesnoff. He went on to write on January 9, 1998, "For just as they stole gold and other assets from their victims, the Nazis took art, often from Jewish collectors. Hitler even maintained a special unit that traveled with his armies to loot collections and museums."

Chesnoff pointed out that, for example, France recovered more than 61,000 stolen artworks—many never claimed, and with no serious attempt by the French to find their rightful owners or heirs—and then proceeded to auction off 13,000 pieces and, at the same time, placed 2,000 of the best works on display in French museums without any attempt to locate their owners or publicity that they were stolen paintings.

Thanks in large measure to American writer Hector Feliciano, author of *The Lost Museum* and resident of Paris, the French finally faced the truth and began returning some stolen artworks to the victims' families.

Edgar Bronfman has also gone on record recently that he and his colleagues were concentrating also on recovery of stolen cultural treasures, in addition to the searches they instituted for Jewish gold.

More than paintings were at stake. For as the WJC revealed in the recent past, the postwar Austrian government, as one example, expropriated more than 250,000 precious books, mostly those of Holocaust victims, and distributed the majority to Austrian libraries.

Richard Chesnoff's further evaluation of the way "A legacy of thefts continues to haunt the art world" is telling. "A few journalists are beginning to say the restitution battle is making them queasy—that it's not only about the

Nazis, but about their willing helpers throughout Europe.

"I was reminded of that by the soul-searing revival of *The Diary of Anne Frank*. The play had a profound effect on anyone who saw the original. But this 'Anne,' played powerfully by the young Natalie Portman, touches the truths left unsaid, or underplayed in the earlier, sanitized version.

"Among them, that it was Anne's own country-men—possibly neighbors—who betrayed the family to the Germans and sent them to their deaths. They then looted the Franks's belongings."

According to experts, that agglomeration of what certainly would seem to comprise some of society's most respected people, possess hundreds to tens of thousands of artworks looted from Jewish victims during the Nazi reign in Europe.

The fight was joined by the World Jewish Congress in 1997, which designated renowned art historian Constance Lowenthal to recruit a task force to track down plundered cultural treasures involving artworks, books and even musical instruments. The search was to be a world-wide operation, but at the onset the heaviest concentration was on four primary targets: France, Germany, Argentina, and the United States.

France, because that nation was considered one of the principal hoarders of stolen art—and its government had launched a campaign to identify such pilfered works that might be hanging on museum walls.

Germany, because that is where the looted trea-sures were brought from the countries and peoples the Nazis overran.

Argentina, because that was the favored destination of Nazi underlings who eluded capture at the end of the war.

The United States, where it was deemed, due to its World War II victory and prosperity, a goodly amount of the stolen artwork made its way into private collections and museums.

The WJC had, of course, once again forgotten Switzerland which, when not the conduit, was certainly a large shareholder in the world's Nazi-looted art.

The sudden surge of interest in so much pirated art, most of it from the homes and businesses of Jewish citizens victimized by the Holocaust and by European nations which rode the Nazi's coattails during the years when the plunder was carried out, prompted one of the nation's most respected adjudicators of masterpieces, James N. Wood, director of the Art Institute of Chicago, to voice a solemn note on the problem.

Testifying under oath before members of the House Banking Committee on Capitol Hill on February 12, 1998 (the previously reported hearing), Wood summed up the task that lay ahead, "This is one of the most pressing and difficult questions facing art museums today."

Despite the lack of records and the fact that many years have passed since the Third Reich began eradicating Jews in the 1930s, the recent opening of wartime archives in the United States and Europe, as well as the news on looted art, has given rise to a profusion of claims for the plundered paintings—and many more are continuing to pour in.

Gilbert S. Edelson, the administrative vice president and counsel of the Art Dealers Association of America, pleaded for the unification, or at the least, coordination of groups performing research on lost art—most preferably such distinguished organizations as the World Jewish Congress and the B'nai B'rith Klutznick National Jewish Museum in Washington.

"We should do now what should have been done many years ago," Edelson declared. "There should be a central registry and database where claims for the recovery of looted works could be registered, kept on file, and where the information would be made available to all interested parties."

Almost before Edelson's words faded into the distance, two members of the banking committee—Representatives Charles E. Schumer of Brooklyn and Nita M. Lowcy of Rye, N.Y., both Democrats—introduced legislation that provided five million dollars to private organizations that undertook to help families trace their losses. An equal amount of compensation was proposed for bodies that checked "the provenance of Federal art holdings." Their bill also required anyone who purchased art, including museums, to do a reasonable title search to establish the true origins and ownerships of questioned artworks.

In written testimony to the banking committee, Ronald S. Lauder, chairman of the World Jewish Congress's new Commission for Art Recovery, called for the declassification of additional wartime archives. "We need to press other nations to do the same," he proposed further.

It is to be noted that the only international database for stolen works of art that can help war art theft victims to identify their property and put the art world on notice is the Historic Art Theft Registry of Trans Art International.

In addition, several international publications focus on lost art. Among them, the IFAR Report published by the International Foundation for Art Research cooperates with insurance companies, Interpol, the FBI, and police organizations. Trace 1 contains reports and photographs of missing art objects. The FBI and Interpol compile their own databases of stolen objects.

To take advantage of the benefits of this Historic Art Registry, theft victims must investigate, catalogue, and record their losses. The registry will appeal to private and institutional collectors, dealers, auction houses, appraisers, accountants, and legal representatives. Not a perfect resolution—but one finally promising hope of righting some of the inequities of the past.

At long last, genuine efforts to resolve ownership of all artworks acquired before, during, and after World War II by American and European museums, as well as by global collectors, traders, and distributors, have gotten under way.

PART V

The Insurance Rip-off

CHAPTER 21

Unhonored Claims

Not only gold and personal possessions were forcibly extracted from the Jewish victims of World War II. Three Holocaust survivors detailed in 1997 at an NAIC Fall Presentation their families' experiences.

Margaret Zentner of Little Neck, New York told how her German father bought dowry insurance, an annuity common in Europe at the time, payable when she reached age twenty-one. When Zentner, after surviving several Nazi concentration camps, tried to collect the policy's benefits, the insurance company refused to pay her.

Marta Drucker Corner—a native of Rakovnik, today part of the Czech Republic—was sent with her

whole family to concentration camps, and she alone survived. Her father had several insurance policies. Not one
would be paid to her.

Rudy Rosenberg—born in Brussels—was also sent
with his family to the camps. They had bought, like many
Jewish families, a special insurance policy and were asked to
recommend other Jews interested in purchasing policies for
their children's future. The company refused to pay
Rosenberg.

Like Zentner, Corner, and Rosenberg, after World
War II, some Holocaust survivors and relatives of those
whose lives were brutally taken by the Third Reich tried to
press claims against European insurance companies for
indemnification of property losses and other material
goods seized or destroyed by the Nazis.

The claimants were immediately denied payment
when they were unable to produce death certificates, policy
numbers, or other documentation.

On March 31, 1997, a class action suit was filed in
New York by three law firms, Fagan & Associates,
Anderson, Kill & Olick, and Kohn, Swift & Graf. The
plaintiffs in the case are Holocaust victims or heirs aged
sixty or seventy who are seeking to recover billions of dollars from seven European insurance companies in Austria,
France, Italy, and Germany, some of whom have agency
agreements with Aetna Life and Casualty Company in the
United States. The companies being sued regularly transact
business in New York.

In the suit, the plaintiffs produced insurance documents of their families. Alleged by the plaintiffs is that the

defendants concealed, stole, and liquidated assets of Holocaust victims and then callously refused to honor claims on the grounds that survivors were unable to produce death certificates for the victims.

Eugene Anderson, one of the plaintiffs' attorneys said, "Insurance companies have always been in the denial business. In this case, simply by doing what they do habitually, major insurance companies linked themselves to one of history's great tragedies."

The most shocking aspect about those insurance rip-offs was the revelation that the top executives of the biggest German indemnification agency, Allianz AG, worked closely with the Third Reich to seize policies owned by Jewish citizens, to expand Allianz's business in conquered countries and, above all other considerations, to limit claims growing out of riots the Nazis perpetrated to destroy Jewish-owned properties.

An all-telling document was unearthed in the search initiated by the New York insurance litigator, Linda Gerstel, a partner in the Manhattan-based law firm Anderson, Kill & Olick, who had launched a suit by Holocaust survivors and heirs of victims against Allianz and fourteen other German and Italian insurers to recoup funds Jews had coming to them for losses they suffered during the Nazi regime.

This document blew the lid off the Nazi-orchestrated insurance scam against millions of Jews. It was a single copy of an Austrian State Police report, a fill-in-the-blanks form that was so apparently banal that researchers at first didn't even appreciate its significance, according to

Terrell E. Hunt, president of Risk International, a Houston company engaged in insurance research.

The form, dated 1946, directed the Italian subsidiary of Allianz to turn over to the Reich Treasury the proceeds of a life insurance policy owned by Salomon Israel Korner of Vienna.

According to Hunt, the numbering on the form suggested that it was only one of tens of thousands of such illegal "releases" in the files of the state police in Austria, which was occupied by Nazi forces in March 1938 during the so-called "Auschluss," the unopposed and outright takeover of that country.

"This document is the key for hundreds of thousands of people to make claims," Hunt explained. "Its significance is that it is a standard form on which the Nazis listed the name and address of the insured, the insurance company, and the policy number, which were the details needed to make a claim." And it showed the way at least one insurance company had taken advantage of a Jewish client and deprived him of his claim.

Under the 1933 German law mentioned earlier, the property of Jews who emigrated to other lands was confiscated. After Hitler began his "Final Solution" program against the Jews, those who were forcibly deported to death camps were considered to be "emigrants" under that law.

The lone document was addressed "to the management office for the German Reich" in the Vienna office of Riunione Adriatica di Sicurta, the Italian subsidiary of Allianz, indicating that the Nazis had their own personnel in the office of at least one insurer—if not, more than likely, many others.

The significance of the document recovered from the archives was disputed by Allianz's senior spokesman, Emilio Galli-Zugaro. While confirming that tens of thousands of similar documents existed, he said reparations the German government made to Holocaust survivors and victims' relatives after the war settled all claims.

However, there's not a shred of evidence to show that Germany—or any other government—fully compensated a single Jew after the war for insured losses sustained during Hitler's reign.

The suit filed by attorney Linda Gerstel on behalf of Holocaust victims against Allianz and fourteen other companies might not have materialized as expeditiously if it wasn't for a rare happenstance that occurred in December 1996 in the Manhattan law offices of Edward D. Fagan.

It was shortly before noon when Fagan's assistant, Edith Pollack-Edra, was opening the mail and found one envelope containing a single page from a notepad. She recognized it as a scrawl written by a former Nazi death camp prisoner.

"It listed a batch of numbers," Ms. Pollack-Edra told the author in an interview. "I put two and two together and concluded that they were digits from an insurance policy."

After a few hours of sleuthing on the telephone, Ms. Pollack-Edra got through to the agency that had issued the policy—Allianz AG!

"I read them the policy identification numbers and was told almost at once, 'Oh, we paid that claim just after the war.'"

The response came back so swiftly and curtly that

all kinds of flags were raised for Ms. Pollack-Edra, who wasted no time passing on those details to her boss. Fagan then delved more deeply into the matter and soon found that Linda Gerstel was in pursuit of similar information from Allianz for one of her own clients, who showed her an actual policy with that company.

Allianz's spokesman, Galli-Zugaro, speaking on the phone from his company's office in 1998 in Rome to *New York Times* reporter David Cay Johnston, stood on his insistence that "All reparations paid by Germany to Holocaust survivors and victims' relatives after the war settled all claims."

Then he offered gratuitously to Johnston listening in the paper's newsroom on West Forty-third Street, "During the war it was normal—it is horrifying to say that now, but it was normal procedure then—to seize the insurance policies of Jews and give them to the Nazis.

"All survivors, of which there are not very many, and their heirs and those who could benefit, collected their money back to then from the German government. Until this lawsuit was filed in New York last year, which hit us quite unexpectedly, we had not had a claim made in twenty years."

The suit was filed jointly by attorneys Fagan and Gerstel in New York's Federal District Court (Southern District in Manhattan). The application sought a court order to compel Allianz and the other insurers who issued policies to Jews in the prewar years to open their files so that the lawyers could cull their lists for the names of clients who had gone to them for payment of losses suffered during the Hitler era.

Since the suit was instituted, Galli-Zugaro claimed, "Eighteen-hundred people had called our toll-free hotline, but we found only two hundred valid claims."

Edward Fagan wasn't about to rely on his words. "The suggestion that those people [the 200] were paid by the German Government is just preposterous," Fagan protested. "Allianz and other insurers controlled the information needed to pay claims and relied on technicalities to deny payment or to provide compensation for considerably less than was owed."

The trickery and chicanery European insurance firms employed to fleece Jews with policies that covered losses they might suffer in the event of catastrophic occurrences such as riots, sabotage, or incendiary destruction of their properties and possessions was horrifying.

One stunning revelation that evolved out of that probe was that some Allianz executives became senior officials in the Nazi Government.

They described the way they courted Nazi officials and began making political contributions to the Nazi party, as early as 1932, when Hitler ascended to the dictatorship of Germany.

Kurt Schmitt, the chief executive of Allianz in those early years, became Hitler's first minister of economics and one of his closest confidantes. He even dined frequently with Der Fuhrer.

The testimony elicited by American interrogators also disclosed that Schmitt wore an SS uniform and rubbed elbows with another Allianz executive, Eduard Hilgard, who served the Nazi regime as head of the Eleventh

Industrial Group of the Third Reich, which oversaw insurance companies.

Playing a role in those two positions, Hilgard
divulged how he was uniquely qualified to "help German
insurance companies settle claims for only three cents on
the dollar from Kristallnacht." (These were the nights of
November 8 and 9, 1938, when Hitler's government
allowed gangs of Nazis to rampage across the country,
arresting and killing Jews, and burning synagogues and
Jewish-owned businesses.)

Hilgard's testimony further revealed that the money
was paid by the insurers to the Reich treasury—not to the
victimized Jews—and "by discounting the claims, the insurers saved as much as nineteen million dollars."

Furthermore, "When the Nazis conquered a country, the assets of local insurance companies were taken over
by Allianz and other German insurance companies, as well
as the Assicurazioni Generali, an Italian insurance company."

That information came to light only recently after a
long-secret report from Central Intelligence Agency economic experts was declassified.

The next-to-last word on this subject came from
Galli-Zugaro. "There is no question that Allianz sought to
profit from the war, but the company never sought to
profit from the Holocaust."

Attorneys Fagan and Gerstel have armed themselves with the ultimate weapon that would bring relief to
the Jewish peoples who were robbed of their indemnities
by the avaricious insurers—the awful truth.

The companies who were the targets of the suit lodged in Manhattan's United States Courthouse all had one thing in common, from Allianz AG down to each and every one of the other fourteen carriers named in the litigation papers. They all have operations in the United States.

Allianz owns Fireman's Fund, one of the largest of property and casualty companies in the United States. Then there is a Minnesota life insurance company that does business with the Allianz name. And, too, there are the Jefferson and Monticello insurance companies in New York.

These are the firms that the lawyers now want to open their books for scrutiny in order to see how many Jewish victims or their descendants are owed insurance payments and how much money is coming to them.

The day of reckoning began on January 27, 1998....

CHAPTER 22

Congress Moves
to Punish Insurers

It started as a three-paragraph dispatch from the Associated Press to its worldwide print and electronic media clients:

"European insurance companies that fail to disclose the names of Holocaust victims who held policies with them would be barred from operating in the United States under legislation introduced in Congress yesterday.

"The proposal of Representative Mark Foley (Republican of Florida) seeks to help Holocaust victims recover insurance benefits denied them after World War II.

"Holocaust survivors last year filed a class-action lawsuit in an effort to recover benefits from Europe's biggest insurers."

The third-paragraph reference was to the litigation that lawyers Edward Fagan and Linda Gerstel had instituted.

The ways of Congress more often than not take weird directions that normal citizens may not understand. In a follow-up to the January dispatch, the Associated Press on February 3, 1998 sent to its clients a more detailed account of the action taken in the House of Representatives.

Congressman Foley's name was not mentioned in the second story because of an agreement on the House floor to have Representative Eliot L. Engel (Democrat of the Bronx, New York) pursue that legislative route to recoup Holocaust insurance claims for the victimized Jews.

The bill was announced February 2, 1998 at a news conference held at New York City's City Hall. Also present were New York Democrats Jerrold L. Nadler and Carolyn B. Maloney, and Staten Island Republican Vito J. Fossella.

The AP story on the House action to force insurance companies that sold policies to victims of the Holocaust to pay benefits to them or their heirs reports, "Engel... said some European insurance companies were guilty of postwar injustices against Jews and other Holocaust victims.

"He said that after the defeat of the Nazis half a century ago, survivors who tried to collect claims on policies issued by insurance companies in Germany, Italy,

Switzerland, and other countries often were rebuffed for lack of documentation, like death certificates.

"'Insurers made little or no effort to locate beneficiaries, nor did they establish procedures to assist those with inadequate records,' Engel said.

"'Even worse, in some instances, beneficiaries were able to produce substantial documentation but were still rejected.'

"Some companies 'were complicitous with the Nazis before and during the war,' he said. 'Afterward, they continued their dishonesty by refusing to pay Holocaust survivors or their heirs.'"

The Associated Press reported that Representative Engel did not name specific companies.

The article continued, "A number of European insurance companies, many with affiliates in the United States, have been named as defendants in a class-action lawsuit accusing them of refusing to honor policies. The suit was filed last year in Federal Court."

The article went on to explain Engel's bill. "[It] would require insurers to disclose how many policies they wrote for Holocaust victims and to pay the beneficiaries." Failure to comply by not reporting the information would result in fines of $1,000 a day and would keep the statute of limitations from barring claimants.

Congressman Nadler, interviewed after Engel's bill was announced at City Hall, was irate over the way Jews were mistreated—indeed tyrannized—by insurance companies.

"Those people pulled off one of the largest thefts

in human history," he fumed. "The bill we are pushing for immediate passage in the House calls upon the Secretary of Commerce to receive an accounting from the European insurance companies doing business in the United States within ninety days or pay the thousand-dollar-a-day fine until they do."

More tales of the outlandish treatment of policy-holders were told by New Yorkers with firsthand experience in attempting to receive restitution for provable losses.

Socrates Fokas, a forty-year-old resident of Ronkonkoma, Long Island, reported that officials of an insurer named Victoria zu Berlin informed him that a $4,000 life insurance policy his grandfather bought in 1927 "doesn't exist."

Shaking his head in dismay, Fokas wondered, "How they can tell me that I will never understand—especially since I have a copy of the policy."

Samuel Hersly, a seventyish survivor of the dread Auschwitz concentration camp, found it incomprehensible that Assicurazioni Generali, Italy's largest insurer, "wouldn't even provide me with a copy of my father's policy when I first inquired about it way back in 1951. And since then, the firm has persisted that it cannot compensate me for any loss I may claim."

Guido Pastori, Assicurazioni Generali's director-general, claimed his firm "has no obligation to pay because all of our subsidies were nationalized by communist governments after World War II."

Assicurazioni Generali, which has no known associated underwriting branch in the United States, can thumb its nose at Samuel Hersly with impunity, since the United

States cannot take sanctions against the Rome-based insurer.

But this case was the exception to the realities attendant upon the conspiratorial machinations Europe's insurance companies (with branches in the United States) have perpetrated on Jewish claimants since the war's end.

Other firms, vulnerable to American penalties, set up special hotlines for relatives who'd been invited to file claims.

Perhaps the most laudable attempt undertaken by an insurer to right the wrongs committed by a European firm is the effort exerted by the Fireman's Insurance Fund in the United States, which offered to pay claims of Holocaust survivors who could produce "reasonable proof."

Allianz AG, owner of the Fireman's Fund in the United States, had no choice but to make that offer, if it wanted to escape the $1,000-a-day penalty that loomed for the insurer and also hold on to its lofty, and very lucrative, business in the United States.

On February 11, 1998, the Senate Banking Committee was told by its chairman, Alfonse D'Amato that a plan had been devised to press European insurance companies to pay the claims of Holocaust victims and their heirs.

D'Amato proposed the creation of an independent panel to supervise searches of insurance company files in order to create "a fund to help aging Holocaust victims."

The plan followed months of quiet, unpublicized negotiations with the insurers by Neil Levin, New York State's insurance superintendent, and Elan Steinberg, of the

World Jewish Congress, who had first proposed such action.

Senator D'Amato compared the proposed panel to the one headed by Paul A. Volcker, the former chairman of the Federal Reserve, which had been searching for deposits Jews made before World War II in Swiss banks.

But the insurance plan would differ from that of the Volcker group in that each insurance company that agreed to take part in the plan would have to make a payment to a fund clearly earmarked for Holocaust survivors.

Assicurazioni Generali, the dominant underwriter of policies sold to Jews in Eastern Europe before the war, immediately indicated that it likely wouldn't cooperate and demanded the focus of the action must be shifted away from Generali.

"We look forward to seeing the proposal and to reviewing the issues dealing with Communist expropriation in Eastern Europe," said M. Scott Vayer, Generali's lead attorney. "But we have neither a legal nor a moral duty to pay claims because Communist governments which nationalized our Eastern European offices explicitly assumed responsibility to pay claims."

Vayer was referring to newly-discovered evidence in Moscow, in archives of the former Soviet Union. The search of the archives was permitted by Russian officials and was conducted by Risk International Services Inc., the Houston-based company mentioned earlier, specializing in "insurance archeology." The company conducts searches of repositories "from archives to attics" to retrieve lost insurance documents and determine their significance.

Risk International vice president and counsel,

Douglas L. Talley, let it be known that, "although the search was preliminary, the documents tell us enough about the way the Nazis, with the German insurance industry's complicity, established the practice of confiscating the insurance assets of German Jews."

Talley said he found some of the Moscow documents in February and April 1998, in a folder labeled "Insurance Affairs—Jewish Question."

Of the incidents detailed in the folder, no chapter bearing on anti-Semitic violence ever stained the pages of history any bloodier or blacker than the savage outbursts of unruly mobs, aided and abetted by the Nazis, on the nights of November 9 and 10, 1938. That nefarious night the Nazis smashed and torched some 170 synagogues and thousands of Jewish shops and homes all over the German landscape.

It has taken sixty years to get to the very bottom of those two nights of inhuman rampage known as "Kristallnacht," or "night of broken glass."

It took Risk International's Douglas Talley to bring the sordid details to light after he read a raft of Nazi documents seized by Soviet troops in Berlin in 1945 and later transferred to the repository in Moscow.

In the intervening years there has been no hiding the fact that the Nazi Government confiscated insurance payments to Jews whose property was damaged in Kristallnacht. But specific details about those seizures were lacking totally—until Talley's Moscow venture.

The eye-opening documents showed that German insurance companies not only connived with the Nazis to avoid paying Jewish policyholders, but also often exceeded government guidelines by canceling unrelated life, health, and pension policies on which Jewish citizens had been paying premiums for years.

After the Kristallnacht riots, Nazi leaders Hermann Goering, Josef Goebbels, and Reinhard Heydrich met with Allianz executive Eduard Hilgard, who also represented the forty-three firms comprising the German insurance industry. Hilgard told the trio that "confidence in the industry would suffer if Jewish claimants were not paid, but that reimbursing them could bankrupt smaller companies."

After the war, Allied authorities were dumbstruck to be told by Hilgard that he had helped insurers settle Kristallnacht claims at three cents on the dollar.

Foreign and non-Jewish claims were paid, but Field Marshal Goering confiscated the money due Jewish policy-holders.

Some of the documents retrieved in Moscow were turned over to the New York State Senate Insurance Company. The panel, headed by Guy J. Vilella immediately took steps to pass legislation that would penalize European insurers who did business in New York if they failed to pay claims related to the Holocaust.

That action was in addition to the steps being taken by the House and Senate bodies in Washington.

Twenty other states have begun public hearings into insurance frauds of Holocaust victims. Insurance Commissioner Chuck Quackenbush of California, during a hearing he convened vowed, "The people who lived through the unspeakable horror of the Holocaust can never be compensated for what they suffered. However, we can help Holocaust survivors recover what is rightfully theirs by forcing insurance companies to settle claims for life and property insurance."

Already, other Holocaust survivors had filed a class-action suit in United States Federal Court in Brooklyn, New York, accusing insurance companies in Germany, Austria, Italy and France—including the Italian company Assicurazioni Generali—of not paying insurance claims to Holocaust survivors and their heirs. The claims average $75,000 and up, and attorneys state another ten thousand people may join the class suit.

Ivan Solti, who lives in Encino, California, and whose father was a concentration camp victim, is encouraged but wary. When his mother tried to collect on his father's insurance, "She was told there was the war clause and they could not find it."

The research needed to trace some claims is complex and difficult to carry out. "Kind of like finding the needle in the haystack," said Jim Stevenson, a spokesman for Washington, D.C. Insurance Commissioner Deborah Senn, who is part of a national team investigating Holocaust insurance fraud.

The investigators' findings are filled with murky revelations. Philip Roberto, research director for the Proposition 103 Enforcement Project, said, "The actions of insurance companies during this dark period of history are sickening. Some insurance companies even went so far as to market life insurance policies to Jews in Belgium and other occupied nations, knowing full well that these people would later be killed and paid out policies to the Third Reich."

The week following the introduction of Representative Engel's bill in New York, President Terrell E. Hunt of Risk International testified before the United States House of Representatives Committee on Banking and Financial Services. He talked about his company's pro bono efforts to recover historical documents and other proof so that Holocaust policyholders, beneficiaries, and heirs could recover benefits.

To date, Risk International has identified twenty-one Holocaust policyholders who hold over thirty insurance policies from thirteen insurance companies, some of which have United States offices. Hunt called for Congressional assistance in the form of:

- Federal funding of insurance research cooperatively with states that are already dedicating considerable resources to recover Holocaust-era claims on behalf of survivors or heirs who reside in their states.
- Document retention: Prohibition of any destruction of Holocaust-era documentation such as insurance policies, history of corporate structure/governance, claim practices, complicity with the Nazi government, and financial reports.
- Access to carrier and foreign government archives.
- Education: Educate the United States public and raise awareness worldwide of the need for restitution.

Risk International, wholly owned by Millennial Assurance Services Inc., a privately held Texas-based company, has also given testimony at hearings in Illinois, Miami Beach, Seattle, Los Angeles, and San Francisco.

"Risk International has been pleased," said Del R. Jones, Chairman and CEO of Millennial Assurance Services, "to support the NAIC on a voluntary basis in an effort to return to Holocaust victims and their heirs what is rightfully theirs."

In late August 1998, the Associated Press reported that an agreement was made by the Jewish World Congress, the National Association of Insurance Companies and European insurance companies to resolve unpaid Holocaust-era policies. To carry out this plan, a commission will examine a company's records, figure out how to resolve the claims and determine the company's liability. Also, insurance companies will be required to put money into two funds—a humanitarian fund and an equity fund—to pay off proven claims immediately.

Although many have applauded this pact as a step in the right direction, others, including attorneys Linda Gerstel and Ed Fagan, are wary. Since the agreement is voluntary, Fagan warns that it fails to address many legal concerns and "insurance companies can withdraw from it if they don't like it."

Even with the mixed reviews that this agreement has conjured, another development—a step towards justice served—in the insurance story has occurred. One week before the announcement of the agreement, Assicurazioni Generali—the Italian insurance company whose lead attorney once stated, "we have neither a legal nor moral duty to pay claims"—succumbed to the intense pressure

of world opinion and a multi-billion dollar lawsuit. The
Associated Press reports, "The company agreed to pay
$100 million to settle outstanding claims brought on by a
class-action lawsuit." As Elan Steinberg explained, "There
was a lot of pressure. They didn't want what happened to
the Swiss Banks to happen to them."

Although the company appears to have been
motivitated more by pressure than by the desire to right
the wrongs they inflicted on the victims of Nazi persecution and their families, the result of their most recent
action is still the same: a measure of justice will be served
and some victims and their heirs will finally receive what
is owed to them.

PART VI

Coming to Terms

CHAPTER 23

Contemporary Efforts

Retracing the bloodstained trail of Nazi gold leads all over the world. Yet the journey must be undertaken even as it brings us at each juncture to painful questions and even more painful answers. These confound and accuse not only individuals, companies and institutions but whole governments, challenging their historical identities and international reputations. Yet, unless we reexamine our past, the footsteps of yesterday will echo down the corridors of tomorrow. And those echoes will sound audible recriminations that the searing injustices of history still go unredeemed. A moral accounting must be rendered before it is too late.

Indeed, such a tabulation is made even more necessary by the headlines of today. For the lessons of history
haven't been learned while anti-Semitism and racism are
still very much alive.

Rabbi Marvin Hier is the dean and founder of the
Simon Wiesenthal Center, the international organization
established in 1977 that bears the name of legendary Nazi
hunter and humanitarian Simon Wiesenthal. The organization has relentlessly striven to "perpetuate the memory and
teach the lessons of The Holocaust—as well as ensuring
the future of the world's thirteen million Jews."

To that end, the center's operatives have made significant advances in exposing anti-Semitic attacks against
America's Jewry and exerting every effort to dissipate
"flare-ups of hatred wherever they happen—before they
explode into firestorms."

One of Wiesenthal's principal recent successes on
behalf of the 385,000 member families in its North
American constituency was in mounting a global campaign
that urged officials at the highest levels of government to
disclose the trail of assets stolen from victims of the Nazis
during the Holocaust. The plea went to Switzerland,
Argentina, Turkey, France, Spain, Britain, and the United
States.

Until 1998, Center lawyers had located one bank's
list with data from 1941 on 1,600 accounts (with a total
value of ninety million dollars). That information was
immediately posted on the Internet, and within just a few
weeks Wiesenthal investigators identified sixteen families
whose rightful assets may still be held in secret Swiss bank
accounts.

An important adjunct of the work that Rabbi Hier has instituted at the Center is a relentless campaign to suppress anti-Semitism, which he described as being "alive, well, and thriving throughout the world today."

He went on to state, "What's more alarming, is that it appears to be growing more robust, more strident, more vicious—and more 'respectable'....

"The human race seems to be suffering more frequent attacks of selective memory loss in which the horrors of the death camps recede and ancient hatreds are revived. It would be difficult to imagine a development with more disturbing implications for humanity."

Even as Rabbi Hier uttered these warnings from the prestigious Simon Wiesenthal Center in Los Angeles, an Associated Press dispatch from Dresden on January 25, 1998, chronicled details about a startling uprising by hundreds of leftists and neo-Nazis, who brawled on a train bound for the "Florence on the Elbe," Germany's home of some of the world's greatest art treasures.

The donnybrook was touched off by competing protests over an anti-Nazi exhibit showing that soldiers of the Wehrmacht, Hitler's regular army, committed atrocities alongside the infamous units of the Third Reich, such as the dread SS troops.

Dubbed "War of Extermination: Crimes of the Wehrmacht from 1941 to 1945," the exhibit had been touring in Germany for nearly three years. It was displaying photos and documents to demonstrate that even rank-and-file German soldiers killed Jews and other civilians.

However, many older Germans still viewed the Wehrmacht as an honorable military force that fought for

Carpozi

the homeland—but they hadn't addressed the frequent, often overwhelming charges of brutality and cruelty visited on Jews and other oppressed peoples during the war.

The tumult broke out while the train carrying about 300 leftists en route from Berlin to Dresden, about 110 miles to the south, was set upon in Wurzen, a town in Saxony, some thirty-five miles from its destination.

As rocks and stones pelted the train along the right-of-way, someone pulled the emergency cord that braked the train to a stop. The protesters then battled the passengers for an hour inside and outside the train before police ended the clash and shooed the demonstrators away—after arresting four rightists with baseball bats and blank-cartridge pistols.

Just a day before, a state court approved the National Democratic Party's right to demonstrate against the "War of Extermination" exhibit and, in a simultaneous ruling, allowed the Alliance Against Rightists to stage its own protests.

The court stipulated emphatically that the protests were to be held in separate parts of the city to prevent clashes—but feelings ran so high that what happened on that mid winter's day in Germany made Rabbi Hier's concerns stand out in bold relief....

"We can deny the accumulating evidence that the world is in the early stages of a virulent new strain of anti-Semitism. We can dismiss it as a series of relatively inconsequential incidents and trust that a Holocaust can never happen again.

"Or, we can dedicate and rededicate ourselves to the

effort necessary to snuff out flare-ups of hatred wherever they happen—before they explode into firestorms...."

At just about the time that Germany's pro and anti-Nazi factions were at each other's throats, a small but influential group of politically conservative Jews—aligned with evangelical Christian groups on the issue of anti-Christian discrimination around the world—lodged a complaint against a seemingly unlikely target: A fourteen-minute film being screened at the National Holocaust Museum in Washington, D.C.

The movie, *Anti-Semitism,* is a sober but wrenching account of the history and consequences of that virulent discriminatory practice and describes the role of Christian churches in fomenting sentiment against Jews in Europe.

Led by Michael J. Horowitz, a senior fellow at the Hudson Institute, a conservative research organization, the Jewish critics issued a steamy press release that expressed an abiding concern for "our evangelical Christian political allies," and proceeded with the declaration, "The documentary [film] *Anti-Semitism* is inaccurate and anti-Christian, and we ask that it be altered."

As Museum officials undertook a review of the film, they and their board of Christian advisers maintained that it was accurate and not in need of revision.

"There was intense anti-Semitism within the Catholic and Protestant communities at a region-cultural level which helped bring about the Holocaust," said the chairman of the Holocaust Museum's Church Relations Council, the Reverend John T. Pawlowski, a professor of social ethics at the Catholic Theological Union in Chicago. "To pretend otherwise is to distort history."

The Hudson Institute's Michael Horowitz said he had written the protest after watching the film with evangelical friends and claimed they were "deeply offended by it but who felt that as Christians, they were in no position to complain about a Holocaust Museum film dealing with genocide whose victims were primarily Jews."

The letter's other signatories were Elliott Abrams, Chester E. Finn, and Michael Ledeen, all Reagan Administration officials, David Dalin, a historian who taught at the Jewish Theological Seminary and most recently at Catholic University, and Michael Medved, a film critic and writer.

The letter described the museum as "an irreplaceable institution," but maintained that the film propagated "libels of Christianity" and supported "a profoundly inaccurate thesis: that Christianity and Christian leaders were the initial causes of anti-Semitism and have at all times been its major proponents."

New York Times reporter Judith Miller, who filed a report with her newspaper about this sudden and unexpected dissension in the Jewish community, observed, "Among the signers' other points was that the film failed to note that anti-Semitism predated Christianity, and that it ignored 'Islam's theology and its often violent practice of anti-Semitism.'"

Citing the background for the dispute, Ms. Miller noted that it stemmed from "a broad political offensive mounted by conservative Jews and the Christian right to establish as a public issue the persecution of Christians abroad, often by Muslim governments, many of which also oppose Israel."

The writer went on to analyze the dispute's political

implications. "Mr. Horowitz is among those who helped draft legislation now pending on Capitol Hill that would impose economic sanctions upon such countries as China and Saudi Arabia, where the Clinton Administration has identified patterns of persecution against Christians. The Administration opposes the legislation."

That political backdrop prompted some scholars and museum officials to challenge the motives of the film's critics.

"They're trying to show the evangelical right how credible they are," declared Rabbi Michael Berenbaum, former project director of the Holocaust Museum, who participated in the writing of the film's script.

Miles Lerman, the museum's chairman, put a lid on the whole problem by describing how the museum was going to handle the matter. "While we take all letters and complaints seriously, the Church Relations subcommittee, responsible for such issues, has decided that the film *was accurate and would not be revised.*"

The open examination of the past advocated by the museum, whether prompted by artistic, political, or historical scholarly inquiries and no matter how unsparing, must not be extinguished.

In the supplement to the Eizenstat Report released in June 1998 the telling and potent words of the original foreword are restated: "Ultimately, the United States, our Allies, and the neutral nations alike should be judged not so much by the actions or inactions of a previous generation, but by our generation's willingness to face the past honestly, to help right the wrongs, and to deal with the injustices suffered by the victims of Nazi aggression."

In truth, it is not only the Allies and neutrals but all civilized nations which must work to accomplish this goal. For, according to Elan Steinberg, "Every country prof-ited—or at least individuals and institutions profited—from the plunder and wholesale thievery of the Nazi regime."

There is a tragic history lesson laid bare on the pages of this book. For, as we focused on the neutrals besides Switzerland one by one—Sweden, Portugal, Spain, Turkey, and Argentina—we learned that though Switzerland was Nazi Germany's major banker, all these countries provided essential goods and tools to keep World War II going. In exchange, they received the looted Nazi gold and valuables which came to them from occupied countries in large part, and from the seized possessions of Holocaust victims.

Even more shocking, the Allies—France, England, and the United States—as may be seen by the chapters delineating their war transactions, are not innocent of the taint of Nazi gold. We have seen how the records of eco-nomic succor of allies, neutrals, and belligerents reveal that the selfish motive of profit and the very human desire for survival figured prominently in the actions of government representatives, citizens, and too many nations at the expense of the rights of those who were helpless victims of the Holocaust.

The International Committee of the Red Cross was even used by the Germans. United States intelligence doc-uments allege that its representatives conveyed information to Berlin, sometimes by U.S. diplomatic mail and that assets were placed in pouches to get them to Switzerland. In 1995, the international committee referred to its "moral failure" during the war to denounce what was happening in Hitler's concentration camps to Jews and other minorities.

Nevertheless and despite all this, it must also not be forgotten that in many nations—both friend and enemy— individual people courageously helped some of the refugees escape almost certain death in concentration camps where six million Jews were exterminated. Even Germany had its Schindler. Other nations had their own Schindlers.

Portugal not only allowed Jewish organizations to relocate in Lisbon but enabled 5,000 Jews to get passage to America. Aristides de Sousa Mendes, a Portuguese diplomat acting on his own, issued 10,000 visas before he was dismissed from his post.

Spain, despite its overt actions showing Axis sympathy, helped between 30,000 and 40,000 Jewish refugees to escape and also protected 4,000 Jews with Spanish heritage living in occupied countries in Europe.

Turkey, historically a point of refuge for fleeing Jews since 1492, sheltered 100,000 Jews, and the government rescued refugees from the Balkan nations. In addition, Jewish representatives in Turkey were allowed to arrange for the air passage to Palestine of victims in Central and Eastern Europe.

Argentina's pro-Nazi government took in almost 45,000 Jews, more than any country in their hemisphere.

Sweden aided Denmark in smuggling virtually all Danish Jews—almost 7,000—to safe haven in Sweden, and the heroic Raoul Wallenberg, aided with money from the

United States War Refugee Board, saved 20,000 to 30,000 Jews from certain death in the camps.

Switzerland, whose request to the Nazis to distinguish Jewish passports led to the infamous "J stamp," admitted over 50,000 Jewish refugees. Carl Lutz, a Swiss vice consul, provided letters of protection for 62,000 Jews, while America saved only 21,000. Amid criticism singling it out as the Nazis' main banker, Switzerland is grappling with its now painfully exposed ties to Nazi Germany. The Volcker Commission, also known as the Independent Committee of Eminent Persons, established in May 1996, reflects the formal agreement of the Swiss Bankers Association, the World Jewish Congress, and the World Jewish Restitution Organization. It is overseeing Arthur Andersen, KPMG Peat Marwick, and Price Waterhouse in identifying and recovering dormant accounts of Holocaust victims. The Independent Commission of Experts, also known as the Bergier Commission, is conducting a review of Switzerland's historic ties to Nazism. And, most importantly, as noted earlier, on August 13, 1998, three of Switzerland's major banking institutions announced a 1.25 billion dollar settlement with the Holocaust victims.

In the last few years, as more and more revelations have surfaced about Nazi gold, "a consensus is crystallizing," according to the Eizenstat report, "among nations that this tragic history must galvanize us to do justice in ways that provide both material and moral justice to the victims and survivors of the Holocaust."

This new attitude of coming to terms with a dark chapter in history in which all have played parts has resulted in major efforts. The most electrifying in terms of its effect on the catholic people of many countries may be the Vatican's study released in March 1998, "We Remember: A Reflection on the Shoah," which the Vatican has called "an act of repentance."

There are other less dramatic but equally positive efforts.

In April 1998, Spain completed its study on wartime gold headed by former Justice Minister Enrique Mugica.

Turkey's commission, headed by Minister of State Gurel, Centers on Gold, reported on gold purchases by the central bank of Turkey.

In Sweden, a commission has been appointed to report on inter-governmental monetary gold transactions during World War II. At the London Conference the Swedish Independent Archives Inquiry gave a report detailing the gold transactions of the Sveriges Riksbank on Nazi gold. And in January 1998 Prime Minister Persson began a countrywide initiative for Holocaust education which will highlight a new booklet on the Holocaust to be used to educate all Swedish citizens and which has already gone out to 250,000 households.

The British government led the meeting of forty-one countries in the London Conference on Nazi Gold in December 1997. For the first time, the international responsibility of all the convening countries was focused upon. The result of the conference, among other things, is a pledge from several nations of $57 million to be given to Holocaust victims and the promise of additional funds from other countries. Their goal: to disperse all the money to survivors or their heirs by century's end.

Britain has also established the Nazi Persecutee Relief Fund which will be directed towards those who suffered under Nazism and Communism, as well as other victims. Nine other countries have also contributed to the fund, including the United States.

France has initiated new programs to find out about millions of dollars of looted bank accounts and other assets plundered from Jewish victims during the Nazi Occupation of their country. In 1997, a commission was appointed to investigate Jewish property stolen by the Vichy government for the Nazis. Finance Minister Dominique Strauss-Kahn and Bank of France Governor Jean-Claude Trichet announced in March 1998 they are creating "a surveillance committee."

Argentina is providing bank records to help investigators track down gold cash and art work transferred to Argentina by Nazi agents, and a commission has been established by President Menem and Foreign Minister Guido Di Tella to study Nazi activities in Argentina during the war.

At the London Conference, in December 1997, the Federal Reserve Bank of New York presented its report, and adding major new evidence is the United States major study *U.S. and Allied Efforts to Recover and Restore Gold and Other Assets Stolen or Hidden by Germany During World War II* released in May 1997. In 1998 the supplemental study focusing on the neutral countries was released. In addition, Senator Alfonse D'Amato's hearings before the Senate Banking Committee in the summer of 1998 have added insights into America's role in receiving Nazi gold.

In November 1998, the United States' Washington,

D.C., Conference will attempt to develop principles and processes, to review progress on the gold issue, to deal with art and the other plundered valuables of Holocaust victims, and to renew the drive to open the archives.

Portugal's Prime Minister Antonio Gutennes is making all his government's documents relating to the transfer of Nazi gold to Portugal available to research and has appointed a three-person commission to review Portugal's dealings during the war.

The Netherlands has budgeted $400 million additional moneys for existing Dutch programs to assist war and persecution victims. Fifty thousand Holocaust victims will be given grants and benefits under the program.

Norway, which has never before made financial provisions, has established a $60 million restitution fund for Norwegian Holocaust survivors of what, Norwegian Prime Minister Kjell Magne Bondevik announced, were moral injustices as well as material losses.

A $111 million contribution by Germany over the next four years will build on the $60 billion repartition effort during the last forty years to compensate Holocaust survivors. And, on August 31, 1998, Germany's biggest bank, Deutsche Bank A.G. released a historian's report commissioned by the bank which gave evidence that it had dealt in Nazi gold during World War II, which will certainly strengthen and expand the class suit of Holocaust survivors against both the Dresdner and Deutsche banks. A spokesman for the bank announced it "regrets most deeply injustices that occurred."

Other countries which have or will soon be appointing commissions and/or completing reports on Nazi gold transactions are Belgium, Brazil, Canada, Estonia, Latvia, Lithuania, and Poland. The latter is working on legislation to enable those whose property was seized to reclaim it or receive some compensation.

Nevertheless, though much is being attempted, much remains to be done. As the millennium comes into view, many survivors awaiting recompense have already died while others are at the end of their lives. More die with every passing day. They and their heirs have waited half a century for the world to pay attention and, from the conscience of humanity, make proper restitution.

The time to act must be now, if justice so long delayed is finally not to be denied.

APPENDIX:
THE OFFICIAL LIST OF DORMANT
ACCOUNTS IN SWISS BANKS

The following pages contain the names of some 6,500 people to whom dormant assets are owed and can be proven as having been deposited at a bank in Switzerland prior to May 9, 1945—two days after Nazi Germany surrendered to end World War II in Europe and a day after V-E Day.

U.S. officials of the State and Treasury Departments in Washington, D.C. had demanded nothing less than full disclosure of names of Holocaust victims and of other Jews who were lucky enough to have avoided Nazi German captivity in countries overrun by Hitler's hordes, and who had deposits in Swiss banks prior to the end of World War II.

In August, 1997, the Swiss Federation of Banks— urged on by government officials, issued a list of some 6,500 depositors whose accounts had no activity in the postwar era. Thanks must also be given to the Volcker Committee, formerly known as the Independent Committee of Eminent Persons. The organization was created persuant to an agreement between international Jewish organizations and the Swiss banks on May 2, 1996. The Volcker Committee had charged three international auditing firms with identifying Swiss banks that held the dormant assets belonging to thousands of victims of Nazi persecution.

Over the next year, hundreds of bank employees searched through archival material and ultimately produced a list that came from 123 banks in Switzerland that reported

74,496 dormant assets of Swiss customers and customers of unknown nationality and domicile. However, only 6,500 names indisputably represent Holocaust victims and their heirs.

"Dormant" means that, on what the banks know today, the published assets have been inactive at least since that May date listed above. The Swiss Bankers Association offered this explanation about the way dormant accounts are defined: "Assets for which the bank has not received any communication from the customer or his/her holder of power of attorney since May 9, 1945, which would have been recorded in the files or resulted in an account movement, are considered dormant. Examples of such communications are deposits, withdrawals, or asset management orders. Annual interest payments made by the bank are not considered to be a customer contact."

Technically, under the guidelines set down by the Swiss Federal Banking Commission, banks are required to preserve transaction documents for 10 years. After that period of time, the banks "usually destroy the transaction documents with which they would have been able to determine the last customer contact."

How the accounts of depositors who'd done business with Swiss banks prior to May 9, 1945, were preserved was not explained.

The Swiss Bankers Association recommended that those wishing to obtain further information if their names appear on the list of approximately 6,500 dormant account holders or their survivors, to get in touch with the Swiss banks' American representatives:

Ernst & Young LLP
c/o D.A. Services
P.O. Box 1880
Radio City Station
New York, NY 10101-1880

List of Dormant Accounts

July List of Dormant Accounts

Aalberts, R. Joh.
Acgar, Imdat
Acquadro, Joseph and Henri
Adaïr, Ms
Adam, Herbert
Adleaic, Juro
Adler, Klara
Agatstein, David
Agence Luxembourg Tour.
Agnew-Marriage-Stiftung
Agop Hatcherian
Ahrendt, Henri Hermann Georges
Aisenstadt, Aba
Aisimann, Joe
Akopiantz, Siméon
Alde, Olimpio
Alexandrescu, Titus
Alibaux, Henri
Alimanestianu, Virgil
Allaerts, H R
Allard, Elisabeth
Almosnino Banca
Alonso-Garcia, Valentin
Alsace Editions
Alstaetter, George
Altenloh, Erich
Altenloh, Richard
Altschul, Walter F.
Amandruz
Amard, Georges Louis
Ambroise, Pierre
Amerhauser Gmbh
Ammann, Johann
Ammann Dr., H.L.
Amrein, Ludwig
Amsler, André
Andlauer, Pierre and Betty
Andlauer, Prosper

André, Paul and Marie and Gilbert
Angeloff Dr., Stephan
Angles, Robert
Annsier, J.E.
Annsin, Karl
Antoniades, Euphemie
Anzile, Hugo
Arbeiter Krankenunterst. Verein
Archainbaud, Joseph and Clotilde
Arioli, Paolo
Arlen, Louis
Arlen, Marie
Armand, Roger
Arnheim Dr., Rudolf
Arnold, Charles
Arnold, Ida
Arnoux, Jean and Marguerite
Aronow, Gillel
Arthaud, Benjamin and M. Th.
Asaka, Mitsuro
Asanoski, Asan
Aslan Nessim
Aslangul, G. Mr.
Asmis Dr., Rudolf
Auberger
Aubron-Guérin, Odette
Audibert, Jean Marcel and Claire
Auge, Juan
Augusto, Maria
Auschlager, Paul
Axelrod, Emma Ernestine
Aynen, Ruhr
Bacchetta, Adolfo
Bachmann, A.H.
Bachrach, Wilhelm
Bachschmidt, Alfred
Baierl, Theresia
Bailly, Max
Baldensperger, Auguste and Madeleine
Ballif, Henri
Balog, Jacques

Balthasar, Waldemar
Baltic India Rubber Company
  Quadrat
Baltzinger, Frédéric and Maria
Baptault, Andre and Anne-Marie
Bär, Ernesto
Baranger, Jacques
Baranski, M.C.
Barbé, André Louis
Barbisin, Ortenillo
Baron, Albert
Barrios Y Aparicio De Alcala
  Galiano, Maria
Barth, Anna
Bartos, Ladislaus
Bärtschi, Walter
Barut, M-T and Léon
Bas Dr., Otokar and Berta
Baselli Dr., Ant.
Basin, Antoinette
Bassaget, Augusta
Bassols Y Olivar, Inès
Baud, Hyacinthe
Baudou, Pierre
Bauer, Theresa W.C.
Bauer, Willi
Bauer & Co.
Baumann, Georg
Baumann, René
Baur, Melanie
Bavinchove Van, Pierre Adrien and
  Désirée
Beaucarnot, Marcel and René
Becher, Luise
Becker Dr., Erich
Beer, Frédéric
Beger, Mathilde
Belajewskaja, Natalie
Belisha, Maurice
Bellejame De, Joseph and Yvonne
Bellion, Madleine
Beneck, Yvonne

Benes, Otto and Ida
Beppu, Setsuya
Bérard, Henri
Bereciartua Y Benedicto De, Luis
Bergel, Egon
Berger, William
Bergès, Paul
Berkeley-Calcott, A. Mr.
Berlinger, Elisabeth
Berlitzer, Olga
Berlitzer, Valeria
Bernard, Pierre
Bernett, Heinrich
Bernier, Georges Marie
Bernier, Joséphine
Bernis Comas, Alberto
Berolzheimer, Herta
Berreteaga, Maria
Berry, Carl
Berta, Gabriel
Berthold, Paul
Bertuck, Erich
Bethusy-Huc, Albrecht and
  Anastasia
Bezhani, Erifili
Bezirkssparkasse Gailingen
Bhusch, M.
Bianchi, Umberto
Bienger, Ernie
Bikélas, Dimitri
Billing, Henriette
Bilteryst, Jacques-Jean
Binder, Fredo
Birkel, Gustave
Bitterlin, Jules André and Louise
Blackmer, Kaja Andrea Karoline
Blanc, Berthe
Blanc, Marcel M.
Blanchard, Alice
Blank, Camilla
Blank, Herrmann
Blank Dr., August

Blatter, Lucie
Blech, Charles Emile
Bliznakoff, Nicolas M.
Bloch, Albert
Bloch, Lea
Bloch, René
Blum, Otto
Bluntschli-Meissner, Olga
Bock, Wolfgang
Bodenehr, Adolph Albert
Bodenheim Dr., Herbert
Bodenmann, Giovanni and
    Josephine
Boér De Dr., Alexis
Boerris, Werner
Boeswillwald, Noémi
Bogdan, Cedo
Bogdanowski, David
Böhlen, Alfred
Böhn, Kaare H.
Boissonnade, Max
Bonnardel, Georges-Christian
Boral, Stanislaw
Bordas Vidal, Antonio and
    Salvador
Borgeaud, Denise
Borselli, Marina
Bosch, Adolf
Boskocits, Alice and W.
Boss, Hugo
Bossard, Marcello
Bosshard, Louis Jakob
Bottema, Marie
Boucher, Célina
Boucheras, Jules-Joseph
Boullaire, Robert
Bourdil, Francois-Fernand
Bousquet, Henri
Bouza, Jose
Boyer, Carmen
Brack, Elise
Braegger, Joseph Heinrich

Brahms, Ernst
Brand, Julius
Brauer, Lina
Braun
Braun, Lina
Bräunel, Walter E.
Braunwald, Jean
Bredow, Edith M.O.
Breitel, Edgar
Brender, Gaston
Brest-Dufour, Raymonde and
    Jeanne
Brewster, Elisabeth Imogen
Breynat, Georges and Jeanne
Briand, Jacques Pierre Victor
Bricmann, Christ.
Brisset, Paul and Juliette
Broca, Jean
Broch, Laura
Brockhaus F.A.
Brod Dr., Isidor
Brodsky, H-Jakob
Brolis, Antonia
Brubaker, Robert S
Brückner, Leonard
Brun, Robert
Brunel, Else
Brunner, Luise
Brustlein, Ch. Ms.
Brylinska, Madeleine
Büchi, Elise Louise
Buehler, Edith
Buergi, Ernest
Bullough, John Martin
Bünzli, Richard
Burchhardt, Friedrich
Burdin, Henri
Buresch, Karl Maria
Buschmann, Paul
Cabiglio Dr., Bernardo and Elise
Caetani Di Bassiano, Marguerite
Cairoli, Giovanni

Cakic, Uros
Calafell Y Adroer, Ana and Ignacio
    and Jose O.
Calderon, Francisco
Caracciola Di Brienza
Carey, Amy
Carmen Societate Anonima
    Romana Pentru Transporturi
    Int./Maritime
Carmi, Elisabeth
Carneiro, Jesus Manuel
Carnot, Jean
Carraud, Paul
Carrel, Maria
Carrel, Marius
Carrier, Antonin and Clotilde
Carter Co. SA
Cascardi, Francesco
Catenazzi, Raphael
Cattaneo Dr.
Caubet, Renée and Louise
Cèrmik Dr., Boerivoj
Chalbaud Y Errazquin, Manuel
Chamayou, Léon and Thérèse and
    Antoinette
Chambre, Jeanne
Chamelet, Jeanne
Chapulut, Michel
Charassouchin, Aron Henri Arkady
Chastel, Germaine
Chaudey, Alfred and Anne and
    Pierre
Chavanis, Maurice
Cheize-Alby, Wanda
Chièze, Marie
Christoyianaki, Iphigenie
Ciampi, Angelo
Cibiel, Ernestine
Clapes Bauer, Julita
Cohnstaedt, Hans Jakob
Cohnstaedt, Ludwig and Rosa
Cohnstaedt, Wilhelm

Colin, Eugénie
Colls, Yves-Jacques
Commerce Universal Establ
Conceiçao, Salvador
Connor, Elsa
Conrad, Carla Valérie Lilli
Constans, Paul
Constantinesco, Lydia
Constantinesco, Marie
Constantinescu, Nicolae N.
Cosserat, Jacques and Pierre
Courtial, Eugénie
Courtial, Rudolf
Coutils, Louis
Couturier, L.
Cozon, Edouard
Cozon, Jane
Crepelle, André and Georges
Crescitz, Jean and Madeleine
Cretien, O.and G.
Cretin, Robert Aristide
Cretius, O.and G.
Crnadak, Milivoj
Croset, Helene
Cruz, Antonio
Curé De La Métropole
Cymbalisty, Elsa
Cyprien-Fabre, Marcel and
    Lucienne
Czerkasow, Pawel
Czychi, Eberhard
D'Amphernet, Michel
d'Andigne and De Langle
    Marquise, Olivier
D'Armagnac, Marguerite Marie
d'Arunau De Pouydraguin, Louis
    Marie Gaston and Jean Marie
    Arnaud
D'orville, Renée
Dall, Jörgen
Dallet Dr., Rafael
Danes, Arthur

Dariel, Madeleine
Darragh, John
Dassetrezel, Marie
Daubron, Henri
De Acevedo, Maria Adelia
De Bardi Baronesse, Adelgonde
De Bourbon
De Bellescize, Georges
De Bertrand De Vaulx Vicomtesse,
Thérèse
De Bizien Du Lézard, Guillemette
De Blouay, M.A.
De Bondeli, Albert
De Bony Des Egaux, Leon and
Marie-Louise
De Chasseloup-Laubat, Louis and
Marie Louise
De Chateauneuf, Nouthsaria
De Chavagnac Comte, Xavier
De Chomel, Félix
De Costantini, Franklin
De Crescenzo, Carlo
De Dorlodot Baron, Albert and
Charles
De Escoriaza Y Aurrecoechea
Viuda De Remes, Maria
Joaquina and Ines
Nemesia
De France, Henri
De Galindes, Maude
De Glatigny, Comtesse Josson, J.
and L.
De Gouvea, Nabuco
De Gregori, Guiseppe
De Guichen-Veillard Comtesse
De Jannez, Bertrand
De Jong Zgg
De La Rochefouclaud, Marguerite
De La Sablière, Marguerite Marie
Anna Louise
De La Tour Maubourg, Anne
Louise Marie

De Lafont La Marquise, Charlotte
De Luppé De Cosse Brissac
Vicomtesse, Anne Marie
Mathilde Françoise
De Maillard, Pierre and Jean and
Marie Caroline
De Malet Comtesse De Tanouarn,
Madelaine Marie Pauline
De Marisy
De Martinez, Maria
De Matas De Nicolau, Luisa
De Menthon, Franç. Bernard
Marguerite Marie
De Montety, Hélène
De Namuroy, Jean
De Palma, Raffaele
De Potestad, Maria Eugenia
De Rodat, Adrien and Fides and
Guy
De Rougemont, René
De Saint-Marc, Henri and Andrée
De Salignac Fénelon, Hélion and
Jean
de Sayve, Olivier
De Talhouet, Comte and Comtesse
Alain
De Tanfani Di Montalto, Emilia
De Vaufreland Vicomte, Louis
De Villiers De La Noue, Jean
De Vogue, Jean
De Vulitch, Douschan Pierre Paul
and Antoinette and Vladimir
Antoine
De Ybarra Y Lasso De La Vega,
José Maria
De Zubiria Y Garnica, Carmen
Declides Dite Rousselot, Jeanne
Defferrez, Georges Joseph and
Hortense Jeanne Ghislaine
Déjeant, Paule
Del Solar Y Maestre, Amparo
Delaplace, Fernand and Eugene

Engel, Camille and Marie-Augusta
Engelson, Libo
Enkel, Hermann
Ensesa Gubert, José
Epa Europaeische Patentanstalt
Eppinger, Hans and Georgine
Erias, Carlos
Erikson, Oscar
Ernst, Gertrude
Ernst Dr., Lucy H.
Escauriaza E Jpina, Antonio
Eser, Hermann
Etablissements John Kinsmen
    S.A.R.L.
Europaeische Marketing,
Fabrica De Spirt Jacques Brunner
    Succesori Josef Hemmerle & Co.
Fantauzzi, Crucien
Feder Dr., Alfred
Feenders Dr., Hugo
Feferberg, Salomon
Fehlmann, Jean
Fehringer, Helmut
Feigl, Rudolf
Feiling, Charles Emile
Feldstein, Clara and Avram
Fenner, Peter and Mariette and
    Patric
Fernandez, Fernando Escalante
Ferrère, Marie Valentine and
    Marguerite Maria and Maurice
    Guillaume
Festa, Nicola
Fetz, Edwin
Ficacci Dr., Luigi and Irène
Ficarra, Filippa
Filiol, Marcel and Marguerite
Finaz, Madeleine
Fischer, Emma
Fischer, Hermann
Fischer, J. M.
Fischer, Marie

Fischer, Marie H.
Fischer, Robert
Fischer Dr., Max
Fischmann, Norbert
Fizely, Tusi
Flachat, Pauline and Georges
Flachfeld, Jeanine-Fanny
Fleischmann, Paul
Foa, Marco and Hélène
Foch, Marguerite
Fock, Nadine
Forter, Boris
Fossard, Albert
Frammel Dr., Fritz
Franc, Lucien Antoine and Denise
    Marie Marcelle
Frank, Helmut
Frank Dr., Michael
Franke, Doris and Dagmar
Fränkel, Karl J.
Fraternale, Pietro
Freire Ferrer, Eugenio
Frelon, Madeleine
Frey, Francesco
Friedel, Anna
Friedel, Augusta
Friedel, Auguste
Friedman, Rejla
Frigge, Ottilie
Frlaig, Albrecht
Froehlich, Otto
Frübe, Gertrud
Fuchs, Elsa
Furlaud, Maxime
Fürst, Fritz
Gadgebowsky, Alexander
Gafenco, Blanche
Gaillard, Paul
Galan, Maria
Galicier, Albert
Galicier, Jean Marie Eugène and
    Frédérique

Hirtz, Theophile
Hiss, Alois
Hixson, Marie J.
Hocke, Walter
Hodgskin, T. Ellet and Mathilde C.
Hodler, Hans Peter
Hoechstetter, Louis
Hof, Eduard
Hofbauer, Erich
Hofmann, Alfred
Hofmann, Eugenie
Hoirie De Kowalski, Joseph
Holczer, Eduard
Holl, Charles
Hollas, Helmut G.
Homberger, P.
Hoorneman, Hanneke
Hopp, Erna
Hora, Richard
Hornain, Denise
Horvath Dr., Gabriel
Horvilleur, Simone Brunette
Horwitz, Hilary
Horwitz, Marie
Houdaille, Léon Charles and Jean
    René
Hryniszak, Michaela
Huart Y Benit, Ana
Hubert, Josip and Luni
Hudry Frères
Hunger, Leo
Hutt Dr., Charles
Iglauer, Stefan
Ikeda, Haruo
Illovy, Gustav and Ota
Imbert, Paul and Pierre
Imprimerie De La Lettre
    Enveloppe
Indig, Dr., E.
Iniguez De Montoya, Maria
    Victoria
Isarescu, Ulisse and Sofia

Isphording Dr., Franz
Ito, Kozo
Itzkin, Paul
Iwanicki, Stanislaw
Izaguirre Y Zuazo, Piedad
Jacquinet, Pierre and Marguerite
Jaffary, Charlotte Jeanne and
    Jeanne Eléonore
Jaggi, Johann
Jakimoff, L.
Jakimoff, Léonide
Jaksic, Antica
James, George William Carr
Janmot, Norbert
Jannez
Japy, Edgar
Japy, Fernand and Albert
Jaris, Millicent
Jasz, H.
Jasz, Helene
Jaumandreu Y Puig, Eugenio
Jauneaud, Marcel
Jeger, Peter
Jegi, Fritz
Jenner von, Marie
Jenni, Charlotte
Jimenez, Arnau
Jimenez Y Rosado, José
Job, Paula
Jochum, Mathias
Joest, John
Johnson, Georgia M.
Jones, Cyril R.
Jordan, F.W.
Jouet-Pastre, Frédéric
Juchert, Luise
Jucker, Hans
Judet De La Combe, Albert
Jula, Giuseppe
Jung, Emilie
Junghans, C.W.
Juricko, Matilda

Just Dr., Karl
Kahn, Louis
Kainer Prof., Margret
Kallenbach, Carl
Kammer, Christian
Kammer Brüder Textilindustrie Ag
Kammerer, Emma
Kampmann, Ernest
Kampmann, François
Kampmann, Susanne
Kanayama, Masahide
Kappeller, Emil and Laura
Karaniewich, Fedko
Karner, Anton
Karrer, Olga
Kasapyan, Araksi
Katz, Jacob
Katzenstein, Paul
Kauffmann, Grethe
Kaufmann, René
Kaufmann, Stéphanie
Kaulbach, Rose Marianne
Kay, Louise
Kazak, Fuad
Kehrli, Margaretha
Kelpsch, Stanislawa
Kengelbacher, August
Kernstok, Gina
Kerschbaumer, Irmhild
Keser, August
Keser, Gerhard
Kessin
Kessler, Pierre
Khattar, Ghassan Toufic
Kiebler, Andreas
Kiefer, Thekla
Kien Dr., Georges and Antoinette
    and André
Kiene, Wilhelm
Kieninger Dr., Georg
Killy, Hilda
Klein, Charles and Marie

Klein, Jean and Olga
Klein Dr., Arthur
Kliche, Martha
Klimwieder, Josef
Klinovsky, Jan
Klopsel, Willy
Klotzsch, Otto and Luise
Kneisel Dr., G.
Knoch, Katharina
Knoth, Rudolf and Hilde
Kobi, Eduard
Koch, Georg
Koch, Katharina
Koch, Othmar
Koechlin, Pierre Charles
    Emmanuel
Koelliker, Guido
Koenig, Karl
Koeppern-Kenneth
Koerin, Hilda and Anna
Kolessa Lubka
Koller, Erna
Komorowsky, Xenia
Königswerther Inc. H.M.
Kornfeld Dr., J. (Mr.)
Kostelnhack, Camille
Kostrencic Dr., Nikola
Kowsman Dr., Srul
Kraatz, Friedrich
Kral, Karel
Kral, Leopold
Kramer, Oskar
Krämer, Ingeborg
Kratzel, Albert
Krausz Dr., Leo
Kress, Eleonora
Kretz, Rolf
Kreuker, Adolphe M.
Krizek Dr., Otto
Kroci, Nikola J.
Kroneberg, Lucie
Krüger Dr., Karl

Krukowski Prof. Dr., W. and H.
Krummenacker, Elise
Krupica, L
Kubler Dr., Conrad
Küderle, Fritz
Kuebler, Julie
Kuhn, Louis and Augusta
Kunen Dr., Aug.
Kunz, Jean and Rose
Kunze, Johanna
Kurfess, Emma
Kurmik, Ludwig
Kurz, Marcelle
Kytzia, Josef
Labesse, Georges
Labordère, Marcel and Jean and
    Marie and Luglien
Ladstätter, Peter
Laederich, René
Lagier, Georges
Laharrague, Léon
Laisné, Eugène and Claire
Lal, Mohan
Lambert, Jean
Lambert, Raoul
Lambert, Suzanne
Lamp Dr., Karl
Lampe + Co.
Lamy, Germaine-Marie
Lande, Kurt
Landmann, Colomba
Landmann & Söhner H. Ab
Landsberg, Richard and Hedwig
Landurin, Marie
Lang, Paul
Lange, Fritz
Langendorff, Franz J. and Margot
Langmartsang, Wachuck Samten
Lanza Filingeri, Maria
Lanza Filingeri, Stefano and
    Amalia
Laporte, Marie-Louise

Lardier, Hélène
Laric, Vilko
Larochette, Adrien
Larrea Y Celayeta, Antonio
Lartigue, Daniel
Laruelle, George-Louis and Marie
    and Roger
Lasser, M
Lassnig, Josefine
Laubbacher, A.
Laube, E.
Laucella, Cornelio
Laudon-Aguillon, Marie
Laur, Paul
Laurent, H. and J. and S.
Layer, Albert
Lazarevic, Todor
Lazarus-Waag, Mathieu
Le Blant, Robert
Le Guillou, Jeanne Marie
Le Vaillant De Glatigny Vicomte,
    Jean De Gibon
Leauté, André
Leauté, Henriette
Lebe, Gertrud
Leblane, Lucie
Leclaire, Caroline
Leclerc, André
Ledermann, Anna Maria
Ledoux, Octave
Legoux Arsène
Lehmann, Franz B.
Leitao, Jaime and Maria
Lejneff, Marguerite
Lenclud, Henri and Bernard
Leonhardt, Jeanne
Lervitzky De Aglaide
Lespabel
Lessmoellmann, Thea
Lestang, Paul and Thérèse and
    Solange
Leutelt Dr., Helmut

May, Percy B.
May, Renée
Mayer, Heinrich
Mazel, Marcielj
Mazzoli Menotti, Guiseppe
Mazzoli Menotti Son Excellence,
    Joseph
Meier, August
Meier, L. Sydberg
Meier, W
Meise, Waldemar
Mencos Y Bernaldo De Quiros,
    Mercedes
Mendaro Y Romero De Ybarra,
    Maria Josefa
Mendel, Nancy
Meneghini, Luigi
Menglane, Françoise
Menten Dr., Ernestine
Mercier Du Paty, Marquis De Clam
Merian, Ida
Merkau, Alfred
Metzger, Eugen
Meyer, Christiane
Meyer, E.O.
Meyer, Erika
Meyer, Michael
Meyer, Otto
Meyer, Paul
Meyer, Rolf F.
Meyer Berlin
Meyerhof, Felix
Meyeringh, H G
Meynial, Henry
Mezey, Véronika
Mezière, Victorine Susanne
Michel, Richemond Georges and
    O. (Ms) and Marguerite and
    Germain and Georgette
Michelsohn Dr., Michel I.
Michl, Darko
Miedreich Dr., Franz and Elisabeth

Mielka, Helena
Milicic Dr., Josip Sibe
Milleff Dr., Dimiter
Milleron, Eugène and Marguerte
Millet, François and Jeanne
Mincoff Dr., Nicola
Minichshofer, Ernst
Mock, Elisa
Moesle, J.
Moghadam, Léon
Moholy, Ladislaus
Moitroux, Jakob Hubert
Moll, Carl and Anna
Möllinger, Josef
Moncetz, Geneviève De
Moncorgé, Charles Roger
Monget, Marie
Mönius Dr.
Montel, Violetta La Baronne
Moos, Dominik
Moosbrugger, A
Mora, Anacleto
Morasso, Giovanni
Moreillon-Montadon, Suzanne
Morel De Foucaucourt, Henri
Moreno, Daniele
Morris, Elisabeth
Mortara, Giuseppe and Franco
Mosaureles, Rata
Mosciatelli, Luigi
Moscona, Henry and Henriette
Moser, Adolf
Mosimann, Alice
Moskovic, Felix
Moulierac, André
Moulierac, Madeleine
Moulin, Marie
Moyat, Antonin
Mueller, Alfred
Mueller, Anna Hedwig
Muersch, Ernest and Elisabeth
Muller, Alfred

Müller, Carol
Müller, Emil
Müller, Eugen
Müller, Fritz
Müller, Josef
Müller, Karl
Müller, Trude
Münch, Adolf
Mundt, Gustav
Munk, Klaus
Munnich, Plona V. Sesztina
Nagel, Rudolf
Nagu, Nicolaus
Nagy, Ladislaus
Najman, Nikola
Natkey, Maurice
Naulleau, Jacques Henri Olivier
  and Pauline Marie Désirée
Naumann, K.
Neculitza Von, Demeter
Neubauer, Paula
Neumayer, Rudolf
Neurath, Elfriede
Neussl Sel, Paul
Nice, Maria
Nicolau Gomez, Antinio and
  Alvaro and Luis and Mathilde
  and Carolina
and Gabriela and Dolores
Nicolopoulos, Georges
Nicolopoulos, Nico
Niederkorn, Andree
Niehans, Albert
Nieuwkerk, Annie
Niffenegger, Ernest
Nikolitch, Pedrag
Nilsson, Ragna
Nobel Dr., Lazlo
Noé, Helene
Noetinger, Paul and H.
Nogueira, Clementina
Noguier, François and

Marie-Thérèse
Nouradormikian, Souren
Novak, Wanka
Novo-Lory (Hoirie), Marie Louise
  Joséphine
Nv Nederlandsche Maatschappy
Oberländer, S.
Obrrutsheva, Aglaida
Ogneanoff, Savka
Oïffer, Yvonne and Aviator
Olivas, Jose
Omnifinance SA
Opielinska Dr., Helene
Oppenheim, Uwe Emil
Oprescu, Georges
Osio De, Rosarito
Osman, Babiker A
Oswald, Adolf
Otermin Y Huarte, Rafael
Ott, Camille
Ouvaroff, Catherine
Pacetti, Antoine
Pache, Catherine
Pagniez, Madeleine and Paul
Palaminy De Marquis, Frédéric
  Marie Samuel Eimar
Palivec, Vaclav
Panier Mgr.
Pantic, Milos
Papadopoulos, Konstantinos
Papazian, R. and Ebros R.
Pardany, Eduard
Pardcik, Vera
Pardon, Robert
Paris, Louise
Pariser Dr., Käthe
Parisot, Marguerite and Marcelle
Parmann, William J.
Parnegg, Hermann
Parnegg, Leopold
Paschoud, F. Ms.
Pastoukoff, Catherine

Rupf, Peter
Russo, Rosaria
Ruttkay, W.
Ruyer, Auguste and Marguerite
Sabani, Hajrula
Sabatino, Angelo
Sacher, Friedr.
Sachs, Ella
Sackheim, Hirsch
Sagerer, Hans
Sahuqué, Gabrielle
Saint-Martin, Denise
Saint-Martin, Pierre and Yvonne
Saitschner
Saladin, Gaston and Beatrice
Salerno, Rino and Calvisi Sannitic
Salhi, Fatima
Salmonowitz Dr., David
Salmson, Emile
Salti, Vitali J. and Rachel
Samain Dr., Henri
Samso, José
Sapountzoglou, Marika
Saurel, Ms.
Sauter, Fritz
Sautter, Jean
Savic, Donka
Sazy, Georges
Schaarschmitd, Friedrich
Schaedler, Katharina
Schaeffer, Gerhard
Schäfer, Lina
Schaller, André and Maxime
Schaller, Jules and Georges and
    Jean
Schatz, Albert
Schatzer, Eveline
Schatzmann, Alfred
Schatzmann, Marie
Schaudt, Karl Rolf
Schautt, Gottl.
Schayesteh Khan, Mahamed

Scheithauer, Emil
Schenker and Co
Scheps, H.
Scherb, Thérèse
Scherbak, Paula
Scherneck, Heinrich
Scheurer, Jean and Ivan and
    Suzanne Marie Pauline
Schiaffino, Laurent and Louise
Schiele, Olga
Schigert, Robert
Schiller, Adolf
Schilling, Manfred
Schirmer, Ludwig
Schittkowski, Harri
Schlesinger Dr., Karl
Schlie, Heinrich
Schlumberger, Paul and Georgette
Schmid, J.
Schmid, Paul
Schmidt, Bruno
Schmidt, Charles
Schmidt, G.
Schmidt, Gernot
Schmitz, H.
Schneider, Hans
Schneider, Walter
Schoen, André
Schönberg, Eric
Schönholzer, Franz
Schrab, Paula
Schreiber, G.
Schriefel, Anny
Schubert, Henri and Louis
Schulenberg, Friedrich
Schuller, Joseph
Schulmann, Hélène
Schultz, Ernst
Schulz, Otto
Schulz, Robert
Schützle, Frieda
Schwaiger, Walter

Schwarz, Patricia
Schwarzkopf, Ernst and Ida
Schweizer, Paula
Schwendener, Walter and Suzanne
Seemann, F.
Seevagen, Anne-Marie Léonie
Seidl, Hilda
Seiffert, Elise
Seinnberger, H.U.
Seix Y Faya, Francisco
Selchert, Theodor Carl
Selimi, Eyup
Sembel, Guillaume
Semis, Heinrich
Serveux, Franziska
Severin, Kurt
Seya, P.
Seyd, Charles
Sgalitzer Prof. Dr., Max
Siahou Barouck, Hrahim
Sik, Helene
Silbiger Dr., S.
Simic, Stanoje
Simon, Antoine
Sinauer, Florine
Sinegger, Helene
Singer, Paula
Sirmois, Koudis
Sittig, Karl
Sivrilin, A.
Skampas, Wasilios
Skinner, Shirley Esther
Skoeld, Giovanni Alessandro
Slavonische Kohlen-Handels Ges.
    Kaufmann & Co
Slobotzki, Erna
Slotnarin, Wilhelmine
Smith, Alan John R.
Smith Dr., J.
Soc. Caradium
Société Etablissement Rios
Societe Pour Le Developement

Soden Von, Adele
Sohler, Francesco
Soloweitschik, Wladimir
Somazzi, Carlo Gabriele
Somazzi, Vincenzo
Sonnenberg, Alfred
Sosnik, Anton
Soullier, Louis
Soupault, Robert
Soyer, Claire
Spaeth, Luigi
Sperber, Max
Sperling Dr., Teodor and Peppi
Spiro, Bruno and S.
Spoerry, Henri and J.
Sraffa, Angelo
Stadelhofer, Adolf
Stäheli, Eugen
Staiger-Schaefer, Lydia
Stambach, Victor
Stanesco, Lucie
Starke, Frank
Statescu Prof., Victor
Staub, Emile
Staub, Pauline
Stecker, Maria
Stefan, Alois
Stefanoff Jr., Sava
Steffanizzi, Giuseppe
Stehle, Lucie
Steil, Anna
Steinbrugge, Camilla
Steinbrugge, Elsa
Steinlin, Robert
Stéphanovitch, L.V.
Stewart, D. M.
Stierle, Hilda
Stifel, Asta
Stiffler, K. and L.
Stoller, Samuel
Stoopman-Glaser, A. J. M.
Stratmann, Carl

Ujj, Marie
Ummard, Minna
Ungar, Alexander
Universa Frankfurt
Unlimited Investments AG
Urban
Urquijo Y Aguirre, Tomas
Vajda, Armin
Vajda Dr., Andreas
Valade, André and Simone and
    Marie-Louise
Valdji, Tibere C.
Valkay Von, Bartholomeus
Van, Necati
Van Diepeningen, Franz
Van Loo, Nicholas E.
Van Versen, William
Vazou, Marie
Veberic, Joseph
Venzmer, Federico
Vereinigte Rebanlagen
Vesely, Marie
Vestergaard, Jens
Vetter, Hubert
Viellard, Albert
Vigo, Clara
Vilain, Jean and Marthe and
    Marguerite
Villandy, Albert
Villarino, Jose
Villiers De La Noue, Yvonne
Vischoff, Hoirie
Visconti Graf, Francesco
Viuda De Lachambre, Maria
Vogel, Berthe
Vogel, Franz
Vogel, Manfred
Vögeli, Jos. Ed.
Vögeli, Oscar B.
Vogl, Karl
Von Avenarius, Theodor
Von Dem Bussche Freiherr, D.

and Eleonora
Von Dirsztay Dr. Baron, Andor
Von Dorsten, Wilhelm
Von Drabich, Günther
Von Franken-Sierstorpff Graf,
    Clemens
Von Glasenapp, Käthe
Von Hibler, Gedeon
Von Langen, Ed.
Von Luterau, Marie
Von Münnich, Aladar
Von Ow, Wilhelm
Von Sonntag, Eugenie
Von Ujszaszy, Stefan
Von Vacchiery, Ida H.
Von Weiss, Ferdinand
Vorlaender, Hans
Vriesman Dr., Emilie
Vulitch De, Douchan and
    Antoinette and Vladimir
Wadd, Kenneth T.
Wagner, Hans
Wähler, Konrad Reinhard
Wähler, Max Bruno
Walch, Stefanie
Waldenmeyer, Robert
Walder, Wilhelm
Walliser, L.
Wallner, Johann
Walser-Wald & Cia
Walther, Marcel
Walz, Albert
Walz, Hermann and Josefine
Wanner, Lilly
Wasilewski Dr., W.
Wassmer, Anna
Watelle, Donat Paul
Watson, Rupert C.
Wattenwyl von, Louis
Wattenwyl von, Reinhard
Weber, Jean
Weber, Renée

Weber, Stephan Emanuel
Weber Dr., Walter
Weick, Jeanne
Weidenhaus, Lucie
Weil, S.H.
Weill, Léon
Weinreich, B.O.
Weiss, Emil H.
Weiss, Louise
Weiss, Robert
Wekerle, Hermann
Wendland Dr., Hans
Werner, Lisbeth
Werner, Theodor
Wertheiner, Frieda
Wessel De Shaw, Alice
Wessing, Rud.
Wetter, Max
Wickswat, H. Ms.
Widerkehr, Louis-Pierre and Léna
Widmann, Frieda
Widmer, Jacob
Wiener, Henry
Wiese, Otto
Wilhelm, Marie
Wilkils
Wilski, Stefan
Winckler, Theo
Winkler, Théo and M.
Winth, Maria
Wintuhalter, Leo
Wirbel, H.
Wirth, Friedrich
Wisiak, Helene
Wittlich, Joh.
Wittlin, Vreneli
Witzner, Ladislaus
Wöhrle, Juliette
Wolde, Ludwig

Wolf, Emil
Wolf, Susi
Woschnagg, Max
Wubbe, Constance
Wygnanki, Bruno
Xenakis, Nicolas J
Yannaghas, Eustache and Eugénie
Ybarra Y Lopez De Calle, Carmen
Yebra, Luis
Yellen, Fern
Yildirim, Ahmed
Zaeppfel, Louis and Jean and
    Jeanne
Zamolo, Umberto
Zampaglione, Joseph
Zander, Jane Muriel
Zehnder Dr., M.
Zehne, Herta
Zeising, E. and H.
Zelinescu, Victor
Zeller, Hortense
Ziebarth, Gerd
Ziegler, Elisa
Zimmermann, Fred
Zimmermann, René
Zimmermann, Richard
Zollino, Eva
Zoltan, Ella
Zorc, Vladimir
Zoubareff, Alexander
Zu Eltz Gräfin, Sophie
Zuber, Ernest and Olga
Zuber, Louis
Zucker, Louise
Zuckerberg, Max
Zuggal, Artur
Zürcher Dr., K.
Zvibel Dr., Jean
Zwick Dr., Karl G.

**October List of
Dormant Accounts**

A Rocha, Federico
Abati, Luigi
Abrial, Henry & Ellise
Acikalin, Hadidjé Djevad
Adam, Franz
Adam, Maria
Adenegg, Josef
Agatensi, Maria
Agid, Bernard
Agid, Robert
Agostini, Natalie
Agosto, Angelo Silvio
Ahr, Anny
Aichinger, Théo & Ginette
Aichmiger, Karl
Albertanti, Gianni
Albertella, Gisella
Albietz, Adolphe
Albrecht, Paula
Albuquerque De, Lezina A.M.
Alessandri, Josef
Alhadeff, Vittorio & Renia
Aliprandi, Joseph
Allan, Germain-Marie-A.
Allegrini, Catterina
Allix, O.
Allo, Edmund
Alterini, Luisa
Altweg, Hans
Amann, Albrecht
Amberg, Anita
Amberg, Marlies
Amighetti, Alfredo
Amman, Käthe
Ammann, Emma
Ampenoff, Wesevolod
Amrein, Marie
Amrhein, Marie
Anders, Alice

Andreis, Renata
Andreu, Maria
Andrews, Harald
Andreys, Marcel
Angenbrand, Karl
Angerer, Franz Joseph
Angeretti, Ambrosiano
Anibas, Luise
Anselm, Josephine
Aprell, August
Aquilini, Gerolamo
Arheit, Walter
Aries, Eugène & Delia
Arioli, Dorine
Arm, Charles
Armbruster, Ernst
Armser, Armand
Arnaud, Laure
Arnold, Joseph
Arnold, Johannes
Arnold, Therese
Arnoux, Henri
Arvengas, Gilbert & Simone
Aspesi, Gianni
Au von, Emma
Aubes, Louis
Auburtin, Alfred Louis Auguste
Aufrichtig, Salomon
Augsburger, Jacob
Aule, Edouard
Aurieux, Marcel
Ausset, Jules
Autenrieth, Annemarie
Avout d', Guy
Azoulay, Mouchi
Babey, Joseph
Babin, Marcelle
Bäbler, Yvonne & Lucien
Bacchetti, Gino
Bach, Martha
Bach, Carl
Bach, Rosa

Bachellerie, Alexis
Bachmann, Maria Veyelise
Bachmann, Elise
Bachmann, Karl
Bader, Henri & René
Badetz, Albert & Berthe
Badina, Lorenzo M.
Baechler, Hugo
Bagland, Pierre & Maurice
Baier, Irene
Baier, Liselotte
Balandier, Clara
Baldo, Elvira
Ballay, Christine
Balluff, Wilhelm
Balmer, Mina
Balocca, Robert
Balsamova, Helene
Balser, Georg
Bamert, Rudolf Gregor
Banaconza, Dante
Banaszezik, Stanislaus
Bandelier, Rosine
Bandelier, Henriette
Banderet, Ilise
Banderet, Henri Charles Louis
Bangerter, Hugo Ernst
Banholzer, Ernest
Bannwarth, Felix
Bano de, Karl
Bantel, Hermann
Bantle, Johanna
Banz, Emma
Barbaroux, Vincent
Barbieri, Hans
Barbieri, Alice
Barbisch, Eduard
Barmasse, Louis
Barnett, Constance
Barp, Fioravanti
Barrera, Pablo
Barret, Gustave

Barrett, Anna
Barschz, Marie
Barth, Pauline
Barth, Hans
Barthelet, Julie
Barthelet, Philomene
Barthelet, Marie
Bärtschi, Henri
Barufini, Maria
Barzucas, Evanghel
Basler, Anna
Bass, Maria
Basset, Adèle
Bassino, Jean-Claude
Bastaroli, Esilda Catherine
Batistella, Imelda
Battier, Sophie
Battistolo, Louis Joseph
Baud, Alexandrine
Baud, Emmy
Bauer, Karl
Bauer, Carl
Bauer, Simon
Baulet, Annette
Baumann, Emil
Baumann, Johanna
Baumann, Leonie
Baumann, Leo
Baumann, Kreszentia
Baumann, Marie
Baumer, Claude
Baur, Elisabeth
Baur, Albert
Baur, Cresenz
Baur, Honorine
Baus, Gerd
Bautz, Hedwig
Baverel, Francis
Baverel, Joseph & Maria
Baveres, Marie-Cesarie-Lina
Baveres, Marie-Sophie-Luisa
Bavezel, Constance Marie

Bayer, Olga
Bayon, Los.
Bazelli, Eugénie
Bazialli, Rosina
Bazzotti, Libero
Bebie, Elise
Beccarelli, Giuliana
Béchaux, Cécile
Bechter, Anton
Beck, Marie
Beck, Ottilie
Becker, Juliane
Becker, Christian
Bedetti, Carmen
Beer, Fritz
Beffroy de la Greve de, Blanche
Begagon-Aronson, Simon
Beggiato, Hedwig
Beghini, Humbert
Beglé, Frida
Beguin, Paul & Georgette
Behrend, Melanie
Behringer, Sofie
Behrmann, Frédérique
Beledinty, Rene
Bellasio, Bertha
Bellasio, Giulia
Bellasio, Paola
Bellenot, Marthe
Belli, Angelo
Belli, Elena Maria
Bellini, Caroline
Belmore, Herbert W.
Benaglio, Guido
Benecke, Hans
Benedetti, Hans & Luise
Benedetti, Ida Costanza
Benedikt, Ruth
Benkovic, Ivo
Benlian, Haig T.
Benlian, Meguerditch T.
Benz, Pauline

Bercowitsch, Alex & Anna
Berger, Gottlieb
Berger, Rosalie
Berger, Frieda
Berger, Louise
Berger van, Erika
Bergmann, Herta
Bergwald, Jules
Berlinka, Simon
Bernard, Julia
Bernard, Marie-Antoinette
Bernard, Marthe Henriette
Bernardinello, Dino
Bernasconi, Bianca
Bernasconi, Auguste
Bernecker, Anna
Bernezzo di
Bernhardt, Julius
Bernhart, Franz
Bernigau, Theobald
Bernuzzi, Ismaele
Berrard, Pelagie
Berthet, Marie-Louise
Berthold, Kurt
Bertle, Rosalie
Bertolini, Carl
Bertsch, Bertha Alice
Bertschinger, Robert
Berwanger, Berta
Besancenet De, Pierre
Besson, Georges
Besson, Léon
Besson, Lucie
Bethge, Ed.
Bethke, Paul
Betschler, Klara
Betz, Mathilde
Beurdeley, Marcel & André
Bey, Lucie Jeanne
Beyerbach, Ludwig
Biagini, Luigi
Bianchi, Giacomo

Bianchi, Teresa
Bichelkistner, Johann
Bichsel, Francois
Biedermann, Frieda
Biederpost, Martha
Biering
Biermann, Helene
Bierwirth, Maria
Biétry, Emile
Bigger, Mathis
Bigler, Ida
Bilek, Karoline
Billian, Anna
Billig, Marie Nicolle
Billod, Cesar
Billod, Ernest
Billod, Felix Alcide
Billod-Morel, Clarisse
Billois, Joseph
Bina, Enrico
Binda, Giuseppina
Binder, Ida
Binetruy, Esba
Binetruy, Hector
Binetruy, Regine
Binova, Marie
Biotti, Rosa
Birchler, Lucie
Birmelin, Karl & Adele
Birnstiel, Elisabeth
Bisasson, Leonie
Bischoff von, Hilda
Bitterlin, Paul
Bittner, Hugo
Bizzozzero, Orlando
Bjurstroem, Gust
Blachere, Josephine-Louise
Blahüschek, Marie
Blaikner, Julie
Blain, Ernest
Blanc, Paul & Madeleine Marie
    Françoise

Blanchard, René
Blanchard, Jean Louis
Blauel, Albert
Blazy, Felix
Bleck, Margaretha
Bleicher, Albert
Blenk, Marianne
Bloch, Max Albert
Bloch, Fernand
Blocher, Catharina
Blotzheimer, Ernst
Blouet, Georges
Blum, Frieda
Blum, Nathan & Emile
Blum, Emil
Bobilier, Louis
Bobillier, Victorine Adelaide
Bocat, Marguerite
Bocat, Odette
Bocquenet, Solange
Bodenheimer, Lidy
Bödler, Anna
Boegli, Elsa
Boero, Leo
Boeswald, Marie
Bogdany von, Ilona
Böglin, Emil
Bohle, Andres
Bohler, Emilie
Böhm, Heinrich
Bohneberg, Ursula
Böhnert, Theodor
Bohny, Karl Maximilian
Böhringer, Anna
Boibessot, Henri Sylvain
Boillon, Lucien
Boillot, Mariette
Boillot, Julie
Boiron, Charles & Antoinette
    Jeanine Elisabeth
Boiteau, Edouard
Boldrocchi, Adele

Bolgar, Georg
Bollack, Germaine
Bolle-Vermot, Aline
Bolletti, Giovanni Battista
Bolliger, Hans
Bolognini, Margot Marlene
Bonaparte, Lucien
Bonardi, Vittorio
Boncourt, Maria
Bondioni, Franz
Bonetti, Benedetto
Bonhomme, Louis
Bonifazi, Joh.Gg.
Bonifazi, Joh.Gg. & Barth.
Bonisson, Germaine
Bonizzi, Adolfo
Bonjean, Marie
Bonjour, Marie Emma
Bonnet, Aline
Bonnet, Gustave Marie
Bonneton, Jean
Bono del, Alberto
Bontadi, Hermine
Bontognali, Edi
Bontognoli, Bruno
Bopp, Philipp August
Böpple, Else
Bordet, Joseph
Borel, Jean
Borell, Eugen
Borga, Edi
Borloz, Jean Eduard
Born von, Elisabeth
Born von, Ruth
Bornstein, Lora
Borsch, Dora
Bortoli de, Nella
Bösch, Maria
Boschi, Ettore
Bosisio, Stefania
Bossard, Nina
Bosse, Hugo

Bosser, Michel
Bosshardt, Sophie
Bottaro, Carlo Giovanni
Boucher, Louis & Marie
Bouchet, Fabien
Bouclier, Bernard
Bouclier, Marie
Boudet, H. & C. & G. & G.
Boudsdruw, Guert
Bouilloux-Lafont, Jacques Louis
    Marcel
Boukalova, Vlasta
Bourdin, Marcel
Bourgeois, Marie
Bourgeois, Maria
Bourgeois, Hortense
Bourgeois, Hermine
Bourgoin, Emile
Bourgoin, Lucie
Bourlot, Marie
Bourquard, Pierre
Bourquin, Clara
Bourquin, Edouard
Bourru, Georges Etienne Antoine
    Mario & Lucie
Bourry, A.
Boussel, Elise Mathilde
Boussinot, Jean-Abel
Boutelier, Margrit
Boutet, Marguerite Gilbrin
Boutherre, Lucien
Bouthiaux, Suzanne
Bouttelier, Margrit
Bouvet, Marie-Louise
Bouvier & Co.
Bovet, Emma
Bown, Humphrey & Herbert &
    Margherita
Boye, Heinrich
Bozo von, Andor
Bracchi, Pierre
Brack, G. Egon

Brack, Heinrich
Braendlein, R.
Brand, Marie
Brand, Käthi
Brandeis, Mathilde
Brandl, Georg
Brasching, Helene
Bratschi, Alfred
Bräuer, Erna
Braun, Andrée & Pierre
Braun, Eugenie
Braun, Mina
Bräuning, Georg
Brechbühl, Frieda
Brechbühl, Ernst
Brecht, Erna
Bredschneider, Gertrud
Breger, Otto
Breghin, Viktoria
Brégier, Georges
Brégier, Marcel
Brégier, Robert
Breguet, Robert
Bréguet, Louis Gustave
Breh, Aug.
Brehme, Anna
Brembilla, Josephine
Brembilla, Lina
Brendle, Emilie
Brenk, Arthur
Brenneisen, Marianne Lisa
Brenneisen, Albert
Brenner, Berta
Bretschneider, Helene
Brianti, Rosa
Brigel, Klara
Brin, Marie
Brinkhuizen, Julien
Brion, Camille
Brizzi, Eugenio Alfredo
Brizzi, Davide
Brocard-Pellet-Soret,

Stephanie Marie
Broccard, Jules
Brodbeck, Alice
Broggi, Carlo
Brombacher, Wilhelm
Brondel, Georges
Brondel, Henri
Brösamle, Ernst
Brown, Caroline E.
Bruché, A.
Bruckner, Jeanne
Bruderlein, Lucie
Bruederlin, Marcelle
Bruetsch, Gertrud Lina
Bruhwiler, Edwige
Brühwiler, Gertrud
Brumann, Sophie
Brunner, Klara
Brunner, Hedwig
Brunner, Thomas
Brunschwig, Marcelle
Brunswig, Paul
Brustio, Cesar
Buchegger, Sebastian
Bucher, Anny
Buck, Werner
Buck, Elisabeth
Buck, Bertha
Buelow, Ionna
Caan-Becker, Magda Minna
Cabrières, Renée & Yvonne
Cabrières de
Cabut, Marie
Cachelin, Yvette
Cacheux, Joséphine
Cadei, Giuseppe
Cadra, Giuseppina
Caffi, Umberto
Cagnoni, Francesca
Cairoli, Emilio
Cairoli, Rino
Calame, Marthe

Calame, Eugène
Calame, Charles
Calamia, Anton
Caldera, Josue
Calderari, Louise
Calmelet, Georges
Cammera, Catharina
Camporelli, Leo
Campos, Alfredo
Camps, Juan
Canali, Edith
Candrian, Caspar
Caneri, Rosa
Canot, Olga
Cantenazzi, Raphael
Cantoni, Jérémie
Capitani, Maria
Capoferri, Eliana
Caporali, Domenico
Cappeli, Carlo
Cappelletti, Flora
Caprara, Pierre & Lea
Caraban, Numa
Caravatti, Johann
Carbo' y Sanfelin, Esteban
Carboni, Marie
Carli de, Florindo
Carrara, Armando
Carulli, Natalina
Carulli, Romana
Casali, Livia
Casartelli, Angelo
Casartelli, Albertina
Caspari, Nataline
Cassard, Fernand
Cassis, Pierino
Castagna, Costante
Castelli, Marie
Castelli, Isolo
Catani, Stella
Catenazzi, Giovanni
Cattin, Emélie & Léa & Mathilde

Cattola, Alfonso
Cavallasea, Verena
Cavina, Bruno
Cecetto, Anton
Cemal, Huesnue Tary
Cenci, Franca
Centinara, Alessandro
Centmaier, Conrad Joh.
Ceresa, Bernardo
Ceruti, Ferdinand
Cesaro, Alice
Chabert, Suzanne
Chabloz, Jeanne
Châlon, Auguste
Champreux, Laure
Chaneck, Charles-Francois
Chanon, Julie
Chapoutot, Irma
Chapoy, Rene
Chapsal, G. & Georges &
    Geneviève Delepoulle
Charbonnier, Elisabeth
Chardar, Pierre
Chardon, Adrien Fernand
Chartoir, Caroline
Charvet Cuvelier, Marie
Chatelan, Emma
Chavannes, Léon
Chavarri, Benigno
Chavrolet, Anna
Cheneval, Joséphine
Chenus, Georges Frédéric
Chevassus, Marcle
Chevenement, Othilie
Chevillat, A.
Chiesa, Josephine
Chilton-Möri, Stefi
Chouillou, Marguerite
Choulon, Marcel & Misciz
    Françoise
Chour, Michel
Chrissoghelos, Andrei

Dalloz, Philippe
Dallyyegh, Oscar
Damelet, Eugene
Damien, Marie
Damur, Marie
Daneele, Gilbert
Dard, Marguerite
Dardel, Charles Eric
Dardel, Philippe
Daucourt, Marcel
Daudey, Edouard
Daufelt, Hans
Davidescu, Vasile
Davidovitch, Gregor
Däxle, Therese
Debaisieux, Raoul
Debove, Arsene
Deflorin, Louis-Henri
Deforge, Paulette & Jean-Lucien &
    Jacques & Elisabeth
Defossez, Willy
Degen, W.
Deirmendjoglou, Jean B.
Deisenhofer, G.
Deiss, Anna
Delacroix, Lea
Delacroix, Louis
Delagrange, Jacques
Delaurens, Elisa
Delbecchi
Deleule, Henri
Deleule, Marie
Deleule, Georges
Deleule, Michel
Dell'acqua, Carlo
Della-Torre, Elise
Delsol, Raoul
Demanche, Blanche
Demmel, Ursula
Demmler, Gottschalk Wilhelm
Denis, Fannelie
Denz, Josephine

Depierre, Claude
Depierre, Felix
Depierre, Marcelle
Desailloud, Roger
Desaules, Paul
Desforges-Meriel, Paul Aristide
    François Jean Clément
Deshayes, C.
Dessandier, Eugen M.
Dessaules, Clemence
Desserich, Anna
Dessert, Pierre
Deuticke, Hans
Deutsch, Robert
Devaux, Paul
Devos, Mathlide
Dick, Esther Sylvia
Dick, Louise Henriette-Renée
Dickstein, Elias
Didier, Henri
Diefenbacher, Ernst
Diehl, Augusta Gusta
Dietrich, Albert
Dietsche, Oscar
Diezel, Mary
Dihlmann, Gustav
Dilger, Lina
Dillat, Louise Gandérique
Dinki, Karl
Djeddah, Ezra Joseph
Djordejevic, Nenad
Dodbiba, Sokrat
Dogge, Anna
Dogwiler, Evelyn
Doillon, Gustave
Dold, Jacob
Dommann, Maria
Dommeyer, Mary
Donati, Maurice Louis
Donati, Alice
Donnebaum, Isidor
Donnet, Charles

Doormick, Rene
Dörler, Lina
Dornier, Clara
Dornier, Clara
Dornier, Leonie
Dornier, Ferdinand
Dornier, Fernard
Dornier, Marie
Dorsch, Heinrich
Doyon, Maria
Dracoulis, Calliope H.
Draghi, Pierre Auguste
Drake, Lily
Drechsel, Katherina
Dreher, Elsa
Dreher, Klara
Dreisbach, Anny
Drescher, Rudolf
Dreyer, Alfred
Dreyfus, Sylvain
Drouhot Avoué, Bernard
Drudi, Angelina
Dübendorfer, Hans
Dubois, Adele
Dubois, R. & E.
Dubois, Antoine Marie-Thimotee
Duca, Louis
Duchalek, Franz
Duchemain-Mauduit
Dückstein, Jety
Ducret, Marcel
Dufour, Germaine
Duguet, Paul André
Dühmig, Gustav
Dühring, Marie
Dumitrescu, Stefan G.
Dumm, Jakob
Dumont, Andrée
Dunarex SA
Dupont, Fauchette
Dupraz, Victor
Durand, Jeanne

Durig, Henri Emile
Durig, Louise
Durig, Helene
Dürnhamer, Anny
Dürst, Margaretha
Dürst, Rudolf
Duspaquier, Thierry
Dussauge, Auguste
Dustert, Karl
Duval, Albert
Duval, Agathe
Duvoisin, Robert
Dworack, Klara
Dyer, Mary-Elizabeth
Ebel, Bertha
Eberhard, Josephine
Eberle, Franz
Eberle, Karl
Eberlé, Agnès Elizabeth
Eblin, Paul
Ebner, Joseph
Ecabert, Georges
Ecclissiarchos, Demetre
Eckerle, Mina
Eckl, Betty
Edel, Rudolf
Edelmann, Frieda
Eder, Anna
Eggenschwiler, Jakob
Eggenspieler, Henri
Egger, Bertha
Eggli, Gottfried
Egler, Hans
Egli, Emma
Egli, Otto
Eglin, Alfred
Eglin, Marie
Eha, Theresia
Ehinger, Rosa Vinzenzia
Ehmann, Emma
Ehrecke, Emil
Ehrenzweig, Jeannette

Ehrlich, Minna
Eichhorn, Edda
Eichmeyer, Walther
Eichninger, Maria
Eichta, Ignace
Eickels von, Liselotte
Eidenbenz, Elise
Eiermann, Karl
Eisen, Valentin
Eisen, Hede
Eisinger, Hedwig
Elsässer, Armin
Emmel, Helene
Emmenegger, Christine
Ender, Franz
Enderlin, Hedwig
Endres, Ida
Engel, Paul
Engel, Jacques
Engeler, Theresia
Engelhardt, Elisabeth
Engelmann, O.
Engesser, Eduard
Engesser, Martha
Engler, Yvonne
Engler, Olga
Engler, Oscar
Enionin, Marguerite
Enoc, Marie
Enzler, Marie
Epstein, Rubin
Erb, Jakob
Erculiani, Giacomo
Eriesson, Nils Axel
Erne, Marie
Erne, Anna
Erny, Julia
Esposito, Jeanne
Eurisch, Frieda
Euvrard, Auguste
Fabbricotti, Maria
Faber, Marie

Fachinetti, Primo
Fader, Anny
Faé, Louis
Fagiano, Carolina
Fagschlunger, Annemarie
Failenschmied, Anna
Faivre, Louis-Jules
Faivre, Louis Jules Ulysse
Faivre, Jules
Faivre, Marie
Faivre, Emilie
Faivre, Philomene
Faivre, Jules
Faivre-Vierret, Leon
Fakler, Theresia
Fall, Ernst
Faller, Jules
Fallet, Isabelle
Faloppa, Rosanna
Fanchini, Peter
Fanti, Achille
Fantinel, Helena
Fantini, Amédée
Fantino, Giuseppe
Fantino, Ines
Fantoni, Achille
Färber, Edith
Fardel, Robert
Fareano, Marie
Farine, Blanche
Farineli, Lucien
Farkas, Eva
Fassina, Italia
Fassler, Mary
Fassy, Berthe
Fassy, Jeanne
Faure, Felice
Faure, Felix
Favre, Georges
Favre, Félicité
Favre, Joseph-Eug.
Favre, Henri Emile

Fawa, Emma
Fehling, Fernande
Fehr, August
Feige, Alfred
Feiner, Alfons
Felber, Anna
Feld, Wilhelm
Felix, Angèle
Ferihumer, Andreas Heinrich
Ferran, Julia
Ferrari, Socrate
Ferrario, Teresa
Ferreras, Teresa
Ferro, Decino
Ferroni, Luciano
Fessel, Frieda
Feuchtenbeiner, Anna
Feuerle, Friedrich
Feyler, Wilhelm
Fichet, L.
Fierobe, Paul & Letitia & Félicité
  & Ernest
Figuet & Co.H., Galerie
Fillenz, Albert
Fillinger, Walter
Filter, Emilie
Fink, Herrmann
Finkbeiner, Emma
Finkbeiner, Christine
Fintescu, Paul
Fischer, Franz
Fischer, Arthur
Fischer, Boris
Fischer, Lydia
Fisher, Henrietta S.
Flamm, Otto
Flanders, Marcel
Fleischer, Line
Floru, Jon I.
Fluck, Frieda
Flückiger, Ernst
Flury, Roger

Foessel, Mina
Föhner, Luise
Föhner, Rosa
Foltete, Charles
Foly, Charles
Fondation De Famille Zourous
Fondini, A.
Fontana, Johannes
Fontana, Anuntiata
Fontanelli, Adolphe
Foon Dalbegue, Alexandre
Forlin, Erich Gottlieb
Formanek, Jean
Fornage, Marie
Förnbacher, Martha
Fornet, Jean
Förster, Victor
Forstmann, Gustav
Förtsch, Werner
Foscarini, Ada
Foucault, Marcel Henry Alexandre
  & Marie Georgette
Fournier, Reine
Fournier, Therese
Fournier, Francis
Fox, Gaston
Fox, Charles
Franceschetti, Guilio
Franchini, Laura
François
Francone, Charles
Frank, Anna
Frank, Rosina
Franke, Elisabeth
Franklyn, Annie
Franz, Albert
Franz, Denise
Franzetti, Luigi
Frattini, Charles
Frattini Borghi, Gina
Freeman Bourbon de, M.J. & J.W.
Freeman Bourbon de, Marie J. & M.S.

Freitag, Walter
Frenn, Elisabeth
Fresacher, Lina
Fressle, Anton
Frey, Jakob
Frey, J.
Frey, Marie
Frey, Louisa Rose
Frey, Edwin
Freyhardt, Nathalie
Freymann, Gustave & Mathilde
Fricker, Nicolle
Friedli, Lydia
Friedli, Walter
Friedli, Willy
Friess, Ernest
Friessner, Oskar
Frischhut, Karl
Fritz, Jakob
Fritz, Paula
Fröbe, Emil
Froelich, Rudolf
Fröhle, Rosa
Fröhlich, Bertha
Frontini, Mario
Frontini, Virgilio
Frugoni, Emilie
Frühholz, Hans
Fuchs, Hulda
Fuchs, Anna Luzia
Fuchs, Berta
Fuchs-Schmid, Karoline
Fuchsbaumer, Anton
Fuess, Nadiège
Füglister, Albert
Führmann, Leonhard
Füllemann, Walter
Fürstenberger, Elisabeth
Furtwängler, Erik
Fusi, Carlo Albino
Fusina, Silvio
Fuss, Georg

Fux, Alfred
Gabrieli, Palmira
Gadagne de, Hélène
Gaedtke, Amanda
Gaerte, Susanne
Gagliardi, Maurice
Gähr, Henriette
Gailer, Adolf
Gaillard, Paul
Gaillard, Lucie
Gaille, Emile
Gailloud, V.
Gaiser, Joseph
Galafahsi, Vincenzo
Galeazzi, Jsidor
Galimberti, Angelo
Gallia, Antony
Gallichi, Sidney
Galliker, Josef
Gamb, Angela
Gambarini, Anna
Gampigotto, Luise
Gandet, Elisa
Gandolfo, Marthe
Ganter, Maria
Ganz, Sofie
Ganz, Rudolf
Garatti, Carlotta
Garattini, Anna
Garattini, Frieda
Garcia, Domingo
Garcon, Helene Elise
Gareis, Wilhelm
Garzia, Guiseppe
Gasparoni, Amalie
Gastaldi, Dominique
Gastell, J.K.
Gatta, Simone
Gatti, Bruno
Gattoni, Maristella
Gaud, Andre
Gaud, Marius

Gauderer, Ernst
Gaus, Susanna
Gavazzini, Carlo
Gave-Baumgartner, Anna
Gay, Jean Marie
Gay, François
Gebele, Johann
Gebert, Karl
Geggus, Margaretha
Gehrig, Friedrich
Gehring, Julius
Geiger, Sophie
Geisert, August
Geisert, Lydia
Geisinger, Peter
Geissbühler, Ernest
Genoud, Euphrasie
Georgesco, Jean
Georget, Maurice & Germaine
Gerard, Hermine
Gérard, Léon
Gerber, Ulrich
Gerber, Renee
Gerdeck, Johanna
Gergurevic, Lydia
Gerille, Francois
Gerlach, Emil F.
Gern, Cesar
Gerosa, Antonio
Gerosa, Carlo
Gerosa, Charles
Gerrat, Ruth
Gerstl, Marie
Gessert, Gustav
Getaz, Susette
Geyer, Walter
Geyer, Eugen
Geyer, Jadwiga
Giacomin, Ester
Gianesini, Giovanni
Giangrossi, Ribella
Giesberger, Jeanne

Giesin, Anna
Giffard, André Edmond Victor &
    Julie Juliette Romain
Gilardoni, Marie
Gillhausen, Elli
Gillier, Simone & Jean
Gilligmann, Jacqueline
Gillot, Antoine
Gindre, James
Gintzburger, Pauline
Giolo, Sophia
Giordanengo, Augusto
Giordani, Raffaele
Girard, Marie-Louise
Girard, Marcel
Girard, Camille
Girardot, Francois
Girardot, Joseph
Girardot, Louis
Girardot, Maria
Girardot, Fernand Arthur
Girerd, Sylvain & Pierre & Charles
    & Anais
Girod, Samuel
Giroud, Camille
Gisiger de, Rufina F.
Glardon-Gattolliat, Lea
Glassbrenner, Elsie
Glattfelder, Joseph
Glauser, Anna
Gletter, Anton
Glockner, Rudolf
Gluntz, Frédéric
Gmachemer, Max
Gmür, Seraphine
Gobba, Carlo
Godefroid, Aenne
Godfroy, Yvonne
Godi, Marzia
Godon, A.
Göggel, Adolf
Gogl, Matthäus

Göhlinger, J.
Göhringer, Lisette
Goldenberg, Antoinette
Goldenberg, Kagos
Goldmann, Jakob
Goldmann, Marguerite
Goldmann, Ludwig
Goller, Frida
Gollob, Hedwig
Golovtschiner, Michach
Goltz, Irma
Gompf, Hans Joachim
Goos, Mathilde
Goosz, René
Göpfert, Marie Rose
Gordon, Gregor
Gosetto, Antoine
Götsch, Rosa
Gottini, Lydia
Götz, Johann
Götz, Philipp
Goulandris, Nicolas John
Gourdin, Abbé E. & René
Gournay de, François & Germaine
Goy, Albert
Gozla, Amelia
Grabher, Rosa
Graf, Anna M.
Grafen vom, Helene
Graizier, Louise
Grambacher, Sylvain
Grandjean, Marguerite
Grandvoinnet, Jules
Grandvoinnet, Leonie
Grandvoinnet, Arthur Camille
Granitzer, Mathilde
Grassi, Angelo
Grau, Friedrich
Grauper, Agnes
Graven, Antoinette
Gravin, Hippolyte
Gray, Marie

Grébot, Emilie
Greco, Assunta
Gregorini, Maria
Greif, Elise
Greil, Hans
Greiner, Kurt
Greiner, Walburga
Greiner, Johann
Greiner, Marie
Greiner, Paulina
Grélat, Josephine
Grelet, Louis
Grell, Harry
Gresset, Henry
Grether, Elisabeth
Grether, Hermann
Grether-Richert, Christian
Gretzinger, Anna
Gries, Pierre
Griesbach, August
Griesser, Heinz
Grigolette, Sante
Grimbichler, Alphons
Grimm, Otto
Grissemann, Joseph
Groenweghe, Maurice
Gröhn, Max
Grolee, Maurice
Gronner, Rodolphe
Gros, Marie
Gross, Alois
Grosse-Muri, Lina
Grossenbacher, Adolf
Grosskost, Marie
Grousson, Jean
Grube, Erwin
Gruenfeld, Renée
Grün, Anna Verena
Grün, Verena
Grüner, Clara
Grupp, Otto
Grüter, Robertine

Gsell, Gaston
Gsell, Peter Josef
Guala, Anton
Guarda, Therese
Gübhard, Max Walter
Gubri, Guido
Guckelberger, Louise
Güdemann, Marie
Gueritte, Marie
Guerne, Lucien
Guetermann, Willy
Guggenbühl, Josef
Guglielmo, Testoni
Guichon, Félix-Eugène
Guidi, Romano
Guigon, Charles
Guigon, Marie
Guillet, Ewa Marie
Guinard, Madeleine
Guippeville de, Marie Thérèse
Guitton, Louise Léontine
Günther, Ernest Gustave
Gunzenhauser, Fritz
Gurschler, Hermann
Gurtner, Karl
Gutekunst, Frieda
Guth, Léon
Guth, Georgette
Guth, Jean
Guthmann, Nathan
Gutmann, Max E.
Gutmann, Otto
Gutmann, Felix
Gutter, Alfred
Guttmann, Maurice
Guy, Constant
Guy, Edmond
Guy, Flavien
Guy, Henri
Guy, Louis Marie Francois
Guyot, Alfred
Guzik, Adolph

Gwiss, Anna
Haab, Fritz
Haab, Mathilde
Haag, Frieda
Haar, Lina
Haas, Friedrich
Haas, Emma
Haas, Gottfried
Haberer, Erich
Häberle, Emma
Häberli, Clara
Hacker, Fanny & Ed.
Hadjilazaros, Etty Christistus
Häfele, Franz
Häfelé, Hélène
Hagen, Carl
Hager, Alfred
Hager, Oskar
Hahn, Alfred
Hahn, Rosa Aloisia
Hahn, Willy
Hailer, Ch.
Haim, Josef
Halama, Gertrud
Halasz, Josef
Hall, Rene
Haller, Elsa
Haller, Jos.
Halmos, Eugen
Halter, Hans Werner
Hammacker, Anna
Hampl, Julie
Hampp, Paul
Hanan, Victor
Handrinos, Helene
Hangarter, Otto
Hanisch, Berta
Hänni, Raoul
Hänni, Albert
Hannschild, Hermann
Hari, Jean-Claude
Hartje, Jean-Ernest

Hartkopf, Julie
Hartleb, Mina
Hartmann, Emil
Hartmann, Rosalie
Hartung, Robert
Hassid
Hassner, Theresia
Hatlich, Hanns
Hattiger, Gustave
Hattiger, Frederique
Hauff, Lina
Hauffe, Inge
Hauffe, Sus.
Haug, Anna
Hauptmann, Anna
Hauptmann, Anna
Hauser, Anna Michelina
Hauser, Otto
Hausis, Rosa
Häusler, Carl
Häusser, Louis-Chrétien
Hauthal, Martha
Haverkamp, Heinrich Jost
Hébertot, Jacques
Hediger, Karl
Heer, Johanna
Hefti, Franziska
Hefti, Fritz Ernst
Hegmann, Jeanne
Heid, Mathilde
Heidinger, Franz
Heidmann, Charlotte
Heiler, Celine
Heim, Jakob
Heim, Berta
Heine, Balbina
Heinrich, Peter
Heintzschel, Hermann
Heitz, Armand
Heitzmann, Josef
Helbing, Paolo
Held, Ernst

Held, Hans
Heldstab, Martha
Helle, Frieda
Hellemans, Hugo
Hellstern, Elisab. & Franziska & Antonie
Hellstern, Elisabeth
Helmlé, Ernst
Helsinger, Ernst
Hemetsberger, Mathias
Hemmerle, Fritz
Henne, Olga
Henneberg, Elisabeth
Henneberg, Albert
Hennet, Pierre
Henze, Robert
Herb, Gottlob
Hermanaux, Markus
Hermann, Ernst
Hermann, Jakob
Hermann, Carolina
Herold, Adolf
Herold, Carl
Hérold, Anna
Herr, Erhard
Herrmann, Christoph
Herrmann, Johanna
Hersperger, Wilhelm
Hertel, Thilde
Hertenberger, Marie
Herter, Marta
Herzog, Emil
Herzog, Robert
Heseler, Julius
Hess, Gustav
Hesselle de, Lothar
Hetzel, Lydia
Heumann, Hugo
Heussler-Reiss
Heyer, Anton
Hiemeyer, Lina
Hierholzer, Mathilde

Huckert, Emile
Huckert, Marie Louise
Huebscher, Robert
Hug, Eugène
Hug, Robert Eugen
Huguenin, Lea
Huguenin, Edgar
Hulmann, Louis
Humann, Hans
Humbert de, Louis & Yvonne
Humblat, Camille
Hummel, Julius
Hummel, Hildegard
Hunter, Edward Wiliam & Mabel
  Elisabeth
Hurle, Camille Simon
Hürlimann, Hedwig
Hurst, Martha
Hutter, Josef
Ides, Jac.
Idjlal, Abon
Ihle, Jakob
Iltgen, Martha
Imbs, Luise
Immer, Karl
Immerdauer, Adolf
Infantado Del
Ingli, Oskar
Invernizzi, Armando
Iseli, Karl
Isola, Giovanni
Issler, Hedwig
Jäckle, Elsa
Jäckle, Marie
Jacobsen, Marcel
Jacquet, Alfred
Jacquier, Adèle
Jacquier, Clément Marcel
Jacquin, Jacqueline-Arlette
Jacquin, Jeanne Arlette
Jacquot, Suzanne
Jacquot, Marie-Sophie

Jacquot, Auguste
Jacquot, Susanne
Jacquot, Roger
Jäger, Klara
Jäger, Maria
Jäger, Eugenie
Jagielski, Viktor
Jahn, Max
Janett, Niklaus
Janssen, Carl Heinrich
Jaquier, Marta
Jaroczynski, Alfred
Jasper, Alwine
Jassinger, Hans
Jau, Louis
Jeanbourquin, Marie
Jeanbourquin, Louis
Jeanneret, Fanny
Jeannin, Georges
Jeanperrin, Ida
Jeger, Emma
Jegher, Carl
Jelmini, Francois Attlio
Jenn, André
Jenny, Laure-Rose
Jenseh, Lydia
Jenter, Sofie
Jeppsen, Gustav
Jeunet, Emile Francois
Jeunet, Marie
Jobez, Anne-Marie
Jochum, Alois
Johé, Karl Friedrich
John, Ellen
Johns, Margarete
Johnson, Arthur Ellis
Jones, Elisabeth Marjorie
Joray, Martin
Jörg, Edith Meta
Joss, Heidi
Josselewitz, Moise
Jost, K.

Jovignot, Victor & Marcelle
Jozefiak, Michel
Juillerat, Justin
Jung, Angela
Junod, Jeanne
Juppet, Antionette
Juvet, Georges
Kadel, Adam
Kaden, Oskar Fred
Käfer, Hilda
Kaftan, Hans
Kahn, Jules
Kaiser, Theresia
Kaiser, Margrit
Kalt, Karl
Kaltenbach, Jakob
Kaltenmark, Ella
Kaltenrieder, James
Kamann, Margrit
Kaminski, Georgette & Marc
Kamm, Balthasar
Kammerer, Eduard
Kammerlander, Melanie
Kampinsky, Henriette
Känel, Christian
Kanngiesser, Friederich
Kanohfsky, Chaim
Kanohfsky, Riwa
Kansy, Elisabeth
Kantlehner, Wilhelmine
Kanz, Josef
Känzig, Edwin
Känzig, Karl
Känzig, Willi
Kapfer, Emma
Kapper, Karl
Kappey, Joseph
Karl, Ludwig
Karlaganis, Georgios
Karlaganis, Gertrud
Karle, Richard
Kart, Hedwig

Karwicki, Joseph-Dunin
Kasztan, Kostancyja
Katz, Abraham
Kaul, Lucienne
Kaupp, Friedel
Kech, Margrit
Keck, Karoline
Kecskemeter Merkur AG
Keim, Irma
Kelbert, Georges
Keller, Marie
Keller, Adèle
Keller, Charles Eugene
Keller, Sofie
Keller, Eugène Marcel
Keller, Arthur
Keller, Emma
Keller, Jda
Keller, Luise
Kelly, E.
Kelm, Walter Ernst
Kempf, Marie
Kenfely von, Stjepan
Kenzler, Anna
Kerdudo, Marcel
Kern, Erna
Kern, Jean-Baptist
Kessler, Charles
Kessler, Adeline
Kessler, Verena
Kiefer, Karl
Kiefer, Hans
Kielmann, Julie
Kienast, Anna
Kiene, Marie
Kiener, François
Kierszkowsky, Mina
Kihm, Robil
Kilkowski, Frieda
Kimmerle, Ludwig
Kintore of
Kirchhoff, Lotti

Kiriacesco, Radu
Kirmann, Thérèse
Kirner, Klara
Kirsch, Erich
Kitsiki, Constantin
Kitzelmann, Marie
Klaiber, Johanna
Klaus, Peter
Klee, Rudolf
Kleeblatt, David
Klein, Jolan
Klein, Marguerite
Kleindessner, Johanna
Klethi, Eugen
Kliatschkin, Bella
Klieber, Anton
Kloos-van d.Horst, A.
Klöppinger, Margaretha
Klugmann, Laura
Knap, Ludwig
Knauss, Wilhelm
Kneier, Keta Anna
Knieling, Marie
Knobel, Babette
Knobl, Katharina
Knollseisen, Elisa
Köb, Arno
Koch, Antonia Fanny
Koch, Senta
Köck, Karl
Köck, Marie
Köckeis, Hermine
Kofmane, Marta
Kohler, Lina
Kohler, Eugen
Köhler, Anna
Köhrig, Franziska
Koll, Marie
Kollmann, Friederike
Kolmanic, Erika
Kolmanic, Hermine Martha
König, Camille

König, Alfred
Kopanjo, Vaso
Köpfler, Katharina
Kopp, Josef
Kopp
Kopsch, Otto
Korn
Korotaeff, Nikolaus
Kotz, Paul
Kozerski, Adolf
Kräh, Karl
Krähenbühl, Christian
Kramer, Lydia
Kramer, Georg
Krämer, Therese
Kranck, Helene Olga Virginie
Kranz, Josef
Krassing, Thomas
Krassototzky, Gertrud
Krauss, Paul
Krauss, Fritz
Krausz, Ladislaus
Krautinger, Marie
Krebs-Claudon, Edouard
Kreiner, Emerich
Kremos, Alexander
Kremp, Josef
Krenger, Fritz
Krenn, Otto
Kress, Rosa
Kretzulesco, Rodolphe
Krieg, Maurice
Kroneberg, Lucie
Kropf, Rosine
Kroupensky, Paul
Krüger, Hellmut
Krüger, Helmut
Krüger, Willi
Kubelik, Jiri
Kubler, Jules
Kübler, Charles
Kübler, Jules

Kuendinger, Wilhelm
Kueny, Marie Lina
Kugler, Alfred
Kuharzewski, Jan
Kuhn, Maria
Kuhn, Alice
Kühn, Gertrud
Kuhnle, Albert
Kummer, Berta
Kumpf, Marie
Kündig, Alice
Kunovjanek, Franz
Kunschke, Klara
Kunz, Klara
Kunz, Philipp
Kunzelmann, Ernst
Künzig, Toni
Kupka, Jenny
Kuppel, Julien
Küpper, Thomas
Kürschner, Kurt
Kustermann, Karl
Kuttler, Albert
Kuzelka, Luise
Kwiatkowska, Anastasia
Labet, Ludivine
Labourey, Georgette
Lachat, Paul
Lachat, Michel
Lacher, Frieda
Lacmann, Otto
Lacroix, Capitaine
Ladame, Francois
Ladner, Josefine
Lagjevic, Georges
Lagrange, Michel & Fanny &
    Suzanne
Lambardot, Augustin
Lambert, Victor
Lambert, Emile
Lamble, Eugene
Lamidien, Edwige

Lammerich, Carlo
Lamouille, Henri
Landel, Jeanne
Lander, Joh.
Landet, Elisabeth
Landet, Louise
Landmann, Columba
Landolf, W.A.
Lang, Therese
Lang, Joh.Bap.
Lang, Yvonne
Lang, Berta
Lang, Margarete
Lange, Fritz
Langen van, Katharina
Langenbacher, Walbury
Langrod, Jurek
Lanoir, Roger & Marguerite
Lanzinger, Marie
Laplace, Claudius Joseph
Lapp, Fritz
Lardi, Adelcise
Larrick, Patricia
Lassale, Alfred
Lassard, Jean
Latour, Jean
Latscha, Eugenie
Lattner, Anna
Lauber, Erwin
Laumann, Renate
Laun, August
Lauprete, Giuseppe
Laurent, Bettina
Lautensack, Olga
Lavabre, Henri & Pierre
Laville, Paul
Lay, Hermann
Lebherz, Richard
Lebras, Therese
Lechevalier, Albert
Leclerc, Albert
Ledochowski, Franz Maria

Lefort, Léon & Juliette
Legler, Frida
Lehmacher, Paul
Lehmann, Martha
Lehmann, Julie
Lehmann, Samuel Raoul
Lehner, Josef
Lehner, Klara
Lehner, Rosa
Leibacher, Walter
Leibbrand, Marie
Leiber, Konstantin
Leiber, Leo
Leicht, Heinrich
Lelovic, Thibor
Lengeler, Rainer
Lenz, Karl
Leoni, Peter
Lepeule, Francis
Leprince, Rene
Lerat, Charles
Léri, Aline
Leroj, Adelheid
Leroy, Elisabeth
Lessan de, Léontine
Lessan de, Nicole
Lessan de, Robert
Leszezynska, Anna
Létang, Fortunio
Leumann, Max
Leverd, René & Jeanne Louise
Levoni, Dante
Levoni, Laura
Levy, Florin
Levy, Charles
Lévy, Felix
Lewandowski, Donald
Leyer, Josefa
Leyfert, Siegmund
Libsig, Rene Paul
Liebi, John William
Liepert, Berta

Lilie, Walter
Lilienstein/Lülienstern, Leon
Limardo, Luisa
Linder, Emilio
Linder, Johanna
Lindner, Anna
Lindner, Friedrich
Lindner, Lisbeth
Lindstadt, Johanna
Lingg, Barbara
Linke, Alois
Linkenheim, Wilhelmine
Lintzer, Pierre
Lironi, Michelina
Litschig, Marcel
Lloyd, Mary
Lobstein, Mathilde Valérie Jeanne
Locatelli, Annette
Locatelli, Joseph
Locatelli, Baptiste
Locher, Hilda
Loewenstein, Berthold & Ida
Loewy, Max
Löhle, Fritz
Lohmeyer, Johannes Friedrich
Lohner, Konrad
Lohrer, Andreas
Loose, Emma
Loose, Ernst
Lopez, Aquilino
Lopez, Germann
Lorch von, Edith
Lorenz, Therese
Lorenzi, Battista
Lorenzi, Ines
Löschberger, Andreas
Lothar, Hans
Loutenbach, Thiébaud
Louvrier, Elisa
Löw, Jos.
Löwenstein, A.
Löwenthal, Jenny

Lüchtrath, Lissy
Lüdke, Paul
Luethi, Walther
Luft, Christian
Luisetti, Jean
Lüling, Julius
Lumbe, Eugenie
Luppi, Emma
Lürs, Heinrich
Lüscher, Jakob
Lutz, Anna
Lutz, Hans
Lutzmann, Helmut
Lux, Emil
Lux, Theresa
Maag, Jacob
Mabon, Robert
Mabut, Marie
Mac Arthur, John R.
Macconi, Severino
Machart, Michel & Alphonse
Machimbarrena y Gogorza, J.
Macias, Silvio
Mäder, Werner
Mäder, Dora
Maestra Della, Enrico
Maestrello, Tranquillo
Maestri, Clotilda
Maggiolo, Luigia
Magistris, Jonny
Magnani, Mary Hélène
Magnin, Louis
Magnin, Vitaline
Magoria, Pia
Magrini, Sandro
Mahault, Yvonne Marguerite Elise
    & Pierre
Mahon, Gabrielle Elisabeth
Mahurroud Djelaleddine
Maier, Bertha
Maier, Josef
Maier, Karthe

Maier, Berta
Maier, Luise
Maillot, Catherine
Maingueneau, Henri
Maire, Rene
Majba, Wilhelmine
Major, Emil Andre
Makon, Janetta
Malartic, Henri
Malende, Lina Frieda
Malet de, Félix François &
    Marguerite Marie
Malniqvist, Erhard
Malyschew, Nicolay
Mändle, Lucy
Mangold, Franz
Manné, Ernestine
Mannich, Theodor
Mantese, Mario
Mantz, Yolanda
Manzolini, Anacleto
Marcelle, Jean
Marchat, Julie
Marchetti, Jacques
Marci, Martina
Marcolli, Emma
Marechal, Chalres-Auguste
Marechal, Maria Irene
Mareischen, J.
Marendaz, Nicole
Mariani, Benigno
Marina, Dario
Marinotto, Heidi
Mariotte, Pierre & Marcelle &
    Sergeux
Markoff, Dimitry
Marmet, Louis Nizier
Marnarelli, Pasquale
Marsanti, Mario
Marsauche, Albert
Marschall, Willy
Marschon, Aloïs

Marschon, Max
Marte, Katharina
Martegani, Enrico
Martelli, Raimonda
Martin, Ramon
Martin, Louis
Martin, Fritz Ferdinand
Martin, Armand
Martin, Victoria & Lily
Martin, Leon
Martin, E.
Martin, Wilhelm
Martin, Frédéric
Martin, Carl
Martinek, Ernst
Martinelli, Heinrich
Martinetti, Marguerite
Martinoli, Oresk
Martinoli, Renato
Marucco, Louis
Mas, Concepcion
Mascalchi, Santi
Maseret, Juliette
Masetti, Luciano
Massalon, Marguerite
Massari, Albano
Massari de, Marianne
Masson, Blanche
Mastnak, Paul
Matarazzo, Francesco
Matarazzo, Rosa-Marie
Matassaro, Michel S.
Matei, Jon
Mathes, Lina
Mathys, Emma
Matli, Ferdinand
Mattenberger, Marie
Matter, Alfred
Mattes, Friedrich
Mattes, Rudolf
Matthey, Rose
Matthey-Doret, Pierre

Matthissen, Hanna
Matzer, Rosa
Maucher, Agathe
Mauclair, Marie
Mauer, Rud.
Maugain, Camille
Mauge, Madeleine
Maul, Alfred
Maul, Karl
Maurer, Rosa
Mautner, Anna
Mavromichalis, Photini
May, Othmar
May, Adrienne
Mayer, Margrit
Mayer, Beatrice
Mayer, Fanny
Mayer, Clara
Mayer, Joseph
Mayer, Karl
Mayer, Otto
Mayr, Wieland
Mazur, Eljasz
Mazzeri, Stefano
Mc Arthur, Angele Laure
Meda, Nice
Medici, Edmondo
Mehlin, Louise
Meienberger, Betty
Meier, Hedwig
Meier, Emma
Meier, Hermann
Meier, Leo
Meier, Franz
Meier, Gertrud
Meister, Eduard
Meister, Sarah
Melli, Ariste
Mellwig, Paolo
Mencisnkiene, B. L.
Mendozza, Maria
Menegini, Armando

Mengsdorf, Emma
Menotti, Therese
Menweg, Albert
Merk, Mina
Merk, Marianne
Merk, Monika
Merk, Thaddäus
Merlo, Charles
Merlot, Adele
Meroni, Angelo
Merz, Christian
Meschenmoser, Julius
Meschenmoser, Julius
Messerli, Christian
Metzger, Jacques
Metzger, Anny
Metzger, Heinrich
Metzger, Johanna
Meusburger, Anna
Meusburger, Karl
Mex, Willy
Meyer, Roger
Meyer, Gebhardt
Meyer, Elise
Meyer, Reymond
Meyer, Emil
Meyer, Diedrich, Wilhelm
Meyer, Kurth
Meyer, Eduard
Meyer, Alfred
Meyer, Auguste
Meyer, Frederick William
Meyer, Josephine & Jeanne &
    Antoine
Meyer, Christiane
Meyer, Charles
Meyerhoefer, Elisabeth
Meyre, Mina
Meyrignac, Anne
Meyrignac, Madeleine
Meyrignac, Marguerite
Meyrignac, Jean

Meyung, Emma
Mezzadri, Anna
Miceli, Francesco
Michaille, Emile
Michel, Henri
Michel, Marie
Michelfelder, Rosa
Michelizza, Santina
Michels, Robert
Michelson, Philipp
Middelmann, Friedr.
Mieg-Reber, Agnès Elisabeth &
    Daniel
Mieg-Reber, Daniel Jacques &
    Daniel
Miglionini, Angela
Mikeler, Eugen
Mikulaschek, Martin Walter
Miller, Johann
Miller, Hedwig
Millet, Simone
Minéry, Eugène
Minoretti, Anton
Miseré, Henri & Marie Anna
Missieritch, Maroussia
Missios, Michel
Mitschele, Albert
Mittellach, Maria
Mock, Elsa
Möckel, Elise
Moeltgen, Max Hubert
Mogel, Josef
Möhle, Lina
Möhrle, Marie
Möhrlen, Christoph
Moille, Leon
Moinat, Célestin
Moise, Julia
Molin, Isidor
Molinier, Henry
Möller, Frieda
Möller, Paula

Ord van der, Alida
Ord van der, Louwrens
Ord van der, Maria
Ord van der, Pieter
Ord van der, Trouwtje
Oriez, Edouard Léonard
Oriez, Emile
Origgi, Ernesta
Origgi, Paolina
Orlandi, Peter
Orsat, Pierrette
Ossola, Carla
Ostendorf, Jaquina
Ostermeyer, Alsa
Ostinelli, Maria Luisa
Othenin-Girard, Max Victor
Otschakovsky, Ghers
Ott, Flora
Ott, Babette
Otto, Karl
Ottoerström, Ernst
Ouchkoff, Alexis
Oustric, Marie & Emile
Ozelsberger, Marie
Paans, Henry Dirk
Paauw De, Christine
Pabst, Gottfried
Paccot, Clotilde
Pagan, Henriette
Pagnier, Joseph
Paleni, Frederic
Palkovics, Eduard
Palovic, Julius
Panayotoff, Alexandre
Panayotoff, Mara B.
Pantillon, Auguste
Paraschivescio, Alexander
Parel, Marie-Esther
Parent, Eugène
Parg, Marta
Parma, A.
Paroisse de Glères

Parrighetti, Jean
Parth, Ernst
Pascal, Marie
Pasqualetto, Antonio
Pasteur, Antony
Pasteur, Marie
Pasteur, Raymond
Pastori, Anna
Pategg, Sophie
Patel, Léon
Patois, Eugéne
Patton de, Marie
Pautke, Helene
Pavan, Josef
Pavid, Léandre
Pavlic, Emma
Pechtel, Wilhelmine
Pégeot, Zépherin
Péguet, Marguerite
Péguet, Max
Peling, Emmanuel & Marie
Pellet, Paul
Pelletier, Berthe
Pelletier, Charles
Pelletier, Joseph
Pelloth, Katharina
Pelloux, Hélène
Pelucchi
Pelucchi, Lina
Pelucchi, Savina
Penacini, Michel
Perigault, Madeleine
Périssé, Eloi
Perk, Elsa
Perkhofer, Josef
Perrelet, Oswald
Perrenoud, Georges
Perret, Jean
Perrey, Emile
Perrey, Louise
Perrier, Yvonne
Perrin, Eric-Bernard

Perrin, Joseph
Perrin, Jules
Perron, Elia
Perrot de, Roger
Pesavento, Rocco
Peter, Emil
Peter, Hugo
Peter, Ludwig
Peter, Rudolf
Peters, Luise
Petersen, Anna
Petit, Richard
Petit, Julia
Petit, Valentine
Petit, Mario
Petit-Maire, Arthur
Petitclerc, Marie
Petitclerc, René
Petithuguenin, Gustave
Petithuguenin, Louise Marie
Petithuguenin, Marie-Louise
Petitpierre, Georges Jules Henri
Petrass, Irene
Petrolini, Elvira
Petrovic, Georg
Peyraud, Marie
Peyrot, Valine Jeanne Cécile
Pfeiffer, Alphonse
Pfeninger, Albert
Pfirstinger, Felix
Pfister, Emil
Pfister, Katharina
Pfisterer, Martha
Pfleghaar, Anna
Philbert, Henri
Philipp, Marie
Philippe, Carlos
Philipps, Kenneth
Piaget, Helene
Piana, Georg
Pianca, Rosa
Piazza, Domenico

Piazza, Stella
Picard, Jules
Picard, Robert & Blanche
Picca, Luigina
Picq, Eugene
Pierini, Carlo Antonio
Pierquin, Jean
Pierrat, Gabriel & Aline
Pierre, Eugene
Pierrot, Cathérine
Pierson, Raphael
Pillod, Louis
Pinchenzon, Dina
Pinchetti, Annunciata
Pinos, Juan
Pinter, Marie
Pirchner, Joseph
Pirini, Francesco Manuele
Pirot, Anne Hortense
Pissot, Sophie
Pittin, Ida
Pivont, Alfred
Planett, Johanna
Platen, Hermann
Pleskacz, Josef
Plouvier, Paul
Plüss, Liesbeth
Pobelle, Alphonse
Podesta, Dionigi
Podesta, Quirino
Podgorschek, Valerie
Poeze De la, M.B.L.L.
Pohlmann, Auguste
Poiblanc, Emile
Pointboeuf, Francois
Poire, Cecile
Poivret, Marcel & Yvonne
Poletti, Miriam
Poletti, Natalina
Poli, Antoine
Pöll, Fanny
Polla, Emilie

Pollak, Vandor
Pomsel, Annemarie
Ponti, Claudio
Popowitsch, Swetislav
Poppen, E.
Pories, Raymond
Porta, Ervine
Porzio, Mario & Angela
Pospichal, Anna
Posselius, A.
Pourrat, Henri
Prada, Pietro
Prager, Paul C.
Prager, L.
Pranger, G. J.
Prejbeanu, Const. S.
Premetz, Marie
Prémonville De Maisonthou de,
    Jeanne Marie & Olivier
Pressler, Albert
Pressler, Antonia
Prestel, Ottilie
Prétat, Jules
Prétat, Adèle
Pretre, Marie
Preuss, Werner
Prevost, Marcel & Jeanne
Prévôt, Emilie
Priebsch, Bertha
Probst, Maria
Prochinig, Emma Magdalena
Profit, Gaston & Marthe
Prongué, Antoine Pierre Joseph
Proprenet, Louis
Protter, Albert
Protzies, Emilie
Prusak, Gustav
Pugin, André
Pugni, Celso
Puigventos, Josef
Puschek, Jda
Puthon, Louis

Putzer, Andreas
Quain, Julia
Quarti, Walter
Quélain, Jules
Querqui, Dino
Quirk, John-Douglas
Räber, Antoine
Rabisson, Endel
Racchi, Remo
Radelfinger, Emmy
Radinger, Lydia
Radisson, M.C. & J.
Rafati
Raggi, Giov. Battista
Raggi, Ginetto
Raid, Lina
Rainvillers de, L.
Rais, Françoise & Henri & Marie
Rakoneza, Gesela
Rakovski, Niklaus
Ralli, Jenny A.
Ramel, Andrée
Rampone, Marie
Ramsperger, Josef
Rapiné, François
Rappaport, Jenny
Rappe, Celine
Raschle, Marie
Raselli, Michele
Rast, Emma Karolina
Rata, Emile
Rath, Veronika
Ratti, Eugen
Ratti, Helene
Ratzenböck, Wilhelm
Rau, Trudi
Räuber, Ernst
Rauch, Elfriede
Rava-Fenton, Violet
Ravani, Paolina
Ravicini Galli, Raphael
Réal

Reali, Carletto
Reati, Mario
Rech, Joseph
Recke, N.
Recordati, Giovanni
Recordon, Alice
Redaschi, Giulia
Rees, Karl
Regeczy von, Bela
Regenass, Rosa
Regis, Stella-Anna
Reheis, Benedikt
Rehklau, Carl
Reich, Maria
Reich, Josef
Reich & Friedmann
Reichart, Kunigunde
Reichel, Walther Siegfried
Reichenbauch, Willi
Reichert, Helene
Reichhart, Emilie
Reichle, Werner
Reichle, Hedwig
Reif, Willy
Reiff, Robert
Reihle, Elise
Reimers, Helmut
Rein, Franziska
Reinhardt, Emma
Reinhardt, Sophie
Reiser, Lina
Reitsberger, Katharina
Reize, Paul
Rejmankova, Bozena
Rejod, Tibustino
Remy, Hélène
Remy, Carl Heinz
Renaud, Joseph-Jules
Renaud, Henri
Renaud, Marie
Renfer, Marguerite
Renggli, Baptist

Renier, Stefania
Renner, Hedwig
Renner, Jean-Francois
Renner, Pauline
Renz, Katharina
Reppert, Otto
Resch, Elisabeth
Resenterra, Luigi & Angela
Rest.de la Pépinière
Reuel, Josef
Reumayer, Loni
Reusch, Josefine
Reutebuch, August
Reyes, Carlos
Reyes, Margaret
Reymond, Maurice Louis Philippe
Reynier de, Rene
Rezzonico, Silvio
Ricard, Suzanne Adrienne
Richard, Elisa
Richard, Robert
Richard, Angele
Richardot, Amelie-Marthe Marie
Richer, Jean & Jeanne
Richter, Alfredo
Rick, Sophie
Ricken, Frieda
Ridder De, Louis
Ridinger, Anna
Rieben, Jules
Rieben, Andre
Rieben, Catherine
Rieben, Colette
Riedi, Rudolf
Riedle, Eugen
Riedlinger, Emma Barbara
Rieger, Robert
Riese, Eberhard
Riesselmann, Betty
Riester, Ida
Riesterer, Berta
Rigamonti, Giordano

Rigassi, Guido
Rill, Marie
Rindelbacher, Josef
Ring von, Karl
Rinke, Elli
Riss, Lucy
Risser, Alfred
Ritter, Hans Adam
Ritter, Karl
Ritz, Paul
Ritzmann, Jacques
Rivaroli, Yvonne
Riz, Francesco
Rizotto, Aldo
Röber, Emilie
Röber, Max
Robert, Adolphe
Robert, Henri & Isabelle
Robin, Charles
Rocca, Gilardo
Roche, Lyliane
Röckl, Hedwig
Rodella, Antonio
Roder, Heinrich
Roesti, Clara
Roger, Germaine
Roger, Marcel
Rohoni, Johann
Rohr, Oskar
Rohrbach, Eugen
Rolland, Madeleine
Rolli, Alois
Rollinger, Cécille
Romagnoli, Catharina
Romain, Alexandre
Romain, Philomène
Romanello, Josefine
Romanello, Viktor
Rombach, Albert
Romiger, Josef
Rommel, Emma
Römmich, Philipp

Romy, William
Rona, Jenoene
Roncoroni, Ermanno
Rönneburg, Elisabeth
Rontscho, Emile
Röschard, Richard
Rosenfeld, Moritz
Rosenow, Johannes
Rosenthal, Anita
Roser, Georg
Rossegger, Marie
Rosselet, Henri
Rossi, Ittalo
Rossi, Therese
Rossi, August
Rossiaud, Fernand
Rossmann, Hanni
Rost, Franz & Mina
Rota, Stefano
Roth, Sophie
Roth, Josef
Rothe, Marcel
Röthlisberger, Rodolphe
Rothmayr, Josef
Rott, Horace
Rottman, Anny
Roueche, Alfred
Rougemont de, Franciska
Roussel-Galle, Marcelin Leon
Roux le, Felix
Rouyez, Albert
Rubinstein, Michel
Rudel, Johanna
Rüdy, Berta
Ruedin, Paul
Ruegg, Hans C.
Ruehl, Philipp
Ruf, Joseph
Ruf, Frieda
Ruff, Irma
Rugarsky, Dusan
Ruggeri, Rocco

Rukavina von, Friedrich
Rümmele, Lina
Rummelhart, Josephine
Runser, Johann
Runser, Ludwig
Ruoff, Ernst
Rupf, Peter
Rupp, Karl
Rupp, Friedrich
Ruppert, Emil
Ruppert, Ernst
Russ, Margar.
Ruteau, Edmond Emile &
   Madeleine Charlotte
Rutgers, Clarissa
Rutgers, Liliane
Rutgers, Mirella
Rutishauser, Rud.
Ruziczka, Fritz
Rypko, Chaim
Ryser, Emma
Saade, Raymond
Sabatini, Nello
Sache, Marcel
Sachs, Fritz
Safarowsky, Robert
Sala, Stephan
Salles, Georges & Robert
Salma, Bruno
Salomon, Marie-Louise
Salomon, Theo
Salvi, Bonaventure
Salvi, Joseph
Salvi, Jolanda
Salvi & Peregrinelli
Salviti, Avenire
Samsinger, Walter
Sanchez de Larragoiti, Antonio & Ana
Sanchioni, Rodolfo
Sandberg, Leon
Sander, Gertrud
Sandi, Jacqueline

Sandi, Maria
Sandi, Serafino
Sandoz, Lydia
Sandretti, Louis-Arthour
Sandrin, Léon
Sanguinetti, Ettore
Sarbach, Georges
Sarkinoff
Särnström, Lars
Sarrafian, Hagop
Sartorelli, Angiolina
Sartori, Domenico
Sartori, Demenico
Sartorio, Carlo
Sassi, Bruno
Sassot, Succ.R.
Sattira, Emil
Sattler, Karl
Saulnier, Gaston
Saurer, Arthur
Sautaux, Adelheid
Sauter, Hans
Sauvan, C.
Savary
Savoldelli, Elise
Saxer, Anna
Scagliotti, Felice
Scala, Elisabeth
Scalabrino, Jeanne Virginie
Scalabrino-Friserri, Paul & Caroline
Scarpellini, Armando
Scarpellini, Peter
Schaarschmidt, Ernst Louis
Schaber, Emilie
Schächtelin, Hans-Peter
Schächtelin, Walter
Schäfer, Anna
Schäfer, Max & Elisabeth
Schahl, Agathe
Schaich, Johann
Schairer, Willy
Schanz, Elise

Schanz, Lydia
Schanz, Louise
Schapiro, Jeanette & Jacob
Schär, Marie
Scharping, Friedrich
Scharping, Johanna
Schatinowsky, H.
Schattmeier, Eduard
Schätzer, Julius
Schaub, E.
Scheer, Karl
Scheerle, Marie
Scheftel, Reneta
Scheftel, Sabina
Scheidecker, Pierre
Scheiner, Simi
Scheli, Rosen
Schell, Agnes
Schellinger, Emma
Schellinger, Klara
Schenck, Albert
Schenk, Anna
Schenkel de, Christine G.
Scherer, Mathäus
Scherrer, Georges
Scherrer, Franz
Scheuer, Ludwig
Schiagno, Albert
Schick, Georges
Schick, Lore
Schickler, Hilmar Johann
Schidel, Franz
Schiechtl, Johann
Schiff, Eugen
Schiffner, Carl
Schiffter, Elfriede
Schild, Anna
Schiller, M. F.
Schiller, Cäcilia
Schiller, Emma
Schillig, Joseph
Schillinger, Fränzl

Schillinger, Wilhelm
Schiltz, Paul
Schimmer, Hansi
Schindele, Rosa
Schindlbeck, Otto
Schlatter, Georges H.
Schlecker, Josefine
Schlegel, Mathilde
Schlegel, Theodor
Schleicher, Pauline
Schlichterle, Hermine
Schlittler, Jakob
Schlotterbeck, Johannes
Schluch, Emma
Schlüter, Hermann
Schmalz, Fritz
Schmid, Rudolf
Schmid, Gottlieb
Schmid, Albert
Schmid, Ferdinand
Schmid, Cresenzia
Schmid, Gottfried Hugo
Schmid, Stefanie
Schmider, Marie
Schmidlin, Louise
Schmidt, Bruno
Schmidt, Hugo & Hilde
Schmidt, Albertine
Schmiedhäusler, Agnès
Schmitt, Carl
Schmitt, Carola
Schmitt, Leopold
Schmitt, Karl
Schmitt, Elisabeth
Schmitt, Kath.
Schmitter, Patricia
Schmitz, Guido
Schmitz, Chs.
Schmutz, Paul
Schnabel, Albert
Schnarrenberger, Erna & Lina &
    Isolde & Gisela

Schneider, Margot Rosmarie
Schneider, Lorenz
Schneider, Ulrich
Schneider, Josef
Schneider, Lotty
Schneider, Marie
Schneider, Anna
Schneider, Elias
Schneider, Frieda
Schneider, Reinhard
Schneider, Berta
Schneider, Gustav
Schneider, Paul
Schneitenberger, Karl
Schnepper, Frieda Anna Olga
  Laura
Schoch, Thomas
Schoen, Henri
Schoerger, Gisella Johanna
Schöffler, Herbert
Scholl, Jean
Scholl, Franz
Schöllhorn, Emma Maria
Schomer, Karl-Heinz Arnold
Schömig, Margaretha
Schöndienst, Jean
Schöpf, Adolf
Schopper, Michael
Schori, Adolf
Schorr, Karl Friedrich
Schott, Emilie
Schramm, Franz
Schramm, Franziska
Schramm, Wilhelm
Schranz, Carl
Schreiber, August
Schreiber, Elfriede
Schröder, Julius
Schröter, Joachim
Schrott, August
Schubert, Max
Schueepp, Jakob E. & Bertie

Schufer, Philipp
Schuh, Paula
Schuler, Emma
Schuler, Maria
Schüler, Lisbeth
Schulhof, Karl
Schultheiss, Ernst
Schultz, Hans
Schultz, Louise
Schulz, Karl
Schurr, Carlos E.
Schuster, August
Schuster, Roman
Schuster, Wilhelm
Schuster, Wilh.
Schuster, Karel
Schütte, Margreth
Schuttel, Clovis
Schwab, Marianne
Schwab, Lucie
Schwab, Jakob
Schwab, Selma
Schwabe, Walter
Schwake von, Clamor
Schwarber, Klara
Schwartz, Josefine
Schwarz, Georg
Schwarz, Marta
Schwarz, Berta
Schwarz, Mina
Schwarzbrod, Aloise Paul
Schwarzer, Hilda
Schweckler, Leon & Leonie
Schweizer, Emma
Schwennicke, Paul
Schwertfeger, Ida
Schwickerath, Hugo
Schwitzer, Alice
Schwob, Euphrosine
Sedenko, Constantin
Seelig, Elisabeth
Seemen von, Hans G.

Sefossi, Eugenio
Seger, Rudolf
Segodnia, Alice
Seifert, Anna
Seigneur, Frédéric
Seiler, Gottfried & Elisabeth &
    Margrit
Seiler, Veronika
Seiler, Emma
Seitz, Gottfried
Seitz, Lydia Anna
Sekulin, Hans
Seligmann, Fanny
Senka, Samuel
Senn, Magdalena
Senn, Betty
Sereno, Jakob
Serman, Emilio
Severi, Elino
Seymour, William & Ernest & Leo
    & Hermann
Shaler, Lee
Siberfeld, Georges
Sichel, René
Sigmund, Marie
Silva Prado de, Octavio
Silvestrini, Angelo
Simomelli, Rina
Simon, Paul
Simon, Josef
Simon, Fernand
Simon, Jeanne
Simon, Charles
Simon, Emil
Simon, Laure Jeanne Adele
Simon, Otto
Simonin, Anna
Singer, Wilhelm
Siri, Domenica Teresa
Sittmann von, Marg.
Sitzler, Lina
Skarzynski, Hedwig

Sloma, Julius
Smania, Gertrud
Sobsic, V.
Sochaczewski, Gutmann
Societe Française de Portefeulille
    en Liqu.
Sogno, Pierre
Sölb, Elsa
Soldenhoff, Alexander
Sollberger, Johannes
Solomon, Nicolas
Sommer, Francine
Sonderegger, Gottfried
Sonderegger, Ruza
Sonntag, Franz
Soudan, Georges
Soukhotine, Lydie
Sourmais, Cyrille
Souroudjieff, Strachimir
Spanjerberg, Johann Henri
Späth, Hermann
Speck, Friedrich
Sperber, Georges
Spetzler, Angela
Spielmann, Hans
Spinner, Emanuel
Spinner, Leo
Sprai, Leo
Springer, Karl
Springer, Marie
Springinsfeld, Emma
Spühler, Johanna
Spycher, Johann
Staar, Anna
Stach, Helene
Stadelmaier, Anna
Stadelmann, Josef
Stadler, Bertha
Stadler, Franz
Staehle, Bruno
Stähle, Maria
Standl, Therese

Stange, Erich
Starck, René
Staresina, Michael
Stark, Marceline
Stark, Georg
Stark, Matthäus
Stättmüller, Marie
Staub, Charles
Staufer, Hermann
Steckel, Alfred
Stefani de, Aldo
Stegemann, Christian
Steib, Alb. Fr.
Steidle, Marie
Steiger, Anna
Steiger, Georg
Stein Von den, Runhillt
Steinbihs, Kurt
Steiner, Trudy
Steiner, Mathilde
Steinwartz, Marie
Steinwurzel, Jsidor
Stepanck, Karl & Lotte
Stephan, W.
Sterchi, Rudolf
Sternbauer, Olga
Sternberger, Stephanie
Stettler, Christian
Steullet, Charles
Stickel, Adolf Christian
Stierlin, Martin
Stihl, Wilhelm
Stingl, Kaethe
Stintzi, Alice
Stock, Georg
Stoessler, Trude
Stofflett, Alois
Stoffregen, E.
Stöhr, Magdalena
Stoll, W.
Stoll, Philomène
Stolle, Gertrud

Stoller, Gustav
Stolte, Ruth
Stoltenberg, Helene
Stoltenberg, Sofie
Stoltenberg, Elsa
Stolz, Walter
Stolze, Elisabeth Charlotte
Stoppani, Federico
Storch, Wally
Storz, Alice
Stotz, Ursula
Stötzner, Ida
Stouff, Louis
Strack, Engelbert
Strassberger, Maria
Strasser, Henri Alois Joseph
Straub, Hermann
Straubinger, Anna
Straus, Siegfried
Strecha, Alois
Streibich, Anna
Streicher, Alois
Streicher, Frieda
Streng, Luise
Stressler, Maria
Streun, Fr.
Stritzl-Cuttat-Tinguely von, H.
Strizziotti, Joseph
Stroh, Marie
Strojny, Marian
Strossier, Marie
Struad, Olga
Strub, Hermann
Strube, Leopold Georges
Strunck, Andrée
Strzys, Johann
Stücklin, Frieda Kath.
Stucky, René
Studer, F.
Studler, Carmen Marie
Stummer, Karoline
Stump, Karl

Stumpf, Johann
Stupp, Hanna
Stüssi, B.
Stutzmann, Robert
Sudan, Gabriel
Surowiec, Walter
Sury, Werner
Süsstrunk, Jakob
Sutter, Hermann
Sutter, Ruth
Sutter, Rosa
Suzaschi, Joseph
Svalduz, Angelo
Svatos, Marie
Svatosová, Marie
Swallow, John-Albert
Swars, Johann
Szandtner, Ernst
Szemere, Leo
Sztowicek von, Dora
Szuchanck, Floris
Tabet, Farid
Tacchi, Edoardo
Tacchi, Renate
Tacchi, Silvia
Taddeo de, Alma
Tagini, Claudine
Tagliabue, Emilio
Taillard, Felix Honest
Taillard, Arsene Virgile
Taillard, Lucie Sophie
Taillard, Marie Cecile
Taillard, Marie Leontine
Tapia, Laureana
Taracasanu, Marie G. H.
Tardan, Marthe
Taroovalle de, Roberto
Tarozzi, Jane
Tarrade, Marie-Christine
Tassy, Auguste & Germaine
Tattegrain, Eugénie
Tavecchio, Stella

Tazzari, Maria
Teabody, Olive W.
Tela, Pina
Tepe, Ruth
Terraz, Eugene
Tessmann, Bertha
Tettamanti, Bruna
Teufel, Rosa
Teunissen, Gerrit Jan
Thaesler, Ottilie
Thaler, Alma Elvira
Tharin, Clara
Theodoniades, D.
Theodoroff, Théodore & Hélène
Theurillat, Berthe
Thibaut, Henri
Thiel, Fritz
Thiel, Jacques
Thieulin, Raymonde
Thiévent, François & Gabrielle &
    Elise
Thines, Hedwig
Thoma, Emilie
Thoma, Emil
Thoma, Anna
Thomann, Willy
Thomas, Emile
Thommen, Ernst
Thon, W.
Thonen, Elise
Thöny, Hans
Thorold, A. F.
Thouvenin, Louis & Camille
Thura, Robert & Gabrielle
Tillmanns, Walter
Timeos, Ernst
Tina, Johann
Tinelli, Rene
Tinghir-Conklin, Nevarte
Tireb, Sophie
Tirolle, Francois
Tissot, Emma

Tjiongboenhok, Deetje
Tocchio, Elisa
Tock, Mathilde
Todd, Bronte
Todd, Helen
Todeschini, Baptiste
Todeschini, Joseph
Tognola, Tulio
Tolle, Gretl
Tomarkin, Jeannette
Tomat, Leonard
Topowridze & Iwaschhin
Torelli, Marie-Hélène
Torelli, Barbara
Torres, Miguel
Tosetti, Jean & Anna
Toth, Anton
Touache, Marie
Touret, Louis
Tourmit, Abel
Träg, Elsa
Tralamazza, Maria
Trautz, August
Trepp, Marie
Triboulot, Charles
Trickes, Johannes
Trieb, Eduard
Tron, Leo
Trösch, Fridolin & Paulina
Trotti, Sonia
Trümpy, Erna
Tschann, Jeanne
Tschornia, Hans Paul
Tua, Anastasie
Tuescher, Armand
Turka, Anna
Turotti, Anna
Turuvani, Thadee
Tuscher, Jean
Überschlag, Josef
Udriet, Jean
Ueberschlag, Achilles

Ugazio, Josef
Ugdulena, Gregorio
Uhle, Max
Ulberich, Elisabeth
Ulianow, Wladimir
Ullrich, Franz
Unfried, Ernst
Uttenweiler, Franz Xaver
Vaccarezza de Gregori
Vajani, Paolo & Laura
Vajkai, Ferdinand Nandor
Valensa, Leon
Valentino, Joseph
Valerio, Emilie
Vallot, René & Suzanne
Valsecchi, Lina
Valtcheva, Marie
Van der Sand, Gabriel
Vandevliet, Gustave
Vane, Marie
Vanier, Louis
Vanossi, Battista
Vanzini, Beatrici
Vassal, Pol & Marie Thérèse
    Lacaille
Vaughly Phocas
Vaurin, Heinrich
Vautherot, René
Vautherot, Raoul
Vautherot, Auguste
Vecchia Della, Francesco
Veitinger, Marie
Verbeke, Maurice
Verdel, François Maurice
Verdel, Josephine
Vergnano, Jean
Vergnes, Céline Paule
Verhuven, Marta
Vermot, Charles
Verny, Victor
Veronelli, Armando
Verri, Aldo & Ida

Veschetti, Giseppina
Vetter, Peter Paul
Vetter, Anna
Veumann, Adolf
Vibert, François Eugéne
Vicini, Sante
Vicuna Ormaza De, Ramon
Vidal, M. & J.
Vielle, Madeleine
Vignier, Marius
Villard, Paul & Blanche
Villavecchia de, R. Ricart
Villiger, August
Vincent, Louise
Vincenzi, Theresa
Vinogradoff, Berthe
Violett, Emma
Vionnet, Jules
Vipret, Rosa
Vitali, Maria-Luisa
Vittorio, Verde
Vivenza, Marie Marguerite
Vles, Arthur & Maria Manuela
Voelkel, Gerda
Vogel, Emil
Vogg, Marie
Vogt, Fanny
Vögtlin, Wilhelm
Voirol, Séraphin & Marie
Voisard, Amélie
Vollmer, Dorothy
Völlmy, Theophil
Vonachen, Rosalie
Vonbun, Ida
Vonfelt, René Paul
Vorberg, Gert
Vossler, Ernst
Vossler, Max
Votta, Augustina
Vouga, Francoise
Vredenburch van, Jonkheer H.
Vuez, Leon

Vuez, Paul
Vuillemin, Marie
Vuillemin, Laurent Ulysse
Vuillet, Samuel
Vuilleumier, Olga
Vulliez, Charlotte
Vurpillot, Florian
Wachter, Johann
Wachter, Marie
Wachter, Xaver
Wacker, Jean
Wacker, Auguste
Wacker, Fritz Josef
Waelbroeck, Caroline
Wagenbauer, Creszenz
Wagner, Carl
Wagner, Jeanne
Wagner, Felicia
Wagner, Elise
Wagner, Justine
Wagner, Rosa
Waizenegger, Ottilia
Waizenegger, Wilhelm
Waizenegger, Casimir
Waizenegger, Bertha
Waizenkorn, Margaretha
Walczak, Theophil
Walder, Albert
Walder de, Georges
Waldvogel, Theresia
Walker, Marie-Louise
Walker, Eugenie
Walker, Johannes
Waller, Isidor
Wallinger, Mathilde
Walter, Rudolf
Walter, Ferdinand
Walther, Edith
Walther, Johannes
Walz, Alice
Wandermann, Hch.
Wapler, Jean-Jacques

Wäschle, Franz
Wäschle, Joseph Carl
Watermann, Gertrud
Webb, Marie
Weber, Andre
Weber, Josef
Weber, Magdalena
Weber, Roger
Weber, Johann
Weber, Jean
Weber, Margrit
Weber, A.
Weber, Mina
Weckenmann, Joseph
Wedekind, Elisabeth
Weghaupt, Elisabeth
Weh, Katharina
Wehl, N.
Wehrli, Albert Emile
Weigand, Otto
Weil, Flore
Weil, Louis
Weil, Erich
Weil, Miriam
Weil, Ruth
Weil, Elisabeth
Weill, Cecile
Weiner, Mathilde
Weingärtner, Albert Peter
Weiser, Paul
Weiss, Anna
Weisz, Henriette
Weitbrecht, Gerda
Weixelbaum, Judith
Welchlin, Emma
Welchlin, Luise
Welf, Camillo
Welk, Lisel
Welte, Berta
Wenk, Elsa
Wenzel, Fritz
Wermeille, Ernest

Werner, Wilhelm
Werner, Julia
Werner, Erna
Werra De, Charles
Werth, Max
Werve van der, Philippe
Wessely, Peter K. H.
Westreicher, Josef
Wetzel, Elisabeth
Wetzstein, Carl
Wiand, Mathilde
Wicker, Josefine
Wickswat, H.
Widler, Carl
Widmann, H.
Widmann, August
Widmer, Margaretha
Widmer, Josepha
Wiedenschler, August
Wiedensohler, Josephine
Wiedmayer, Emma
Wiegner, Klara
Wieilly, Joseph & Rosalie
Wieland, Elisabeth
Wieland, Felix
Wieland, Gerhard
Wieland, Werner
Wiemers, Hans
Wiesauer, Anna
Wiggenhauser, Pauline
Wild, Karl
Wildtraut, Paul
Will, Carl
Willeitner, Hermann
Willeke, Karl
Willner, Rosa
Windler, Anna
Wingren, Karl Edwin & Jennie
Wininger, Théophile
Winkler, Erna
Winne, Josef
Winter, Marie

Zlatin, Lubomir
Zöller, Lina
Zons, Erwin
Zons, Friedrich & Anna
Zorn, Charles
Zournatzis, A.
Zuccotti, Bortolo

Zucker, Franz
Zurcher, Jeanne
Zuretti, Charles
Zusatz, Fernande
Zwicker, Helena
Zwicky, Ellen

BIBLIOGRAPHY

Agence France-Presse. "Historians Point Figure at Deutsche Bank over Nazi Gold." @ *Thunderstone*, July 31, 1998.

_____. "Report Criticizes Sweden Over Nazi Gold Purchases." @ *Thunderstone*, July 9, 1998.

Ain, Stewart. "Gold Stash—Possibly from Jews' Teeth—Unearthed." *New York Jewish Week*, September 27, 1998.

Akinci, Ugur. "US Accuses Turkey of Pocketing Looted Nazi Gold." *Turkish Daily News*, May 9, 1997.

Alcalá, Jesús. "Swedish Companies Purged Jews." trans. Stephen Croall, *Dagens Nyheter* (Sweden), June 8, 1998.

Associated Press. "Argentina Tells WWII Gold Secrets." *Salt Lake Tribune*, November 28, 1996.

_____. "Catholic Church Supported Nazis in WWII, Report Says." *Daily New Miner* (Anchorage), February 5, 1992.

_____. "Congressman Proposes Law to Force Payment of Policies." *The Boston Globe*, February 2, 1998, Latest News.

_____. "Maurice Papon Ordered to Pay Compensation." *The Nando (North Carolina) Times*, April 3, 1998.

_____. "Nazis Protected by Spain." *Beloit (Illinois) Daily News*, March 31, 1997.

_____. "Newly Released Documents Detail British Planning to Kill Adolf Hitler." *The Ottowa Citizen*, July 23, 1998.

_____. "Portuguese Bank Probed for Nazi Treasure Trove." *The Standard-Times*, January 11, 1997.

_____. "Spain Hid 2 Tons of Nazi Gold at End of WWII." March 16, 1997.

_____. "Swiss Banks Helped Nazis Plunder Gold." *Beloit (Illinois) Daily News*, January 13, 1997.

_____. "U.S. Claims Vatican Had Nazi Role."@ *Mosquitonet*, July 27, 1998.

_____. "U.S. Senate Panel Probes Holocaust Survivors Missing Money." *The Nando (North Carolina) Times*, April 23, 1996.

Associated Press and Reuters News Service. "Vatican Drawn into Scandal Over Nazi-era Gold." *CNN*, July 22, 1997.

Barrett, Devlin. "Swiss Will Pay $1.45 Billion to Nazi Victims." *New York Post*, August 13, 1998.

Barsamian, David. "How the Nazis Won the War." *Secrets, Lies and Democracy*, 1994.

Baryli, Waltraud. "Nazi Gold Inventory Found in Vienna." *Agence France-Presse*, November 30, 1997.

Bell, Andrew. "Swiss Confirmed as Main Nazi Bankers." *BBC News*, December 2, 1997.

Blomberg, Göran. "Directors Ran the Nazis' Errands." trans. Stephen Croall, *Dagens Nyheter* (Sweden), May 20, 1997.

Blum, Howard. *Wanted! The Search for Nazis in America.* New York: Quadrangle Press, 1977.

B'nai B'rith Center for Public Policy. "'Nazi Gold': An Update." July, 1997.

_____. "Portugal's Prime Minister Tells B'nai B'rith it will Establish Commission to Investigate its Financial Dealing with Nazi Germany." April 7, 1997.

Board of Economic Warfare. "A Country by Country Summary of Recent Developments in the Blockade Enforcement Program." RG 169. National Archives and Records Administration, September 1943.

Board of Economic Warfare. "Blockade Enforcement Manual." RG 169. *National Archives and Records Administration,* June 1943.

Bohlen, Celestine. "Holocaust Repentance Issued; Jewish Leaders disappointed in Vatican Statement." *The New York Time,.* March 16, 1998.

_____ "Vatican Repents Failure to Save Jews from Nazis." *The New York Times,* March 17, 1998.

Bradsher, Greg. "Searching for Documents on Nazi Gold." *The Record (New Jersey),* May, 1997.

Bransten, Jeremy. "Europe: Stolen Jewish Gold Continues to Tarnish Reputations." *Radio Free Europe/Radio Liberty* (Prague), January 28, 1997.

Briscoe, David. "Vatican Harbored Nazi-Era Gold: Damning Document Found." *Reuters News Service,* July 21, 1997.

Broomby, Rob. "Ford 'Profited from Nazi slave labor.'" *BBC News.* February 23, 1998, World: Americas.

Brown, Stephen. "Croat Death Camp Suspect Ready for Argentine Court." *Reuters News Service,* April 8, 1998.

Bushinsky, Jay. "WJC: No Breakthrough with Vatican on Nazi Gold." *The Jerusalem Post*, February 19, 1998.

Business Wire. "Insurance Archeology Firm Testifies Before U.S. Congress on Nazi Confiscation of Jewish Insurance Proceeds." @ *Pathfinder*, February 12, 1998.

Caister, Nick. "Argentina: Commission Investigates Nazi Links." *BBC News: Nazi Gold*, December 2, 1997.

Carter, Chelsea. "Insurers near Pact on Holocaust Payout." *Associated Press*, August 25, 1998.

Châtel, Vincent and Chuck Ferree. "The Forgotten Camps: Drancy (France)." August 23, 1998.

Chesnoff, Richard Z. "Fifty Years Too Late, a Reckoning." *U.S. News and World Report*, March 17, 1997.

Clarke, William. "Nazi Gold: The Role of the Central Banks—Where Does the Blame Lie?" *Central Banking*, vol. VIII, no. 1, summer 1997.

Cohen, Debra Nussbaum. "Response to Vatican Paper: Open the Holocaust Archives." *Jewish Telegraphic Agency Inc.*, March 16, 1998.

Cohen, Roger. "France to Look for Property Stolen from Jews during World War II." *The New York Times*, January 28, 1997, International.

_____. "Trial of Ex-Vichy Undermines Gaullist Mythology." *The New York Times*, October 22, 1997, International.

Commission for Religious Relations with the Jews. *We Remember: A Reflection on the Shoah*. March 16, 1998.

Commission on Jewish Assets in Sweden at the Time of the Second World War. *The Nazi Gold and the Swedish Riksbank*. Stockholm: The Swedish Ministry for Foreign Affairs, July, 1998.

_____. *Sweden and the Nazi Gold.* Stockholm: The Swedish Ministry for Foreign Affairs, December, 1997.

Consumer Project, The. "Consumer Group Demands Insurance Companies Honor Claims of Holocaust Victims." November 24, 1997.

Cook, Robin. *Britain in the USA: Press Conference by the Foreign Secretary.* New York: British Information Services, May 19, 1997.

Cook, Robin and Madeleine Albright. "Nazi Gold: Joint UK/US Statement." *Britain in the USA.* New York: British Information Services, May 19, 1997

Cooper, Rabbi Abraham. "How the World Plundered the Nazis' Victims: Who Profited from the Nazi Genocide." *Response,* Winter 1996/97.

Cowell, Alan. "Biggest German Bank Admits and Regrets Dealing in Nazi Gold." *The New York Times,* August 1, 1998.

_____. "Europe Revises Its War Stories." *The New York Times,* July 6, 1997.

_____. "Nazis Reportedly Stole More Victim Gold Than Estimated Earlier." *The New York Times,* December 2, 1997, International.

_____. "U.S. Urges Prompt Action on 'Nazi' Gold." *The New York Times.* December 5, 1997. International.

Danow, Mitchell. "Vatican Urged to Probe Facist Loot." *Jewish Telegraphic Agency Inc.,* July 25, 1997.

Davis, Douglas. "Britain Refusing to Compensate Holocaust Victims for Seized Assets." *Jewish Telegraphic Agency Inc.,* March 31, 1998.

D'emillo, Frances. "Vatican Document on Jews Defends

Pius XII; Angers Some Jews." *Associated Press*, March 17, 1998.

Dobnik, Verena. "Jersey Gives Swiss Banks the Cold Shoulder." *The Star-Ledger* (New Jersey), July 3, 1998, sec. A.

Dobrzynski, Judith H. "A Bulldog on the Heels of Lost Nazi Loot." *New York Times*, November 4, 1997.

Dorf, Matthew. "Holocaust Survivors Could Benefit in Wake of U.S. Report on Nazi Gold." *Jewish Telegraphic Agency Inc.*, May 7, 1998.

Dumay, Jean-Michael. "French Complicity in the Antijuive Policy." *Le Monde* (Paris), October 1, 1997.

Edinger, Bernard. "Nazi Collaborator Lashes Out at French War Crimes Trial." *Reuters News Service*, March 18, 1994.

Edward Reed to Secretary of State, Buenos Aires. RG 59. Decimal Files 1940-44, December 14, 1942.

Eisenthal, Bram. "Bank of Canada Launches Probe into Reported Link with Nazi Gold." *Jewish Telegraphic Agency Inc.*, July 15, 1997.

_____. "Investigation: Canadian Officials Knew About Wartime Laundering." *Jewish Telegraphic Agency Inc.,* July 29, 1997.

Federal Department of Foreign Affairs. *Gold Transactions in the Second World War: Statistical Review with Commentary.* Center for Security Studies and Conflict Research. June 4, 1998.

"Ferro-Alloys and Their Effect on Steel in the German War Industry, 1943 and 1944." RG 169. National Archives and Records Administration, June 1944.

Fleck, Fiona. "Germany Lost Nazi Gold Files-Official." *Reuters News Service,* July 22, 1998.

Florida Department of Insurance. "Witnesses at Holocaust Presentation." Washington D.C.:NAIC Fall National, September 22, 1997.

Finger, Seymour Maxwell. "American Jewry During the Holocaust.*" American Jewish Holocaust,* March 1984.

Follain, John. "French Church in the Dock at Nazi War Crimes Trial.*" Reuters World Report,* March 24, 1998.

Foreign & Commonwealth Office General Services Command. "Nazi Gold: Information from the British Archives." *History Notes,* no. 11, September 1996.

Foreign Relations of the United States 1940, vol. V. Washington: U.S. Government Printing Office.

Foreign Relations 1942, vol.II. Washington: U.S. Government Printing Office.

Foreign Relations 1943, vol. II. Washington: U.S. Government Printing Office.

Foreign Relations 1944, vol. VII General. Washington:U.S. Government Printing Office.

Fusi, Paolo. "Nazi Gold in Thuringia." *Zum Gesamtangebot Hintergrund,* Nov. 14, 1997

FYI-Israel in the News. "Nazi Gold Investigation Continues." *The Jewish Post of New York,* July 21, 1997.

Gardiner, Beth. "Papers Suggest Swiss Banks Laundered Nazi Gold." *The Seattle Times,* January 13, 1997, World.

Georgieff, Anthony. "Europe: Documents Reveal Sweden's Ties to Nazi Gold.*" Radio Free Europe/Radio Liberty* (Prague), January 27, 1997.

Giacomo, Carol. "U.S. Report Cites Neutral Countries in Aid to Nazis." *Reuters News Service,* June 2, 1998.

Goggin, Maureen, Walter V. Robinson. "Murky Histories Cloud Some Local Art.*" The Boston Globe*, November 9, 1997, Nation/World.

Goldsmith, Belinda. "Swedish War Government, Central Bank Rebuked over Nazi Gold." *Reuters News Service*, July 9, 1998.

Goñi, Uki. "Bormann Buried in Bariloche?" *The Sunday Times* (London), June 23, 1996.

_____. "'Nazi Gold' Clues in Argentina?" *La Nación* (Buenos Aires), May 11, 1997.

Goodstein, Laurie. "How Boyhood Friend Aided Pope with Israel." *The New York Times*, March 29, 1998.

Gordon, Michael R. "Russian Parliament Overrides Yeltsin Veto Concerning Looted Art." *The New York Times*, May 17, 1997, International.

Goshko, John, M. "Aid of Neutral Nations Kept Nazis Fighting." *The Salt Lake (Utah) Tribune*, June 3, 1998.

Gowland, Rob. "Banks' Nazi Connections Exposed." *The Guardian* (United Kingdom), June 19, 1996.

_____. "Banks' Nazi Connections Exposed.*" The Guardian* (United Kingdom), June 19, 1996.

Haskel, David. "Argentina Opens Central Bank Accounts to Jewish Probe." *Reuters News Service*, November 27, 1996.

Headden, Susan, Dana Hawkins and Jason Vest. "A Vow of Silence." *U.S. News & World Report*, March 30, 1998.

Heath, William. "Central Bank Turns Over WWII Gold Transfer Records to Jewish Group." *Associated Press*, 1996.

Hedin, Sven Fredrik and Göran Elgemyr. "Sweden Swapped Iron for Looted Gold." trans. Stephen Croall, *Dagens Nyheter* (Sweden), January 21, 1997.

_____. "When Stockholm Glittered with Stolen Diamonds." *Dagens Nyheter* (Sweden), June 8, 1998.

Heintz, Jim. "Report: Sweden Got More Nazi Gold than Previously Known." *Associated Press*, January 21, 1997.

Henning, Christopher. "Nazi Legacy: Britain, Vatican in Jewish Funds Link." *Sydney Morning Herald*, July 23, 1997.

Henning, Christopher. "Vatican Remains Mute on Looting." *The Age* (Melbourne). December 6, 1997.

Henry, Marilyn. "Austria to Return Looted Holocaust Art." *The Jerusalem Post*, March 8, 1998.

Higgins, Alexander G. "Swiss Bank Taken to Task over Nazi Gold." *Associated Press*, May 26, 1998.

Hillenbrand, Barry. "A Paper Chase for Gold." *Time Europe*, vol. 150, no. 24, December 15, 1997.

Hirsh, Michael."The Holocaust in the Dock." Newsweek, vol. 129, no. 7, February 7, 1997.

"Switzerland's Reckoning," *Newsweek*, June 9, 1997.

Hoell, Susanne. "Disputed Trojan Gold Glitters in Moscow." *Reuters News Service*, April 15, 1996.

Hornblower, Margot. "Of Mercy, Fame—And Hate Mail." *Time*, May 25, 1998, vol. 151 no.20.

Jack, Andrew. "Stolen Art: French Government Under Fire." *Culturekiosque Publications Ltd.*, February 19, 1997.

Johnson, Philip. "Britain 'Knew Swiss Kept Stolen Nazi Gold.'" *UK News*, Issue 437, July 29, 1996.

_____. "U.S. Archives Show that, 'Britain Blocked Return of Nazi Loot.'" *UK News*, Issue 467, September 2, 1996.

Kabel, Marcus. "Switzerland Yet to Decide on US Nazi Gold Hearing." *Reuters News Service*, July 13, 1998.

Karon, Tony. "Vatican Releases Holocaust Finding." *Time Daily*, March 17, 1998.

Keeler, Bob. "Act of Repentance." *Newsday*, March 17, 1998.

Kertzer, David I. "Secrets of the Vatican Archives." *The New York Times*, February 7, 1998.

Kessel, Jerrold. "Report: Neutral Nations' Trade Kept Nazi War Machine Going." *Associated Press*, June 2, 1998.

Kettle, Martin. "Nazi War Loot 'Underestimated.'" *The Guardian* (United Kingdom), June 2, 1998.

Kiernan, Sergio. "Argentina Begins Examination of Postwar Relations with Nazis." *Jewish Telegraphic Agency Inc.*, May 14, 1996.

_____. "Argentine Jews Skeptical About Nazi-Looted Gold Probe." *Jewish Telegraphic Agency Inc.*, April 20, 1997.

_____. "Jewish Group to Publish Book on Nazi Activities in Argentina." *Jewish Telegraphic Agency Inc.*, May 19, 1997.

_____. "Switzerland to Investigate Nazi Payments to Argentina." *Jewish Telegraphic Agency Inc.*, June 25, 1997.

Kurtzman, Daniel. "Analysis of Looted Nazi Gold Comes as U.S. Readies Report." *Jewish Telegraphic Agency Inc.*, March 25, 1997.

_____. "B'nai B'rith: National Gallery Knew it Displayed Nazi Plunder." *Jewish Telegraphic Agency Inc.*, November 5, 1997.

_____. "Documents: Swiss Facilitated Transfer of Nazis to Argentina." *Jewish Telegraphic Agency Inc.*, December 9, 1996.

_____. "Swiss Shipments of Nazi Gold Add Fuel to Ongoing Public Furor." *Jewish Telegraphic Agency Inc.*, January 14, 1997.

_____. "U.S. Calls for Closure as Nazi Gold Conference Ends." *Jewish Telegraphic Agency Inc.*, December 4, 1997.

_____. "U.S. Moves to Create Panel to Examine Assets." *Jewish Telegraphic Agency Inc.*, April 1, 1998.

_____. "WJC Claims a Third of Nazi Gold Looted from Individual Sources." *Jewish Telegraphic Agency Inc.*, October 7, 1997.

Lederer, Edith M. "Group Seeks Access to All Files Tracing Gold Looted by Nazis." *Associated Press*, August 25, 1998.

_____. "Nazi Gold Conference Ends." *Associated Press*, December 4, 1997.

Leitz, Christian. "Hermann Göring and Nazi Germany's Economic Exploitation of Nationalist Spain." *German History* 14, 1 (1996).

Lewis, Jo Ann. "Legal Fallout Continues from Looted Art." *The Washington Post*, May 14, 1998, sec. C.

Mackay, Lord of Clashfern. "London Conference on Nazi Gold." *Britain in the USA*. New York: British Information Services, December 4, 1997.

MacLeod, Alexander. "Global Search for Wartime Flow of Nazi Gold Enters a New Phase." *The Christian Science Monitor*, December 8, 1997, International.

Maissen, Thomas. "Switzerland: Dormant Accounts, Nazi Gold and Loot." *Swiss-American Chamber of Commerce*, February 1998.

Marshall, Tyler. "U.S. Document Says Vatican was Repository for Nazi Gold." *The Los Angeles Times*, July 23, 1997.

McGeary, Johanna. "Echoes of the Holocaust." *Time*, vol. 149, no. 8, February 24, 1997.

Memorandum from Samuel Klaus to Oscar Cox. RG 169. National Archives and Records Administration, January 27, 1945.

Moore, Stephen D. "Swiss Banks' Pact Forced by Sanctions," *The Wall Street Journal*, August 14, 1998, International.

Morrow, Lance. "The Justice of the Calculator." *Time*, February 24, 1997.

Myers, Laura. "U.S. Report: Swiss Aided Gold Plunder." *The Washington Post*, May 7, 1997.

Neuffer, Elizabeth, Walter V. Robinson. "Austria Confronts Dark Past By Combing Art for Nazi Link." *The Boston Globe*, March 5, 1998.

Newton, Ronald C. *The 'Nazi Menace' in Argentina, 1931-1947*. California: Stanford University Press, 1992.

Niebuhr, Gustav. "Vatican Document Seeks to Weave Several Themes." *The New York Times*, March 17, 1998.

Nossiter, Adam. "With Cool Energy, Ex-Vichy Official Defends His Past." *The New York Times*, October 16, 1997, International.

Office of the Prime Minister, "Investigation of Vichy-Era Confiscation of Jewish Property." *French Embassy*, February 5, 1997.

"Outline of Inter-American Economic Activities and Their Official Agencies." RG169 National Archives and Records Administration, College Park, Md., October 20, 1942.

Overbeck, Charles. "Nazi Gold Stored at Federal Reserve Bank." @ *Parascope*. October, 1996.

Pellegrini, Frank. "The Vatican Pipeline." *Time Daily*, July 22, 1997.

Plaut, James S. "Hitler's Capital." vol. 178, no.4. *The Atlantic Monthly*, October, 1946.

Powers, Ronald. "U.S. May Be Forced to Open Nazi Files." *The Star-Ledger*, August 2, 1998, sec.1.

"Preclusive Operations in the Neutral Countries in World War II." RG 169. National Archives and Records Administration, March 20, 1947.

Reuters News Service. "Eva Peron May Have Put Bribes in Swiss Banks." *The Irish Times*, June 25, 1997.

_____. "France Asked to Share Burden of Nazi Gold Debts." *The Nando (North Carolina) Times*, January 30, 1997.

Robinson, Walter V. "170 Museums to Review Collections for Stolen Art." *The Boston Globe*, June 5, 1998, Nation/World.

_____. "A Dispute in Miniatures: Sherborn Man Seeks to Keep Art Germany Wants Back." *The Boston Globe*, April 1, 1997, Nation/World.

_____. "An Ignominious Legacy: Evidence Grows of Plundered Art in U.S." *The Boston Globe*, April 25, 1997, Nation/World.

_____. "Art Buyer Fights Holocaust Heirs." *The Boston Globe*, May 18, 1997, Nation/World.

_____. "Art Registry Did Not Inform Met of Claim." *The Boston Globe*, July 25, 1998, Nation/World.

_____. "Italy Calls N.Y Museum's Prized Collection Stolen." *The Boston Globe*, April 17, 1998, Nation/World.

_____. "The 'Lost' Masterpieces: In France, an Uneasy Look Inward." *The Boston Globe*, March 16, 1997, Nation/World.

_____. "Paradox of Peace: Artworks Taken as Reparations Pose U.S. Dilemma." *The Boston Globe*, August 1, 1997, Nation/World.

_____. "Sotheby's Takes Work Tied to Nazis off Block." *The Boston Globe*, November 25, 1997, Nation/World.

_____. "Sweden Probes a Dark Secret." *The Boston Globe*, July 6, 1997, Nation/World.

_____. "Theft Admission Ends Tug-of-War over Artwork." *The Boston Globe*, May 13, 1998, Nation/World.

_____. "U.S. Tracked Influx of Looted Art." *The Boston Globe*, May 9, 1997, Nation/World.

Robinson, Walter V., Maureen Goggin. "Stolen-art Claims Shake N.Y. Museum." *The Boston Globe*, July 24, 1997, Nation/World.

Rohde, David. "The Lawsuits Pile Up, Matching the List of Atrocities." *The New York Times*, September 13, 1998, The World.

Rubin, Seymour. "Allied-Swedish Accord on German External Assets, Looted Gold and Related Matters." Bulletin, July 27, 1947.

Ruth, Arne. "The Wallenbergs Helped the Germans." trans. Stephen Croall, *Dagens Nyheter* (Sweden), November 28, 1996.

Sancton, Thomas. "Unforgiven." *Time* (Paris), October 20, 1997.

Sanger, David E. "Documents Show U.S. Melted Down Nazi Victims' Gold." *The New York Times*, December 1, 1997. International.

_____. "Nazi Gold Was Recast and Issued in the U.S." *The New York Times*, November 2, 1997, International.

_____. "Nazis Looted Almost 9 Billion in Gold." *The New York Times*, October 7, 1997.

_____. "U.S. Commission to Look for Holocaust Assets." *The New York Times.* April 2, 1998, International.

Schuman, Joseph. "Report: Former Chirac Deputy Oversaw Shipment of Jews in 1942." *Lubbock Avalanche-Journal* (Texas), February 1, 1997.

Seidel, Carlos Collado, "Zufluchtsstätte für Nationalsozialisten? Spanien, die Alliierten und die Behandlung deutscher Agenten 1944-1947." *Vierteljahrshefte für Zeitgeschichte*, 43 (1995): 131-157.

Senate Banking Committee. *Swiss Banks, the 1946 Washington Accords, and Current Developments in Holocaust Restitution.* Washington D.C.: U.S. Government Printing Office, July 22, 1998.

Sims, Calvin. "Argentines Searching for a World War II German Submarine: Did It Carry Nazi Booty?" *The New York Times*, November 29, 1996, sec. A.

_____. "Jews Now Hail Argentina for Anti-Nazi Efforts." *The New York Times*, April 18, 1997.

Sisk, Richard. "U.S. Eyes Vatican for Nazi Gold Plot." *The New York Daily News*, July 23, 1997.

Specter, Michael. "In Latvia, the First Token of Swiss Remorse: $400." *The New York Times*, November 19, 1998.

Speer, Albert. *Inside the Third Reich*. New York: Macmillan Press, 1981.

Spiegelman, Arthur. "Swiss Banks to Go It Alone in Holocaust Talks." *Reuters News Service*, July 16, 1998.

_____. "U.S. Bank Accepted Nazi Gold," *Reuters News Service*, November 1, 1997.

_____. "Vatican Bank Dealt with Reichsbank in War-Document." *Reuters* News Service, August 15, 1997.

_____. "WWII Documents Bolster Nazi-Red Cross Connection." *Detroit Free Press*, August 30, 1996.

Syndicated News Service. "Argentina to Probe its Banks for Nazi Gold." *Jewish Post of New York*, April 18, 1997.

_____. "Nazi Gold." *The Jewish Post of New York*, September 19, 1996.

"Transfer of Swiss Gold to Portugal and Spain: Communique from Spain." January 12, 1946.

"Totalitarian Activities–Argentina Today." RG 60. National Archives and Records Administration, June 1943.

U.S. and Allied Efforts to Recover and Restore Gold and Other Assets Stolen or Hidden by Germany During World War II. Washington, DC: U.S. Government Printing Office, May 1997.

U.S. and Allied Wartime and Postwar Relations and Negotiations with Argentina, Portugal, Spain, Sweden, and Turkey on Looted Gold and German External Assets and U.S. Concerns About the Fate of the Wartime Ustasha Treasury. Washington, D.C.: U.S. Government Printing Office, June, 1998.

Usher, Rod. "The Double Victims." *Time*, August 25, 1997, vol. 150, no.8.

Valasis, Adriana D. "Sweden: Dirty Money." *Europ Magazine*, no. 89, April 2, 1998.

Ward, Stephen and Ian Locke. "Holocaust Gold: Credit to the Nation." London: Research Department of the Holocaust Education Trust, September 8, 1997.

Warner, Joan and John Parry. "Swiss Banks: The Noose Tightens." *Business Week,* July 27, 1998.

Weinberg, Gerhard L. *A World at Arms: A Global History of World War II.* Massachusetts: Cambridge University Press, 1994.

Whiteside, John. "Search for Nazi-Looted Art." The Profits of Plunder. *Reuters,* February 12, 1998.

Whitney, Craig R. "Vichy Official Found Guilty of Helping Deport Jews." *The New York Times,* April 2, 1998, International.

Wren, Christopher S. "Insurers Swindled Jews, Nazi Files Show." *The New York Times,* May 18, 1998, sec. A.

Yanowitch, Lee. "Collector's Heirs Ask Museum to Return Nazi-Looted Painting." *Jewish Telegraphic Agency Inc.,* February 2, 1998.

_____. "France Expands Efforts to Find Nazi-Looted Assets." *Jewish Telegraphic Agency Inc.,* March 10, 1998.

_____. "French Jews Shocked to Learn Museums Hold Looted Art." *Jewish Telegraphic Agency Inc.,* January 31, 1997.

_____. "France Expands Efforts to Find Nazi-Looted Assets." *Jewish Telegraphic Agency Inc.,* March 10, 1998.

_____. "Mitterand Eulogized Amid Controversy Over Nazi Ties." *Jewish Bulletin of Northern California* (San Francisco), January 12, 1996.

Young, Eric. "State Joins Fight to Help Holocaust Survivors, Heirs: Many Say Life Insurance Policies Never Honored." *The Sacramento Bee.* November 25, 1997, Business.

Zagorin, Adam. "Saving the Spoils of War." *Time,* December 1, 1997. vol. 150, no. 23.

CONTRIBUTORS

Those I wish to acknowledge at the outset are Dr. Joan S. Dunphy, editor-in-chief, Shannon Vargo and Rebecca Sheil, assistant editors and Chris Marietti, publishing intern, at New Horizon Press, whose services allowed me to produce the most extensive and accurate account of the subject possible.

The author is also indebted to John Steinbeck, for his incisive translation of the ways men triumph over sin, which is from *East of Eden* and serves as the frontispiece for *Nazi Gold*.

Grateful appreciation goes to the people who contributed to one of the studies that shape the heart of this book including Stuart Eizenstat, Secretary of Commerce and International Trade; William Z. Slany, State Department historian, and the staff members of the following government bodies that participated in the study: Central Intelligence Agency, Departments of Commerce, Defense, Justice, State and the Treasury, Federal Bureau of Investigation, Federal Reserve Board, National Archives and Record Administration, National Security Agency, and the U.S. Holocaust Memorial Museum.

The cast contributing to the American Jewish Commission on the Holocaust is a formidable one, headed by former Justice of the Supreme Court Arthur Goldberg, and supported by vice chairmen: Jacob R. Javits, Abraham Ribicoff; and Harrison J. Goldin; and City College of New York Professor Seymour Maxwell Finger, director of Research and Editor. The members who served on the commission that produced this monumental study include: Rabbi William Berkowitz, Rabbi Balfour Brickner, Sol Chaikin, Marvin Frankel, Dr. Saul S. Friedman, Rabbi Arthur Hetzberge, Ira Hirschman, Elizabeth Holtzman, Philip M. Klutznick, Mrs. Charlotte Jacobson, Mrs Frieda S. Lewis, Professor Martin Meyerson, Mrs. Isaiah Minkoff, Rabbi Israel Mowshowitz, Dr. Martin Peretz, Dr. Harold Proshansky, Simond Rifkind, Rabbi Arthur Schneir, Rabbi Morris Cherer, Jeanette Friedman-Sieradski, Rabbi Ronald Sobel, Jack Spitzer, Mrs. Bernice Tannenbaum, Rabbi Mordecai Waxman and Walter H. Weiner.

The following were also invaluable contributors to the text: U.S. Senators Alfonse D'Amato and Harley Kilgore; Holocaust survivors, Ivanova of Antwerp, Hindy Fekete, Elias Abramson, and Reva Shefer; American Jewish leaders

Howard Squadron, Gideon Taylor, and Rabbi Marvin Hier; Edgar Bronfman, Elan Steinberg, and Israel Bashevis Singer of the World Jewish Congress; Margers Vestermanis of Riga; the Reichsbank's Albert Thoms; U.S. Brigadier General Frank McSherry; Switzerland's Peter Cosandey, Hans Schaffner, Christopher Meili; and Presidents Jean-Pascal Delamuras and Arnold Koller; Avraham Burg of Isreal's Jewish Agency; Attorneys Michael D. Hausfeld, Mel Urbach, and Havier Astigarraga; New York City and State officials: Neil Levin, H. Carl McCall, Alan Hevesi, and Irwin Nick; Scholars, historians, writers, and academics: Dr. Sol Chaneles, Dr. Jan Karski, Christian Gerlach, Professor David I. Kertzer, Rabbi Jack Bemporad, Reverand Richard P. McBrien, Professor Victor Halberstadt, Antonio Louka, Michel Slitinsky, Marc Jansen, Mineke Bosch, and Myrium Eveard; New Jersey Governor Christine Todd Whitman; California Treasurer Matt Fong; Ivan Rooth of Sweden's Riksbank; Argentine President Carlos Saul Menem; Marcelo Stubrin and Juan Jose Ribelli of Argentina; Manouchehr Moatamer; Emilie Schindler; Turkey Minister of State Sukru Sing Gurel; John Cardinal O'Connor and William Cardinal Keeler, Archbishops of New York and Baltimore; Joseph Zwillings of the New York Archdiocese; Vatican representatives Joachin Navarro-Valls and Undersecretary Tauran; Vincent LaVista, U.S. diplomat to Rome; Treasury Minister of Italy Carlo Ciampi; Joseph Cardinal Ratzinger; the Anti-Defamation League's Rabbi David Rosen (Israel) and Abraham Foxman (U.S.); Rosann Catalano; Eugene J. Fisher; Robin Cook; Lord Greville Janner, and G.I.F. Bolton of England; Fernando Brito; Simon Wiesenthal; Shimon Samuels; French President Jacques Chirac; Citicorps's Jack Morris; Ronald Lauder; Willie Kort; Robert O'Brien; Members of the Art Museum Community, James N. Wood, Philippe de Montebello, Glenn D. Lowry, Stephen E. Weil, Gilbert S. Edelson; Judge Laura Drager; Rita Rief; and Austria's Elizabeth Gehrer.

Members of the press and media whose work was invaluable to the author deserve mention. They are: Alan Cowell, David Sanger, Laurie Goodstein, and David Cay Johnston of the *New York Times*; *Time* magazine's Lance Morrow; Devlin Barrett of the *New York Post*; Rob Gowland of England's *Guardian*; the *Boston Globe's* Walter V. Robinson and Elizabeth Neuffer; *Los Angeles Times* South American correspondent Sebastian Rotella; Richard Z. Chesnoff of the *New York Daily News*; Jay Bushinsky of the *Jerusalem Post*; the Jewish Telegraph Agency; the staffs of the Wiesenthal Center's magazine *Response*, the *Washington Post*; French magazines *Le Monde* and *Le Point*; Swedish newspaper *Dagens Nyheter*, British newspapers *Daily Telegraph* and *London Times*, Austrian newspaper *Der Standard*, and Argentinian newspapers *La Manana del Sur* and *La Nacion*.

The author salutes all of the aforementioned contributors to this text and those who have been inadvertently omitted with deepest appreciation and the most heartfelt thanks.

INDEX